TOKYO STYLE FILE

TOKYO STYLE FILE

A SHOPPING GUIDE

Jahnvi Dameron Nandan

CHIEF RESEARCHER
Hisaya Kumano

RESEARCH ASSISTANTS
Chiyo Udagawa
Damion Mannings

KODANSHA INTERNATIONAL
Tokyo • New York • London

Fabric on front jacket courtesy of TexStyle Depots.

Distributed in the United States by Kodansha America Inc., and in the United Kingdom and continental Europe by Kodansha Europe Ltd.

Published by Kodansha International Ltd., 17-14 Otowa 1-chome, Bunkyo-ku, Tokyo 112-8652, and Kodansha America, Ind.

First edition, 2007
15 14 13 12 11 10 09 08 07   10 9 8 7 6 5 4 3 2 1

        Library of Congress Cataloging-in-Publication Data

Nandan, Jahnvi Dameron.
  Tokyo style file : a shopping guide / by Jahnvi Dameron Nandan. -- 1st ed.
     p. cm.
  ISBN 978-4-7700-3055-9
  1. Shopping--Japan--Tokyo--Guidebooks. I. Title.
  TX337.J32T663 2008
  381'.110952135--dc22
                        2007017485

www.kodansha-intl.com

CONTENTS

I have to admit that I have a fashion pedigree that would shame the haughtiest of fashion editors. Born to bespoke-wearing parents, my bespoke-clad childhood meant never having to go clothes shopping. In fact, the only things that I was allowed to buy ready-made were shoes (which I continue stocking with a vengeance!). Like every other child who found themselves drawn to the forbidden, the world of "ready-to-wear" beckoned to me, almost to the point of obsession. I became fascinated with shops—their collections, their window displays, their designer shopping bags, and the sheer pleasure of indulgence.

Fast-forward a bit. I was twenty years old when I arrived at Tokyo's Narita Airport, grabbed my matching pieces of luggage from the gloved baggage handlers, and rushed to my new post-modernist apartment, my new job, my new life. My apartment was located in the center of Harajuku—Tokyo's vibrant fashion mecca. I saw hair bands, eyebrows plucked to a straight-edged line, designer totes and flashy finger rings parading down my street. And that was the men!

Through my job—at a company introducing foreign designers to Japan and vice versa—I began to get a close look at the fashion industry. I found that while stylists in the rest of the world were struggling, my stylist friends here in Tokyo were celebrities. And there was no lack of young and powerful buyers of trendy shops who seemed to be constantly off scouring the world from Stockholm to Santiago, attending all the fashion weeks to handpick collections for their stores. (One buyer from a major interior store, for example, gingerly carried every piece of vintage Baccart he bought in Paris as hand luggage to Tokyo, and immediately placed it on the shelves.)

More than a decade later I am still in that apartment. I am neighbors with Louis Vuitton, Fendi, Issey Miyake, and recent newcomers Bottega Veneta and Dolce & Gabbana.

I sip wine on my balcony and watch pouting Lolitas share the sidewalk with Chanel addicts and other fresh faces with a new LV buy. I ask myself where else one would find a department store dedicated to showcasing the hottest items from Israel, an aromatherapy shop dedicated to jasmine from Tunisia, heavyweight fashion brands marrying cutting-edge architecture, and twelve LV mega-shops under direct control of the brand.

So I put my Prada pencil to my favorite Smythson paper to document the offerings of the world's most fashionable city. The challenge was daunting: so many hundreds, no, thousands of shops spread all over a town with the most complicated address system in the world! Thankfully, I had help. My best friend, fashion designer Kuma, offered to decipher all the addresses. Singer Chiyo cooed into the phone requesting appointments (who could refuse such a sexy voice?), and so we micro-managed our way through town. Shop after shop, collection after collection, I discovered the openness of Tokyo-layering, accessorizing, anti-conservatism, and dressing up to the hilt (or thinking for hours on how to dress down), no matter what the occasion. I learned about the fetish obsession with cult chairs and other accoutrements for the house. I began to revel in Tokyo's freedom of fashion, the fact that no one bats an eyelid if I decide to leave my house channeling Gwen Stefani through my lipstick, ra-ra skirt, and knee high socks.

In the *Tokyo Style File*, I share the results of our labor: over six hundred shops, from the biggest and the best to the smallest and the newest, from the best known to the less-known, to some that I've always considered my own little secrets. My hope is to make the shopping experience in Tokyo as exciting for the reader as it has been for me.

There are a few things to keep in mind. Like this ephemeral city that changes, it seems, on an almost daily basis, Tokyo-ites are famously fickle when it comes to brand loyalties. Shops come and go, collections change, and new designers and mega-brands are constantly making their way up and down the high street at a pace that puts other big cities to shame. How does one make sense of it? Keep track of it? Well, we figured that sticking to the best would ensure that most of our entries would be around longer than the annual spring cherry blossoms.

ADDRESSES/MAPS

Because Tokyo address numbers go around (randomly numbered) blocks rather than down streets, addresses can be mind-boggling—though GPS phones are making life easier. Taxis can get you very close, but you still may have to do some looking. Our maps are as accurate as we could make them, but there are so many alleys and by-ways that you should go out with an adventurous spirit—and be ready to stumble across something that isn't in the *Style File*.

DATA

The data next to the shop name and category is in the following order:

> Address
> Phone number (including Tokyo's 03 area code)
> Web site (when available)
> Shop hours
> Holidays
> Map Number

At the end of the addresses in the data box, you'll often see "(Others)," meaning that other locations selling the brand also exist. It also means that we've gone to the trouble of selecting what we feel is the best outlet with the best selection available. You can find the other locations by checking their web site or asking at the shop.

DENIM

It's not a secret (though it's not that well known, either) that Japan is the source of the most sought-after denim in the world. Most of the best denim brands source their material from mills in Western Japan's Okayama Prefecture. Their strong weave and natural indigo dyes have earned them universal acclaim for their vintage appeal. Check out our denim category for the latest and best in cult denim.

FOR MEN

Tokyo is surely one of the most fertile grounds anywhere for men's shopping, so we've tried our best to include an exhaustive list of men's destinations. From the fantastic Isetan for Men all the way to the avant-garde Via Bus Stop Homme, we believe that the Tokyo shopping experience for men is unparalleled retail therapy.

MADE IN JAPAN

From the genius of Issey Miyake to the giant Yohji Yamamoto and Rei Kawakubo, Japanese designers stock their very best and latest in their Tokyo shops. And if you're looking for newcomers like Ato, Undercover, Sacai, Toga, and the New Romantics (as the latest generation is known), check out the category list on page 262, for a listing of all the Japanese designers—old and new.

PRICES

It's very hard to make definitive statements about prices, since everything from exchange rates to varying tariffs can affect what appears on the tag. But I'll make a few generalizations. The major international brands tend to be more expensive here—especially leather goods. The works of Japanese designers are, understandably, priced better than anywhere else, so this is your chance to fill your closet with "Made in Japan" fashion. The ¥ marks are a general indication of the prices, as follows:

¥	A Bargain
¥¥	Reasonable
¥¥¥	Moderate
¥¥¥¥	Expensive
¥¥¥¥¥	Luxury

All that said, you'll never know what kind of sale or special deal you might stumble across, so keep your eyes open.

"SELECT SHOPS"

We've translated this Japanese-English phrase that categorizes a certain style of shop as "boutique," which we think is more understandable to a foreign audience. A shop that is called a "*Selekuto Shoppu*" in Japanese tends to be one of the cult of shops that stocks the best and the latest of foreign and

Japanese fashions. They are located in the prime real estate areas of Tokyo and are *the* places to head if you're looking for the latest looks.

SIZES

The perennial problem. Yes, sizes tend to be small in Tokyo, and it is a special problem for women. It's often said that clothes are small, shoes are medium and hats are big. We can't do anything about that (but mention sizes when it's relevant), but for those for whom it's a real problem, we can only suggest sticking to the accessories. Thankfully, Tokyo offers an amazing selection. Splurge on what we think is a great choice of bags, hats, socks, and jewelry.

WEBSITES

We've included them whenever possible. The international brand's sites may be the most understandable, but many Japanese brands include English info, and even if they're only in Japanese, some time spent browsing can give you a good sense of what's available.

I will say it again: Tokyo breathes fashion, and the industry's obsession with quality and style means that no one shops better than a Tokyoite. One evening at a cocktail party, I met a European couple that travels all the way to this city every year for Christmas shopping because, they swear, it is the best place to shop on the planet. I've also met students who wear YSL to class, young working women who spend half their salary every month on a new dress, and the boyfriend of a friend who did not have a fixed income but wore only Dior Homme. *Tokyo Style File* is dedicated to them and all the other thousands like them, myself included, who wander Tokyo's streets in search of their own brand of sartorial energy and adventure.

Happy Shopping!
Jahnvi Dameron Nandan
Tokyo

THE SHOPS

109

WOMEN'S DEPT. STORE

2-29-1 Dogenzaka, Shibuya-ku, Tokyo
03-5561-7714
www.shibuya109.jp
🕐 10:00–21:00
📅 Not fixed
🚇 MAP 8-1   ¥

If you've become too sophisticated and world-weary, enveloped by luxury and refinement, this is a must-visit for a much needed jolt to the senses. A few floors of Japanese schoolgirl faves of whatever is the latest trend—off-shoulder dresses with big bows, sky-high denim shorts, celebrity suede baseball hats, metallic stiletto sandals, wraparound dresses and lots of gaudy fake accessories and intimates at unbeatable prices. This is Japanese youth culture at its gaudiest—a step-down version of the Hilton sisters or the footballer wives syndrome. Megafreaky, girly, trance-a-thon: a straight shot of Japanese street style.

10 CORSO COMO COMME DES GARÇONS

MEN'S/WOMEN'S BOUTIQUE

5-3-20 Minami-Aoyama, Minato-ku, Tokyo
03-5774-7800
www.10corsocomo.com/
🕐 11:00–20:00
📅 Not fixed
🚇 MAP 1-1   ¥|¥|¥|¥-¥|¥|¥|¥|¥

The marriage of Carla Sozzani's school of cool with Rei Kawakubo's passion for stellar talent makes this Tokyo's must visit one-stop thrill-shop. Whereas the main Comme des Garçons collection is available at the nearby flagship store, the reason you should come here is to check out the handpicked collections from Homme, Homme Deux, Tao, Tricot, Vivienne Westwood Red Label, Balenciaga, Alexander McQ, Margiela, and Junya Watanabe Comme des Garçons with shoes from Aläia, Junya Watanabe, Tricot, and Tao, bags from Balenciaga, and Jaques le Corre, and leather numbers straight from the equally hot Milanese outpost.

16 AOUT

WOMEN'S BOUTIQUE

5-3-25 Minami Aoyama, Minato-ku, Tokyo
03-5468-0816
www.16aout.com
🕐 11: 00–20:00
📅 Not fixed
🚇 MAP 1-2   ¥|¥-¥|¥|¥

Another starry shop for the consummate buyer. This one manages to keep the prices somewhat low and the interest high. Selections from the latest collections of Alessandro Dell`Acqua, Viktor and Rolf, Haider Ackermann, Golden Goose, Isabel Marant and top T-shirts from Devastee—in short, everything you need to continue your reign as a diehard fashionista. While the collections might be more grandiose elsewhere, there is something in the boudoir-like, at-home-but-no-nonsense fashion experience here that makes you want to come back and check this place out as often as your wallet allows.

17 DIX SEPT DESIGN GALLERY

MEN'S/WOMEN'S BOUTIQUE/ INTERIOR

17-6 Daikanyamacho, Shibuya-ku, Tokyo
03-5428-0335
www.17dixsept.jp/web/
🕐 11:00–20:00
📅 No holidays
📍 MAP 2-1

¥|¥

17 dix sept is a design gallery that contains a heady combination of all that is great in Japanese design, and is perhaps the only place in town that variously includes graphic design, textiles, interiors, sounds, motion graphics, jewelry, accessories, shoes, clothes, and interiors all in one very tiny space. Crystal accessories, kimono belt straps for your mobile phone, fashion diaries, leather clutch bags, beaded shoes, silk scarves, and many other seasonal inspirations mostly handmade and irresistible, especially in the run up to Christmas.

45RPM

MEN'S/WOMEN'S DENIM

6-19-16 Jingumae, Shibuya-ku, Tokyo
03-5468-0045
www.45rpm.jp
🕐 11:30–20:00
📅 Not fixed
📍 MAP 6-1

¥|¥|¥

Tradition at its finest. A must-visit for those who aren't aware that the best denim in the world comes from Japan. Purveyors of traditional Japanese denim in ink and indigo dyes, the shop sells jeans in many different weaves and finishes. The jeans all come in just one basic straight cut style, but in five different hues of blue dyes or in organic indigo dye. These give all the jeans a darker finish, with the fine cloth comfortable on the skin and a delicate weave resulting in a refined look. Ultra pure, dependable, and full of style.

5351

MEN'S/WOMEN'S BOUTIQUE

5-9-15 Minami Aoyama, Minato-ku,
Tokyo (Others)
03-5467-5799
www.abahouse.co.jp
🕐 11:00–20:00
📅 No holidays
📍 MAP 1-3

¥|¥|¥-|¥|¥|¥

5351's aggressive, near-goth jetblack collections offer rock chic with an Italo-Japanese aesthetic: flashy suits, metallic T-shirts, stressed denims, and a lot of leather in the signature tailored styles. Women can find short sporty coats with lace detailing, off-shoulder knits, tube dresses with matching drapes around the neck, and thick chunky cardigans complemented by some really pointy toed leather lace-ups.

ABC MART

MEN'S/WOMEN'S SHOES

1-11-5 Jinnan, Shibuya-ku, Tokyo (Others)
03-3477-0602
www.abc-mart.com/index.html
🕐 11:00–21:00
📅 No holidays
🚋 MAP 8-2   ¥

Whether you're out in the elements or out on the town, ABC Mart will lace you up with shoes that are not high up on the style ladder but great for your budget, making this a haunt for teenagers and those in their early twenties. This is also where guys with big feet can find shoes that fit. Collections from Hawkins, Rockport, Timberland, Merrel, Vans, Nike, and Reebok line the shelves. They have them in women's and junior sizes too.

ACANTA

CIGAR SHOP/
MEN'S ACCESSORIES

Cerulean Tower Tokyu Hotel, 26-1
     Sakuragaoka, Shibuya-ku, Tokyo
03-3780-8335
www.ceruleantower-hotel.com
🕐 10:30–20:30
📅 Not fixed
🚋 MAP 8-3   ¥|¥|¥

Finding the perfect gift for the man in your life is never a breeze, but if the man is a cigar smoker this is the place for you. Apart from cigar cutters, humidors, and matchbox holders from Ashton, Griffin's, Elie Bleu, and Christofle, you can find one of the finest cigar collections in town handpicked from the Dominican Republic and Cuba. Also a great place for fine accessories such as watches, ties, cufflinks, and shoe-care sets.

ACTUS

INTERIOR

BYGS Bldg, 2-19-1 Shinjuku, Shinjuku-ku,
     Tokyo
03-3350-6011
www.actus-interior.com/
🕐 11:00–20:00
📅 Not fixed
🚋 MAP 9-1   ¥-¥|¥|¥|¥

Rustic, retro or rigorously modern—however you decide to decorate your home, this shop will have something for you. The first floor consists of towels, kitchenware and other utility items for the house. But the second floor is where the action is—with furniture from Germany's Tecta, Italy's Porada, and, most importantly, in a tribute to Scandinavian design, a number of sleek metal designs from Arne Jacobsen and wooden chairs from colleague Hans J Wegner. Revel in design purism as only the Germans do, with Poggenpohl—a huge variety of functional kitchenware. It is of great benefit to those who live in an open plan house, and with good looks that would prove irresistible even to the most male of the species.

ADAM ET ROPE HOMME

MEN'S BOUTIQUE

Kokusai Bld 1F, 13-16 Udagawa-cho,
 Shibuya-ku, Tokyo (Others)
03-3476-2974
www.adametrope.com
🕐 11:30–21:00
🗓 No holidays
📍 MAP 8-4   ¥/¥

Arty interiors with sculpture, painting, images, and an art director intent on making the place into a hot destination gives this place a happening sense of cool. Interesting items like couture mouton coats, patchwork jackets, Kenji Ikeda bags, sweaters with a difference, and ankle-high boots with eye-catching lasts might not be the next great things, but the shop offers some nice street looks at equally nice prices.

ADDITION ADELAIDE

MEN'S/WOMEN'S BOUTIQUE

4-19-8, Jingumae, Shibuya-ku, Tokyo
03-5786-0157
www.adelaide-addition.com/
🕐 11:00–20:00
🗓 Not fixed
📍 MAP 5-1   ¥/¥/¥-¥/¥/¥/¥

It's refreshing to see a shop that prides itself on showcasing fashion from unique young mode designers. The men's clothes are where your money should go—look for tailored jersey fabric jackets worn with a chunky knit cardigan, skinny trousers and vests with tails in front. A mixture of trimmings keeps you thinking, like T-shirts adorned with blazer buttons or with shirt collars in satin. Black and night blue is in the shop's DNA and accessories almost always have sharp silhouettes.

ADELAIDE

MEN'S/WOMEN'S/
KID'S BOUTIQUE

3-6-7, Minami Aoyama, Minato-ku, Tokyo
03-5474-0157
www.adelaide-addition.com
🕐 11:00–20:00 (Sun/Hol. until 21:00)
🗓 2nd Sundays
📍 MAP 1-4   ¥/¥

Adelaide means gorgeous avant-garde clothes for men, women, and kids where both style greats and young fashion renegades show their stuff in a super chic arty environment. Fashion leaders Balenciaga clothes and bags for both men and women, along with Lanvin, Rick Owens and Raf Simons. A heady collection of jeans and separates from Intoxica, Wendy&Jim and As Four. A nice collection from Japanese labels Toga and Sacai help establish this shop as the prime venue for the best looks hot off the catwalk. The kids collection from labels like Levi's kids, re-makes from designer Clover, and Richard Kidd is equally elitist and terribly cute. And finally, a small corner upstairs is home to the choicest collection of cosmetics and fragrances, such as Dr Hauschka and Jacques Garcia. This shop will get you approval even from the most sharp-eyed trend hawks.

ADIDAS ORIGINALS

MEN'S/WOMEN'S SPORTS-WEAR/SHOES

Cat Street, 6-14-7 Jingumae, Shibuya-ku, Tokyo (Others)
03-5464-5580
www.adidas.com
🕐 12:00–20:00
📅 Not fixed
📍 MAP 6-2   ¥|¥

Adolph Dassler created this brand way back in 1924, and in this squeaky clean faux-vintage pad you are privy to all that adidas history in a contemporary neon, metallic and sportswear-is-the-hippest-thing-in-the-world vibe. There are Stan Smiths, Halfshells, and Superstar sneakers in many color combinations and training tops, pants, logos and Ts all with the trefoil logo circa 1972. Spring/Summer 2007 saw the Sleek series, a cute, girly collection of sportswear designed by French street artist Fafi especially for Fafinettes (cute, sexy free-thinking girls) while the men get Ali by Adidas, a range of great leisure wear emblazoned with Ali's quotes. If you really want to stick with the more historical offerings then go for the late 60s-style retro sneaker called "Tokyo for Ladies," or the remake of the Stan Smith "Hailet" for men.

ADIDAS PERFORMANCE CENTRE

MEN'S/WOMEN'S SPORTS-WEAR/SHOES

1-19-5, Minami Ikebukuro, Toshima-ku, Tokyo (Others)
03-5960-1300
www.adidas.com
🕐 11:00–20:30
📅 Not fixed
📍 MAP 17-1   ¥|¥

Adidas turns your gym into the hottest catwalk in town. With Stella McCartney's riveting pieces, you can throw away your old tracksuit and trade up to her co-branded collection with this sports wear giant. Girly hoodies for running in a body hugging style with puff sleeves, crimson shorts with multi-colored tank-tops all in a very light breathable fabric. And, at last, a great winter sport collection and exciting swimwear with the right mix of sporty and sexy. Apart from McCartney's collection you can also jump up and down over the infinite array of classic Adidas.

ADORE

WOMEN'S BOUTIQUE

Roppongi Hills West Walk 2F, 6-10-1, Roppongi, Minato-ku, Tokyo (Others)
03-3475-5915
www.sanei.net/brands/adr.php
🕐 11:00–21:00
📅 No holidays
📍 MAP 12-1   ¥|¥-¥|¥|¥

This is a Japanese high street label that feeds the voracious appetites of young Japanese women with whatever is the latest trend of the moment. Whatever the season, the shop stocks dresses in the newest silhouettes. These few seasons see Hitchcock silhouettes with classic feminine details—simple, but luxurious. The first blossoming of spring sees minimal coats with clever design details. A shop like this would, of course, not be complete without the latest styling craze—a range of leggings to be combined with tunic tops.

ADORNOR
WOMEN'S BOUTIQUE

6-28-6 Jingumae, Shibuya-ku, Tokyo
03-5464-7026
www.b6-web.jp
⊙ 11:00–21:00
▦ Not fixed
⌐ MAP 6-3   ¥|¥|¥

The shop from outside is absolutely devoid of any exhibitionist streak but if you are prepared to go the extra mile and step in, you'll immediately notice a pretty collection of the more unique designs from Manolo Blahnik and Casadei shoes. Every season the buyers here select only those models that you will not find elsewhere. The clothes too are pretty, with a tailored quality, and are an interesting mix from preppy to boho to schoolgirl-crossed-with-biker-girl trousers and jeans. Utterly charming, quite contemporary, but don't expect anything groundbreaking.

AFTERNOON TEA
INTERIOR/WOMEN'S BOUTIQUE

1-8-7 Jiyugaoka, Meguro-ku,
   Tokyo (Others)
03-3717-7009
www.afternoon-tea.net
⊙ 11:00–20:00
▦ No holidays
⌐ MAP 11-1   ¥|¥

Afternoon Tea is so famous among Tokyo girls that one could imagine a shop full of cult products. In reality, it is just full of everyday things Tokyo girls love—pretty floral ideas for the house, like matching bath towels, French soaps, sweet-smelling cosmetics, lacy peignoirs, cardigans, dresses, and a neat selection of bags, including the French label Le Tanneur.

AGITO
INTERIOR

Roppongi Hills West Walk 2/3F, 6-10-3
   Roppongi, Minato-ku, Tokyo
03-5770-4411
www.agito-web.com/
⊙ 11:00–21:00
▦ Not fixed
⌐ MAP 12-2   ¥|¥|¥-¥|¥|¥

Agito offers hot design at even hotter prices. The shop stocks some really exquisite furniture, lamps, interior and fabrics—things you would want at any price. Take, for example, the world's finest artificial flowers by Herve Gambs or Sweden's Bookbinders Design, the world's most desired handmade notebooks and albums. There is also an extensive range of the cult fragrance Diptyque and George Fedon's smart gentlemanly leather items, including visiting card cases—an absolute must for all those who inhabit (or visit) this island. And check out the space-age metallic design of the Danish design group Stelton, and their matching USB memory sticks, money clips and card cases. Your dogs too will look particularly good on handmade dog beds from Bow Wow. The shop is a crash course on successful haute living.

AGNÈS B
MEN'S/WOMEN'S DESIGNER

5-7-25 Minami Aoyama, Minato-ku, Tokyo (Others)
03-3797-6830
www.agnesb.com
🕐 11:00–20:00
📅 No holidays
🎵 MAP 1-5 ¥|¥|¥

Agnès b's zenith might have passed, but people addicted to the basics can't just shrug her off. She continues to dress women in her simple modern creations of cardigans, hats, handbags, scarves, shirts, black pants, and jackets that complement each other very well. This wonderfully designed airy store often plays host to artist collaborations and adds excitement and a contemporary buzz to the collections.

AGNÈS B HOMME
MEN'S

5-7-25 Minami-Aoyama, Minato-ku, Tokyo
03-3797-6830
www.agnesb.com
🕐 11:00–20:00
📅 Not fixed
🎵 MAP 1-6 ¥|¥|¥

With agnès b homme, urbane men can quickly add touches of television anchorman elegance in a Parisian, red-wine drinking, skinny silhouette way. Black suits, starched white stretch shirts, jeans, trainers, and leather accessories for both day and night—looks that work best when your preferred mode of transport is, say, a Vespa.

AGNÈS B VOYAGE
MEN'S/WOMEN'S ACCESSORIES

6-3-10 Jingumae, Shibuya-ku, Tokyo (Others)
03-5485-1400
www.agnesb.com
🕐 10:00–20:00
📅 Not fixed
🎵 MAP 6-4 ¥|¥|¥

Minimalists on the go should consider agnès b's affordable, sophisticated luggage. Her understated nylon bags and leather accessories are unfussy- ideal for low-key jet setters—and have taken on a new funky arty image with *bon voyage* logos and pastel colours. But the basics are still around (on the top floor), including trolleys in slate with matching zipper totes. These user-friendly items are logo-free and perfect for frustrating the efforts of the most criminal baggage handlers.

AGOSTO

WOMEN'S BOUTIQUE

Agio 2F, 3-3-12, Ebisu Minami, Shibuya-ku,
    Tokyo (Others)
03-3760-6171
www.agosto.co.jp/
⊘ 11:00–20:00
▦ Not fixed
⌐ MAP 2-2   ¥|¥|¥-¥|¥|¥

Agosto is a fabulously cozy boutique painted in red which sells collections best described as avant-garde chic in super-mode style. These include shirt jackets with big balloon collars, short linen bomber jackets with wool sleeves and lapels, and knits in a wrap-around style. Also stocks London label Preen's latest collection and menswear from Jean Pierre Braganza. Most items are washed out or enzyme processed for a used look. Accessories follow similar patterns, with no beads or anything dainty, but a lot of leather, metal, and chain. To finish off the look, there is also an excellent collection of elegant handmade shoes in lizard and crocodile by designer Joanna O.

AI BY ATSUKO IGA

WOMEN'S ACCESSORIES

Roppongi Hills Hill Side B1F, 6-10-1
    Roppongi, Minato-ku, Tokyo
03-5786-7765
www.zero-rei.jp
⊘ 11:00–20:00
▦ No holidays
⌐ MAP 12-3   ¥|¥

In Atsuko Iga's creations, relationships are at the forefront: all her bags are inspired by her family. This shop does tend to exude warmth and a homely atmosphere, and if you have long been look-ing for something that is fun and inexpensive, you'll be delighted to find a huge collection of bags hanging from every empty space. Leather Bostons, slouchy bags in soft calf skin in greens, reds and blues, totes in woody colors and leather mesh, simple A4-sized business bags in many colors, leather and python shoulder com-binations, along with croco embossing and lots of vintage looks and canvas numbers. Her own line, called Essence of Poison, is more like a cute comedy—with monkey, dog, hare, and cat motifs on pouches, mini totes, and round Bostons. Loads of gift ideas are available too, like the Meaow Boston with a cat's face drawn on the side that make great gifts.

AIGLE

MEN'S/WOMEN'S ACCESSORIES

6-27-8 Jingumae, Shibuya-ku,
    Tokyo (Others)
03-3797-4817
www.aigle.co.jp/
⊘ 11:00–20:00
▦ Not fixed
⌐ MAP 6-5   ¥|¥|¥

They've been outfitting the outdoorsy, wholesome types among us for decades and kitting out the whole family for any adventure under the sun, including yachting and riding. Aigle Japan has spe-cially designed all its gear for the Japanese outdoors—with patented inventions like the ultra quick-drying Dacron QD T-shirts, for conquering the super humid Japanese summers. But if *your* idea of outdoors is just a trip to the neighborhood park in the rain, this 150-year-old company still makes the most fashion-friendly rubber boots in bold colors and foliage prints.

AINZ TULPE
DRUGSTORE

1-13-14 Jingumae, Shibuya-ku, Tokyo (Others)
03-5775-0561
⊘ 11:00—23:00
▦ Not fixed
↑ MAP 5-2   ¥|¥

This ritzy drugstore, filled with bath, beauty and healthcare products, has a cult following in Tokyo. If you are looking for a favorite product and can't find it anywhere else, chances that you'll find it here are extremely high. Products from Neutrogena, anti-cellulite bath salts, and soya-based hair remover cream are particularly great buys. Or—if you have time for just one thing—get the ultra-long eyelash mascara from Shiseido. There's a great variety of products to combat sore feet and incredible massage goods too.

AKRIS
WOMEN'S BOUTIQUE

Imperial Hotel Plaza 3F, 1-1-1 Uchisaiwaicho, Chiyoda-ku, Tokyo
03-3501-2205
www.akris.ch
⊘ 11:00—20:00
▦ No holidays
↑ MAP 4-1   ¥|¥|¥-¥|¥|¥|¥

Extremely conservative but perfectly tailored, as can only be expected of this Swiss luxury label, Akris is best at skirt suits, trouser suits and of late some very chunky knits born at the hands of designer Albert Kriemler. Almost always on the right side of conservative, these expensive suits are favored by socialite ladies in their 50s and 60s; upwardly mobile career women love to pair their jackets with more avant garde skirts, or their perfect trousers with shirts from elsewhere. The 07/08 autumn/winter collection employed leather, chiffon, double-faced cashmere, and some new textiles specially created for the brand for luxe layered looks.

ALAIN FIGARET
MEN'S/WOMEN'S DESIGNER

1-10-1 Yurakucho, Chiyoda-ku, Tokyo (Others)
03-5220-4702
www.alain-figaret.fr
⊘ 11:00—20:00 (Sat/Sun/Hol until 21:00)
▦ No holidays
↑ MAP 7-1   ¥|¥|¥|¥

Alain Figaret brings French luxury tailoring to your shirt collection. Stock up on luxury ready-made business and dress shirts that come with button-down, French, or spread collars, French button hole or standard barrel cuffs, and different sleeve lengths in sizes 37-43 (some designs even come in size 44). Even though the shop is justifiably proud of its excellent range of fabrics, it is the pure cotton that they do best. You will always find colors in a wide palette, including the subtle grey (a true shirtmaker always carries this color whatever the trend or season). There's also a range of matching ties, pocket squares, cuff links and PJs—and a neat range of women's shirts too.

ALAIN MIKLI
MEN'S/WOMEN'S EYEWEAR

T-Place 101, 5-5-25 Minami-Aoyama,
   Minato-ku, Tokyo (Others)
03-5485-1921
www.mikli.fr/
🕐 11:00–20:00
🗓 Not fixed
🔗 MAP 1-7   ¥¥¥-¥¥¥¥

Legendary eyewear from France, known for its precision manufacturing. Each of these frames is crafted by hand and takes up to six months or more to make. Expert in the art of shaping acetate, all the frames are scented with pine cones: a secret method passed from generation to generation. Alain Mikli frames come in a range of colors to suit every personality and feature gravity-defying designs at the temples. Alain Mikli's association with Alux gives you frames with a perfect fit, twice as light as titanium, and a solid one-piece front with bioprotected and polarized lenses for haute protection from the sun.

ALBA ROSA
WOMEN'S BOUTIQUE

6-29-10 Jingumae, Shibuya-ku,
   Tokyo (Others)
03-3498-6333
albarosa-japan.com/
🕐 11:00–20:00
🗓 No holidays
🔗 MAP 6-6   ¥¥

This brand was originally a style phenomenon worn only by the peroxide-hair-and-dark-tan *gyaru* once ubiquitous in Shibuya. The girls grew up, and so did the brand. Now the average Tokyo teenager is in love again with Alba Rosa's posher reincarnation as a celeb-resort-style brand with hibiscus motif, fluorescent colors, and palm-frond wraparound dresses, shirts, T-shirts, shorts, and pants, all eminently suitable for taking the plunge or rocking the boat.

ALBERTA FERRETTI
WOMEN'S DESIGNER

5-16-2 Minami Aoyama, Minato-ku,
   Tokyo (Others)
03-5464-3131
www.sannfreres.co.jp/brands/ALBERTA/
🕐 11:00–20:00
🗓 No holidays
🔗 MAP 1-8   ¥¥¥¥

A Ferretti dress features lavish girly frills and beading for the ultimate in feminine style. Season after season, Ferretti puts forth charmeuse and empire-waisted dresses, draped and ruched in silks, satins and chiffons, incorporating styling details such as long sleeves and tunic silhouettes to keep the looks modern. Crystals peeping from underneath layers of fabric and chiffon floating around the shoulders add to the appeal. With a little help from lingerie and fishnets, something from the selection of frocks at this modest store could really give your evenings an instant new twist.

ALESSI

INTERIOR

3-2-5 Kita-Aoyama, Minato-ku, Tokyo
03-5770-3500
www.cassina-ixc.jp/
🕐 11:00–19:30
🗓 Not fixed
🚇 MAP 16-1   ¥|¥|¥

Top design at pop prices is Alessi's claim, but it is more about pop colors at hot prices. With bar and wine accessories, kitchenware, tableware, electrical appliances, and other sculptural items for the house, Alessi, in their heyday, were in every design lover's home. Their hot sellers are all still sold here: from the Philippe Starck-designed citrus squeezer to the doll-like chrome corkscrew called Anna G. Many design greats have collaborated with Alessi: here you'll find Achille Castiglioni's spiral ashtray and Ettore Sottsass cutlery. While the service is at best dreary and the cafe above should be given a pass, for Alessophiles in town no other place offers a better range.

ALEXANDRE HERCHCOVITCH

WOMEN'S DESIGNER

25-8 Sarugaku-cho, Shibuya-ku, Tokyo
03-3463-1027
www2.uol.com.br/herchcovitch
🕐 12:00–20:00
🗓 Not fixed
🚇 MAP 2-3   ¥|¥|¥-¥|¥|¥|¥

Brazilian designer Alexandre Herchcovitch is the star of the San Paolo fashion week and the Paris pret-a-porter collections for his genius with latex. While rubber skirts and tops are not highly practical ideas for day-to-day wear, his floral themes in natural fabrics with exquisite silhouettes and high waists, sleeveless tops, and tiered frills on skirts, feel like a feast in the Amazonian forest with a free-spirited touch of dressy glamor. The shop also stocks his exclusive collection of jeans. He is involved with the construction of his skinny fit jeans even at the weaving stage, and they are only sold at two shops around the world. Look out also for Herchcovitch's collaboration with British stylist Judy Blame that offers pretty clothes with prints to recharge your wardrobe.

ALFREDO BANNISTER

MEN'S/WOMEN'S SHOES

20-9 Sarugakucho, Shibuya-ku,
Tokyo (Others)
03-5458-5010
www.abahouse.co.jp/
🕐 11:00–20:00
🗓 No holidays
🚇 MAP 2-4   ¥|¥

A made-in-Japan brand of shoes—which means that the quality you get here for the price is great. Party types come here for the men's shoes, such as the *hinomaki guruguru* that you tie around the foot and not the ankle, the sneakers that come with a leather sole, co-respondents in great combinations, and also formal shoes in beige, camel and black. They also make a neat pair of men's knee-high boots that are great for wearing over pants. Some items need to be reserved in advance and other stock sells out as soon as it hits the shelves, so regular visits are a must. Women will find asymmetrically designed shoes and pumps in polka dots or lace that could be lovingly garnished with one of the accessories on sale, such as the flower clip-ons in leather that double as brooches. Women's stuff does take a backseat though, as it is the men's shoes here that are the most interesting in town.

ALLUREVILLE
WOMEN'S BOUTIQUE

Shinjuku Flags 3F, 3-37-1 Shinjuku,
    Shinjuku-ku, Tokyo
03-3225-6088
www.sazaby-league.co.jp/
🕐 11:00–22:00
🗓 No holidays
📍 MAP 9-2   ¥|¥-¥|¥|¥

Allureville's collections for women have a slightly masculine flavor and are unlikely to go out of fashion quickly. Most pieces are the shop's own labels, but you can also find some painstakingly selected imports from Europe, the best of which is the biker brand Belstaff whose diehard series of waterproof jackets is adored by movie rebels and revolutionaries like Brando, Che Guevara, T.E. Lawrence, et al. Great jeans from Cloud Nine and a couple of vintage items thrown in with the right balance of fur, classic sport, and British trad for jackets, shirts and pants coordinates are also sold here. Ageless with a free spirit, the shop keeps dishing out regular winners with the city's style-conscious crowd.

ALTERNATIVE VERSION WR
WOMEN'S BOUTIQUE

3-7-6 Ebisu, Shibuya-ku, Tokyo
03-5724-4511
none
🕐 12:00–20:00
🗓 Not fixed
📍 MAP 10-1   ¥|¥-¥|¥|¥

A fun shop from hard-knock label WR. It's difficult to describe the collections here, as they are shamelessly trendy and precisely what you want. In their own words, the stylists of the shop select only those clothes that designers want to design, buyers want to buy, and the city's girls want to wear now. Things change fast and everything seems like a sample. So these days you'll find extra narrow leggings and all the bold new shapes everyone wants to wear: bell coats, balloon pants, bustles and A-lines with big floating skirts and high snug bodices. Dresses, skirts, jackets, and pants with matching pumps in many colors, and at very reasonable prices. The colors for the moment remain natural and streetwise but would change immediately if the fashion winds blow the other way.

AMADANA

INTERIOR

Omotesando Hills Main Bldg. B3F, 4-12-10 Jingumae, Shibuya-ku, Tokyo
03-3408-2018
www.amadana.com/
🕐 10:00–21:00
🗓 Not fixed
MAP 5-3   ¥¥-¥¥¥

Smooth, slinky, minimal and luxurious. You think lingerie, but we mean Amadana—a brand of elite consumer electronics products that adorn Tokyo's choicest homes. Amadana in downtown Tokyo was an area that specialized in lacquer crafts. Inspired by a tradition of the very best minimal design, Amadana's designer Shuwa Tei unleashes a new school of electronics. Apart from the much fêted sleek bamboo headphones, those with an interior fetish can also take home items like Amadana's toasters that come with a walnut handle, DVD players with surround sound, stylish massage chairs, chocolate colored calculators, neat acrylic weighing machines, deluxe stereos, and walnut telephones.

AMERICAN APPAREL

MEN'S/WOMEN'S CASUAL

15-5 Hachiyamacho, Shibuya-ku, Tokyo
03-3464-1880
www.americanapparel.net/
🕐 Mon–Fri/12:00–21:00 Sat/11:00–22:00 Sun/12:00–20:00
🗓 Not fixed
MAP 2-5   ¥

Straight from downtown LA, this explosive brand is cheap, fun, and famously sweat-shop- and logo-free. If it's style you are looking for, this is not the shop for you. But the slim fitting tracksuits with white piping, plain T-shirts, zipped jackets, head bands, striped leg warmers, hot pants, and basically everything you need for lounging around can be found here at amazingly cheap prices. If you don't feel like going shopping, there's a fine online store, and everything can be delivered to your home.

AMERICAN RAG CIE

MEN'S/WOMEN'S BOUTIQUE

5-8-3 Minami-Aoyama, Minato-ku, Tokyo (Others)
03-5766-8739
www.americanragcie.co.jp
🕐 11:00–20:00
🗓 Not fixed
MAP 1-9   ¥¥-¥¥¥

To the uninitiated, this shop seems confusing—with Chloé, crockery, and candles all under one roof. In reality, this is the latest Tokyo trend, where your house, too, gets accessorized with glam goods, like a huge collection of Diptyque aromas in candles and room sprays, collector porcelain from Fornasetti, orient-inspired porcelain tea sets from Parisienne Martine Goron and reasonable safari Hermès inspired crockery. By the way, that's all meant to go with your Allessandro Dell'Acqua suits, Chloé bags and Louboutin shoes. Even accessories for the iPod are not left behind, so check out the bespoke Swarovski cases. Strangely zeitgeist defining.

AND A
MEN'S/WOMEN'S BOUTIQUE

3-6-19 Kita-Aoyama, Minato-ku,
Tokyo (Others)
03-5774-1505
www.and-a.com/
🕐 11:00–20:00
📅 Not fixed
📍 MAP 6-7

¥¥

Clubbing clothes for a club-going clientele, spread over two beautiful large and extravagant floors. Hushed lighting and a floor lit from below further adds to the shopping-is-a-party vibe. Perfect for the trendy, relaxed, über-urban androgynous lifestyle, the And A label has streetwear in cool colors, ideal for lounging around or biking all over town, a nice collection of sneakers, plus a superb magazine and CD selection.

ANGE
MATERNITY

2-32-3 Jingumae, Shibuya-ku, Tokyo
03-3796-1103
www.shop-ange.com/
🕐 11:00–19:00
📅 Not fixed
📍 MAP 5-4

¥¥-¥¥¥

Ange provides chic for pregnant women in all sizes. Jeans and shorts are what they do best, with stretch elastic bands to fit all midriffs. Their wraparound dresses and simple front-opening coats can be worn well at work and at parties, and come summer the whole collection becomes flirty with cotton and lace. The upper floor stacks underwear in all sizes and while the shop might lack the glam of some other boutiques its reasonable prices, constant sale offerings and pretty collections have made it a haunt for fashionable mums-to-be.

ANGELICO PERRO
VINTAGE

Kurashima Bldg. 2F, 2-3-8, Shibuya-ku,
Tokyo
03-3499-7661
www.angelicoperro.com/
Monday–Friday 11:00–21:00, Saturdays
🕐 13:00–22:00
📅 Not fixed
📍 MAP 8-5

¥¥-¥¥¥

The renaissance of 60s design that began a couple of years ago shows no signs of abating, and in this shop you understand why. The owners collect retro one-off pieces—lamps, jewelry, accessories, and unbelievably cheap, stylish clothes. Check out the Mondrian-inspired clutches, early Pucci dresses, vintage Armani sunglasses, and lamps, lamps and more lamps, from the 40s onwards. The accessories collection in plastic, exotic leather, and chains is definitely worth the price. Suits every occasion from Halloween to housewarming.

ANNA SUI

WOMEN'S DESIGNER

1F Garden Terrace, 6-1-4 Jingumae,
Shibuya-ku, Tokyo
03-3486-1177
www.annasui.com
🕐 11:00–20:00
📅 No holidays
📍 MAP 6-8 ¥|¥|¥-¥|¥|¥|¥

Having been inspired by Coco Chanel and having inspired designers like Marc Jacobs, Sui continues to thrill with her baby doll dresses, skirts layered with crocheted pieces, great coats and even better lingerie and stockings with lots of purple and pink. Think 60s and 70s rock'n roll, punk, and grunge combined with role-play favorites. Her hot-selling killer "redder than red" nail polish and cult make-up are sold here too—a favorite of all Japanese stars (not to mention Madonna and Britney).

ANN DEMEULEMEESTER

MEN'S/WOMEN'S DESIGNER

Omotesando Hills Main 1F, 4-12-10
Jingumae, Shibuya-ku, Tokyo
03-6279-5071
None
🕐 11:00–21:00 (Sundays until 20:00)
📅 Not fixed
📍 MAP 5-5 ¥|¥|¥|¥

If Tokyo ever gets to cast a vote on its all-time favorite designers, the Belgians led by Ann Demeulemeester would definitely be in the top five. This tiny shop (serviced by excellent Ann Demeulemeester clones) features her classic deconstructed and minimalist looks. Lots of stressed leather in biker's coats, slouchy masculine tailoring for women, and chunky knitwear. Feminine pieces like mini frock coats and beautiful skirts have also been making their way into her collection of late, and she is adept at making black come alive with volume, movement, and layering. The same deconstructed looks are translated into men's wear, with low slung trousers stuffed into boots for wearing with, say, a short black coat with silk lapels sometimes trimmed with ribbons or feathers.

ANNE FONTAINE

WOMEN'S DESIGNER

3-18-14 Minami Aoyama, Minato-ku,
Tokyo
03-3797-9717
www.annefontaine.com/
🕐 11:00–20:00
📅 No holidays
📍 MAP 1-10 ¥|¥|¥-¥|¥|¥

This is a great label for many reasons, and one is that you're never distracted by housewares or perfumes. They stick to what they know best—the essential white shirt, and only for women. With the most flattering feminine cut, cinched waist decorated with ruffles, rosettes, epaulettes, or big collars, the shirts are perfectly suited for absolutely any occasion from dawn to dusk. The ones with more character fit like corsets and have plunging necklines. While the white shirt is still her forte, Anne is also adept with black ones and, of late, denim shirts that, amazingly, look as formal as the white. For the holidays, try the baby-doll tops and stunning black halter neckpieces.

ANNE KLEIN
WOMEN'S DESIGNER

Mullion Bldg. 2-5-1 Yurakucho,
  Chiyoda-ku, Tokyo (Others)
03-3575-2233
www.anneklein.com/
⊘ Mon/Tue/Sat 11:00–20:00. Wed/
Thu/Fri.11:00–21:00.Sun/Hol 11:00–
20:00
▦ Not fixed
⌐ MAP 3-1   ¥¦¥¦¥-¥¦¥¦¥¦¥

Quintessential American dressing that doesn't grab the headlines but is all about elegance and subtle quality, which never goes off the trend charts. Even so, Anne Klein has managed to get a lot more drama into the boardroom than ever before, with her hourglass silhouettes, drainpipe trouser suits, dresses with capelets and high cinched waists. Colors, though, remain very classic, in greys, blacks, reds, and whites, with ultra-feminine, soft styling.

ANTE BUENOS AIRES
WOMEN'S BOUTIQUE

Lumine Est B2F, 3-38-1 Shinjuku,
  Shinjuku-ku, Tokyo
03-3341-1827
www.ante-buenosaires-hpfrance.com/
⊘ 11:00–10:00 (Sat/Sun/Holidays
  opens from 10:00)
▦ No holidays
⌐ MAP 9-3   ¥¦¥¦¥

Ante Buenos Aires, brainchild of HP France's super creative team, is meant to showcase all that is hot off the hangers from Buenos Aires. The spotlight is expectedly on Tramando's futuristic fabric creations but a few meters in the lead aesthetically are the beautiful creations of Viviana Uchitel. Once upon a time, Buenos Aires had the world's best living standards and a healthy number of aristos who kept the fire for fashion burning, and Viviana's ethereal creations—half accessories, half clothes in chiffon and bronze colored chains—hark back to this era. She couldn't be more different than Nadine Zlotogora, who uses animal motifs and cartoons to create clothes in eye-popping colors and, sometimes, in mother-and-child combos. Pesqueira sexes up polka dots and sailor stripes in whimsical skirts, wraparound tops, and stringtops. And the collections with the plant motifs and portraits are bound to be traffic stoppers. Lastly, this whole trip to Buenos Aires wouldn't be complete without Argentinian lingerie in candylicious colors with psychedelic lace from Juana de Arco.

ANTEPRIMA
WOMEN'S DESIGNER

5-4-41 Minami Aoyama, Minato-ku,
  Tokyo (Others)
03-5468-3547
www.anteprima.com/
⊘ 11:00–20:00 (Sat/Sun/Hol until
  21:00)
▦ No holidays
⌐ MAP 1-11   ¥¦¥¦¥-¥¦¥¦¥¦¥

Anteprima Designer Izumi Ogino's label takes Japanese minimalism and marries it to Italian taste. The result can only be superbly tailored unfussy luxury knits, dresses, and elegant sweater set combinations that gracefully float around the body. Perfect for work or play, the color palette varies from chocolate to beige, and goes extremely well with her accessories, bags, clutches, and shoes. The shop here stocks Anteprima's Plastiq range of fun wire accessories (handwoven by men) that come in bags of all sizes, pouches, belts, brooches, and key chain forms. While this shop stocks her entire collection, the shop in Ginza is dedicated only to the riotous Anteprima Plastiq accessories collection.

ANTIK BATIK
WOMEN'S/KIDS BOUTIQUE

3-8-18 Kita-Aoyama, Minato-ku, Tokyo (Others)
03-5766-6701
www.antik-batik.jp/
🕐 11:00–20:00
📅 Not fixed
🎵 MAP 6-9   ¥|¥|¥-¥|¥|¥|¥

While the prices here are fractionally higher than back in the label's hometown Paris, the shop is a must for all those who love their statuesque clothes, embroidered kaftans, skirts, gypsy tops and party bags that whisk you away on a luxury trip to India, Pakistan, Morocco, Mexico and other distant shores. There is enough gear for It-children too and if the boho clothes are not your thing, stick to their logo-free beaded bags and pretty clutches. Definitely a must for the wardrobe of every spirited girl in town.

ANTITESI
WOMEN'S ACCESSORIES

5-11-25 Minami-Aoyama, Minato-ku, Tokyo
03-6419-9663
none
🕐 11:00–20:00
📅 No holidays
🎵 MAP 1-12   ¥|¥-¥|¥|¥

If you'd prefer a classic, good bag over an ubiquitious status tote, it's worth exploring the range of carry-alls in one of Tokyo's premier boutiques for mostly Italian (brand) bags. Inspired choices include roomy bags from the fifty-year-old Venetian Plinio Visona, superb messengers for people in motion by David and Scotti, and sweet little somethings from Antitesi's own factory, in beautiful materials and in all sizes, shapes, and prices.

ANYA HINDMARCH
WOMEN'S BOUTIQUE

4-3-11 Ginza, Chuo-ku, Tokyo
03-3567-8677
www.anyahindmarch.com
🕐 11:00–20:00
📅 No holidays
🎵 MAP 3-2   ¥|¥|¥-¥|¥|¥|¥

Classic and chic, this shop recreates the designer's London boutique with accessories, clothes and shoes. Anya is Brit with a Firenze education, which means that whatever she does is fun and functional with a lot of humor and detailing. Most of the bags are classic in taste, never frighteningly sleek but often shiny for a touch of glam. The Bespoke Ebury is where your money should go if you want a day bag, with your own personal handwritten message and name on the inside as decoration if you so desire. Their series of white Bostons are hypnotic and there are many sizzling options for the evening that include golden and silver party clutch bags, and the art deco inspired tote Jasmin.

APART BY LOWRYS
WOMEN'S BOUTIQUE

8-9 Sarugaku-cho, Shibuya-ku, Tokyo (Others)
03-3780-3181
www.apartbylowrys.jp/
⊙ 11:00–20:00
▦ No holidays
⌁ MAP 2-6

¥¥-¥¥¥

French gamine essentials at Made-in-China prices. Apart by Lowry's tries to bring you a slice of Paris style, with knit cardigans, blouses, skirts, mufflers, layered cut and sewn tops, suspender pants, neckwarmers, trench coats, and lots of other simple basics for the days that you don't want to stand out from the crowd. What it might lack in quality it makes up with the prices and spacious wooden décor.

A.P.C.
MEN'S/WOMEN'S BOUTIQUE

11-9 Sarugaku-cho, Shibuya-ku, Tokyo (Others)
03-3496-7570
www.apcjp.com
⊙ 11:00–20:00
▦ Not fixed
⌁ MAP 2-7

¥¥¥

Designer Jean Toitou had the brilliant idea of using old military uniforms and turning them into shirts, trousers, and other highly coveted items that combine street and art-film intellectual styles. Since then, the aptly named Atelier de Production et Creation has built a cult following among mostly arty people who love his style for its nonchalance and great prices. Women can always find beautiful tops in natural fabrics, woolen dresses, basic cashmere sweaters, skirts, and a range of city-friendly shoes. The mens collection has all the basics, including business suits, and true denim lovers will zero in on killer jeans famed for their fit and stressed wash. This shop also stocks actor/designer Waris Ahluwalia's exquisite silver creations in the form of dagger pendants, charms, and fine lapel pins in silver and gold from his label House of Waris.

APOC

WOMEN'S DESIGNER

3-17-14, Minami Aoyama, Minato-ku, Tokyo
03-5770-4500
None
🕐 11:00–20:00
📅 Not fixed
📍 MAP 1-13   ¥|¥|¥-¥|¥|¥|¥

Even though Issey Miyake has handed over the reins of his other brands to apprentices, he still keeps a hands-on approach here. A Piece of Cloth has been revolutionary in garment technology, with their garments cut from tubes of material. Now part of a permanent MOMA exhibit, the clothes here do seem more like collectors' items than fashion produce. The basic deal is that you buy a tube of cloth, then cut it up in marked places, so it can be worn as a skirt, top, hat or bag—all from the same piece of fabric. Available in beautiful shades, often with gradations and prints, APOC has always snubbed trends but remains superbly creative at very reasonable prices.

APRICA

KIDS

18-8 Sarugaku-cho, Shibuya-ku, Tokyo
03-5728-8760
www.aprica.jp
🕐 11:00–19:00
📅 Closed Mondays
📍 MAP 2-8   ¥|¥|¥|¥

Babies who have been carried around in Aprica's super-stylish prams and car child seats are fashion icons before they can spell the word. Stylish mamas refuse to be seen without Aprica's hottest prams with chrome wheels, decorated this season in Russian military-style flaps and bonnets replete with gold military buttons, or the Royal Knot series with everything in extravagant, hand-woven beige lace. For the fast and furious parents, the bright Ferrari child seat available here is a great option. For those who just want to leave with something in hand from here grab their adorable organic cotton blankets and teddies.

AQUAGIRL

WOMEN'S BOUTIQUE

2-8 Sarugaku-cho, Shibuya-ku, Tokyo (Others)
03-5489-3492
www.aquagirl.ne.jp
🕐 12:00–20:00
📅 No holidays
📍 MAP 2-9   ¥|¥|¥-¥|¥|¥|¥

The Aquagirl is light, flirty, feminine, and always ready to party. Modern and classic at the same time, silver, whites, grays, and gold is what she chooses to sparkle in. The all-night-long look in Phillip Lim, Bruce, Gilles Rogier, 20,000,000 Fragments, Zariani, Sacai, Bluegirl, and Jovovich Hawk provide a sweet taste and a leader of the pack attitude. Celebrities and models love coming here not just for the collections but also their impeccable service where you can lounge around in their boudoir among plush sofas, fur carpet and a very slimming gilt mirror.

AQUAGIRL ON THE STREET
WOMEN'S BOUTIQUE

1-20-17 Jinnan, Shibuya-ku, Tokyo
03-3770-9372
aquagirl.ne.jp/
🕐 12:00–21:00
Not fixed
MAP 8-6   ¥|¥|¥-¥|¥|¥|¥

Aquagirl On The Street stocks diffusion lines from Chloé, Dress-camp, Kaon, Tei Jojima and others. The styling remains Aquagirl style which means really feminine with a bit of street attitude. The mood is clubby and very cool Tokyo.

AQUASCUTUM
MEN'S/WOMEN'S DESIGNER

1F Shin Tokyo Bldg., 3-3-1 Marunouchi,
   Chiyoda-ku, Tokyo (Others)
03-5224-3223
www.renown.com/aquascutum/
🕐 11:00–20:00 (Sun/holidays until
   19:00)
Not fixed
MAP 7-2   ¥|¥|¥|¥

Since 1851, their sexy trenchcoats have protected luminaries like Sophia Loren, Greta Garbo, Cary Grant, and Margaret Thatcher from wily weather. With their recent accessories collection, Aquascutum continues to make the world's most consistent umbrellas, scarves, and rain hats, as well as waterproof bags to keep you in style, rain or shine.

ARMANI CASA
INTERIOR

6-14-5 Jingumae, Shibuya-ku, Tokyo
03-3400-8821
www.hhstyle.com/
🕐 12:00–20:00
Not fixed
MAP 6-10   ¥|¥|¥|¥-¥|¥|¥|¥|¥

Since 2000, Armani has been dressing up houses with furniture, rugs, lighting, tableware, and many other desirable items, including cashmere bath gowns and leather beds. Every article is in classic Armani colors—black, beige, grey, and white, and the shop also offers total interior solutions in the event that money is no object. It's also a superb place for gifts: no one has ever been disappointed by Stars, the scented candle studded with Swarovski crystals, or Nettuno, the marble toothbrush holder, or the classic Caldura series of leather and silver notebooks. Houseware at its hautest, nestled in a building designed by top architect Tadao Ando.ARMANI

ARMANI JEANS
MEN'S/WOMEN'S DESIGNER

Roppongi Hills West Walk 2F, 6-10-
 3 Roppongi, Minato-ku, Tokyo (Others)
03-5786-9590
www.giorgioarmani.co.jp
⊘ 11:00–20:00
🗓 No holidays
𝕀 MAP 12-4   ¥|¥|¥

This outlet of the Milanese style giant stocks his jeans collections
for both men and women—but it's not just the jeans that has weekend shoppers filing in. Their collection of casuals, from shirts for
men to sexy T-shirt tops for women, or the occasional long dress
for parties, hot-colored down jackets, and a slouchy bag or two,
ensures that you won't leave the shop without an Armani weave.

ART-BERG DO
WOMEN'S ACCESSORIES

19–11 Daikanyama–cho, Shibuya–ku,
 Tokyo (Others)
03–5458–8986
www.art–berg.co.jp/
⊘ 11:30–20:00
🗓 No holidays
𝕀 MAP 2-10   ¥|¥

Art-Berg Do makes bags and shoes in original stressed leather and
fabric combinations in their own little studios in posh Daikanyama.
This means that they can also get away with cheeky copies of bags
straight from the catwalk. If you shop here, do leave with one of
their many variations of bananas, belt purses, or messengers. Definitely the neatest in the world, these stylish accessories will serve
you equally well whether traveling, shopping, or clubbing.

ARTEMIDE
INTERIOR

On-line shopping and delivery
03-3797-4400
www.artemide.com
                 ¥|¥|¥-¥|¥|¥|¥

Artemide makes multifaceted home lighting that does for your bed-
side what handmade shoes do for your feet. With all the functional
benefits of mass production and all the sculptural beauty that only
A-list product designers can provide, Artemide's products outper-
form any other lamps in the industry. The inverted tumbler shaped
Tolomeo desk lamp and conical Nestore are classic examples of this
style, as they come in the common shape of any table lamp, but
with cutting edge proportions and sleek chrome and other metal
combinations. Mushroom-shaped Nesso by Giancarlo Mallioli in
bright orange is enough to give any room an instant facelift. IBM
designer Richard Sapper's early 70s Tizio desk lamp is the Porsche
of home lighting, an original classic model that should be on
everyone's wish list. With a skeletal frame in dark metal that offers
adjustable angles of light diffused from a nifty little hood, this is
stuff you'd reach out for if your house caught fire. While Yamagiwa
in Akihabara would stock most of their better known lamps, for the
complete floor/wall/ceiling suspension ideas from Artemide, call
this number and have the lamps delivered to your home or office.

ARTH

MEN'S/WOMEN'S HATS

Roppongi Hills West Walk 4F, 6-10-3
Roppongi, Minato-ku, Tokyo
03-5772-1613
www.arth.cc
🕐 11:00–20:00
📅 No holidays
📍 MAP 12-5   ¥|¥|¥-¥|¥|¥|¥

When a ritzy hat shop comes to town (especially an accessory crazed town like Tokyo), all heads turn in the hope of finding something singularly sensational. From the best collection of borsalinos from the namesake label Borsalinos, to Overrides' toques and golf caps, a nice collection of wide-brimmed sun hats, military caps, simple sunhats and baker's boy hats to Philip Treacy's extravagant Ascot numbers (and some simpler denim ivy caps and linen Tyrolean hats), Arth lets your good looks go to your head.

ASH AND DIAMONDS

WOMEN'S BOUTIQUE

6-10-8 Jingumae, Shibuya-ku,
Tokyo (Others)
03-5464-9939
www.ashanddiamonds.com
🕐 11:00–20:00
📅 Not fixed
📍 MAP 6-11   ¥|¥-¥|¥|¥

This shop's kiss n' tell style collections may have you wondering whether to enter or buckle up and run. But, if it is any help, it does bling like nowhere else, so, if you have the courage, step in to be enveloped in a dizzying world of diamante and enamel leather. Ash and Diamonds' cigarette cases, bags, pouches, sunglasses, and chiffon clothes—sometimes in impossible combinations of fuschia, turquoise, emerald, gold and even yellow and hot pink—are loved by Tokyo's hot young things. Don't miss out on their best-selling items—diamante cigarette lighters and matching Frisk mint cover cases. For a watch that purrs sexy, the Patricia Field collaboration, a square watch with straps in light pink, orange, lime, turquoise and bronze is a must-have. Add a blond curtain hairstyle and a sky-high skirt, you're good to rock at the nightspots further down the street.

ATO

MEN'S/WOMEN'S DESIGNER

3-18-9 Minami-Aoyama, Minato-ku,
Tokyo
03-5474-1748
www.ato.jp/
🕐 11:00–20:00
📅 No holidays
📍 MAP 1-14   ¥|¥|¥-¥|¥|¥|¥

In a country where a designer's career tends to be shorter than the seasons, Ato has managed to stick around for more than a decade, making softly tailored romantic clothes for men and women. His colors remain simple and androgynous: black, brown gold and white with the neatest of silhouettes and clean modern lines. His trousers for men are made for all sizes with a perfect fit, neither too slim nor too broad and great for stuffing in boots or for wearing as part of a suit. His slim lapelled jackets make for one of the best designer deals in town. The women's collection is incredibly romantic without being "come hither," with fitted dresses with pocket details, tight mermaid skirts in soft hybrid luxe fabrics and tops with frills and polka dots. Ultra modern and refreshingly free of exhibitionist streaks, Ato's collections might be small in number but big on wearability and superb on price.

ATTIC
MEN'S/WOMEN'S BOUTIQUE

5-2-11 Minami Aoyama, Shibuya-ku, Tokyo
03-5485-1799
none
🕐 11:00–20:00
📅 Not fixed
📍 MAP 1-15   ¥|¥|¥

Stocks the largest collection from cheeky twins Dean and Dan Catena of Dsquared. While they started making clothes for men in 1994, it was only after launching the women's collection in 2003 that they grabbed the headlines. Christina Aguilera, Madonna, Naomi Campbell, Cameron Diaz, and other party animals love their super low jeans, leather pants and huge sweaters. Their more recent collections have surprised everyone with their surprising feminine coyness, flowers, and ladylike gloves, but whatever trick the twins have up their sleeves, their jeans, jackets, and T-shirts always score serious points on the trend barometer.

B'2ND
MEN'S/WOMEN'S BOUTIQUE

1-17-4 Jinnan, Shibuya-ku, Tokyo (Others)
03-3770-2921
www.b-2nd.com/
🕐 11:30–20:30
📅 No holidays
📍 MAP 8-7   ¥|¥|¥-¥|¥|¥|¥

A bijou of a shop that stays clear of cookie cutter looks. Peg-legged Taverniti So Jeans that can be worn with top of the line cashmere from Lucien Pellat-Finet or a Duvetica down. Neil Barret, Giles Rosier, Marani dresses that are sensual, polished and never standard. Collection Privee, which is, of course, the new ultimate in bags, home grown designer Lad Musician (famous as the Japanese Dior) and Mary Magdalene, well known for her street chic remakes that offer softness and an edgy look.

B&B ITALIA
INTERIOR

6-4-6 Minami-Aoyama, Minato-ku, Tokyo
03-5778-3540
www.bebitalia.it
🕐 11:00–19:00
📅 No holidays
📍 MAP 1-16   ¥|¥|¥

Luxury where less is more has always been B&B's credo and is exemplified in its block sofas, minimal beds, wooden dining tables with metal legs and perfectly ergonomical armchairs. The Bambolo '07 designed by Mario Bellini (a remake of the original 1970s model) is just one big cushion modeled into a sofa—could any sofa be more comfortable? Antonio Citterio's JJ chair with Mongolian fur upholstery goes a step further by adding humor to comfort. The brand ensures that every time one reclines on the latest from the bestselling Maxalto series or the Charles, George, Mart, and Marcel collections, they will be as creatively inspired as all the stellar designers who have left their mark on this shop's furniture.

BACCARAT
INTERIOR

3-1-1 Marunouchi, Chiyoda-ku, Tokyo (Others)
03-5223-8868
www.baccarat.fr/
🕐 Mon–Fri 10:00–20:00/Sat.11:00–20:00/Sun, Holidays 11:00–19:00
🗓 Not fixed
🚇 MAP 7-3   ¥|¥|¥

In 1816, Baccarat created its first crystal glass in the village of Baccarat, in the eastern French province of Lorraine, where it still produces all its crystal. Since then its products have graced the tables of princes, presidents, and just about everyone who can afford the world's finest crystal. Bar glasses, stemware, and jugs with classic flat cut sides and a sculptural appearance give any interior a palatial atmosphere. The most popular among these are the Massena stemware with their curved shape and extremely carved base, and the Philippe Starck series in iconic black. But Baccarat has added fun to its collections, with a range of crystal accessories often combined with gold. Cabochon rings and couqillage rings in crystal and precious metal, dangler crystal drops in amber, turquoise and grey, and pretty, heart-shaped pendants that are irresistibly charming to any woman and make great gifts.

BALI BARRET
MEN'S/WOMEN'S DESIGNER

1-4-8 Jinnan, Shibuya-ku, Tokyo (Others)
03-3462-4611
www.balibarret.co.jp/
🕐 11:30–20:00
🗓 Not fixed
🚇 MAP 8-8   ¥|¥|¥

From Paris to Tokyo with love—Bali Barret brings her ultra hip Parisienne style to Tokyo through her collections Paris 01 up to the latest, *Regarde Paris*. Decorated in her favorite color red, this shop is like an haute camping ground featuring tent walls and trunks strewn around the floor. The men's and women's collections are almost identical, with straight cuts and great detailing in monochromatic colors making it a brand that manages to look great, even if worn from head to toe. Add a pair of great quality lace-up shoes from Repetto and Michel Vivien, both also sold in the shop, and you can tap your way through the city's hot spots without making a serious dent in your bank balance.

BALLANTYNE
MEN'S/WOMEN'S BOUTIQUE

4-23-11 Minami Aoyama, Minato-ku, Tokyo (others)
03-5466-7711
www.ballantyne-net.com/
🕐 11:00–20:00
📅 3rd Wednesdays
🍴 MAP 1-17   ¥¥¥¥

Josef Frank's prints of brilliant foliage decorate the walls of this recently opened flagship store, perfectly complementing the colorful combinations of the world's finest cashmere knits by Massimo Alba. These perfect sweaters, with argyle and plaid patterns in peach, red, caramel, and gelato-colored cardigans with pink polka dots and flower motifs, were beloved of people like Jackie Kennedy, who often wore them when she went riding. Adoring Tokyo fans have been waxing lyrical about the new range of cashmere print T-shirts in the palest of greens and blues. With one of the largest collections in the world, this shop is a must visit for those who swear by tradition and authenticity in their fashion choices.

BALLY
MEN'S/WOMEN'S ACCESSORIES

5-4-7 Ginza, Chuo-ku, Tokyo (Others)
03-3573-8130
www.bally.com
🕐 11:00–20:00
📅 Not fixed
🍴 MAP 4-2   ¥¥¥¥

The legendary shoemaker from Switzerland is known as the purveyor of the most hardy, long-lasting, and least fashion-friendly shoe in town. In their übercool makeover they now do strappy open toe sandals and espadrilles in summer, plus flashy colorful pumps in winter. Men's shoes remain traditional, but the accessories and bags in leather with the trademark striped canvas strap are a must and offer an easy transition from informal to formal. As glam accessories designer Brian Atwood has been signed in as creative director, expect to see hotter looks—especially in leather boots.

BALS
INTERIOR

1-10-21 Nakameguro, Meguro-ku, Tokyo
03-5773-5500
www.balstokyo.com
🕐 11:00–21:00
📅 Not fixed
🍴 MAP 2-11   ¥¥¥¥

Fashionistas with dogs, stylish supplements, fresh oxygen and a hundred designer bicycles. That's Bals, Tokyo's largest one-stop shop for all lifestyle ideas. From the dog fashion at design f to the world's finest artificial flowers by French designer Herve Gambs and haute electronics from amadana, this is a level of good taste usually only seen on Conran videos or Martha Stewart. The prices are reasonable by Tokyo standards, and though weekends can get hectic, weekdays are quiet and offer the perfect environment in which to browse.

BANANA REPUBLIC

MEN'S/WOMEN'S BOUTIQUE

Roppongi Hills North Tower 3F, 6-2-31
Roppongi, Minato-ku, Tokyo (Others)
03-5412-6641
bananarepublic.co.jp/
🕐 11:00–21:00
🗓 Not fixed
🚶 MAP 12-6   ¥│¥│¥

Easy (read lazy) shopping with clothes arranged by occasion and in matching coordinates, Banana Republic's collections are known for comfort and wearability. A distinct safari feel pervades the spacious shop floor. Women tread the adventurous path with whites, khakis, neutral colors, chino pants, and summer jackets all simple, basic, and of excellent quality. The Japanese store shows its muscle in the men's department, winning over its American counterpart in accessories such as belts, ties, hats, wallets, and more.

BANG AND OLUFSEN

INTERIOR

6-13-15 Jingumae, Shibuya-ku, Tokyo
(Others)
03-5468-6537
www.bang-olufsen.com
🕐 11:30–20:00
🗓 No holidays
🚶 MAP 6-12   ¥│¥│¥│¥

If Artemide is the Porsche of lighting, Bang and Olufsen is definitely the Porsche of audio. This Danish company, which has been around for decades, suddenly rose to cult heights with their Beomaster 1200 receiver, popular for its precision of design and its welcome controls concealing state-of-the-art technology. Their Beosound 9000 CD player is likely the most consistent accessory in suites and luxe bachelor pads world-wide, and their slice-sized plasma TVs and razor thin telephones are all technological wonders whose performance matches their good looks.

BANNER BARRET

WOMEN'S BOUTIQUE

5-23-6 Jingumae, Shibuya-ku, Tokyo
(Others)
03-3406-1250
www.bannerbarrett.biz/
🕐 12:00–20:00
🗓 No holidays
🚶 MAP 6-13   ¥│¥│¥

No two articles at Banner Barret are alike and this is good for the glamor pusses who shop here often. Minidresses in gold or silver lamé, Marie Green lingerie in lace and peachy colors, basic knits, and lots of silk and lace dresses. The shop calls their collection *noble chic*, with a potent personality pervading every item. Off-shouldered peasant blouses with huge bows, animal print shirts quirkily combined with a lace yoke, denim jumper skirts with big chunky buttons, and coats that combine sportswear with tailored feminine details. Instant touches of the bold and the beautiful for your wardrobe.

BAPE EXCLUSIVE

MEN'S BOUTIQUE

5-5-8 Minami Aoyama, Minato-ku, Tokyo
03-3407-2145
www.bape.com
🕐 11:00–19:00
📅 Non–fixed
👣 MAP 1-18

¥|¥|¥

Hot, clever and overrated, fashion's most iconic ape is the most successfully branded underground label the world has seen in recent years, and this shop is where it all started. What makes this property hot is a limited edition of everything. BAPE sweats emblazoned with the hairy ape, zipped BAPE hoodies, shiny Bapesta sneakers, A Bathing Ape logo jeans (with the logo on the butt or crotch), and even haircuts at their nearby salon or coffee at their cafe. A darling of the hip-hop community and close friends of the Beastie Boys as well as a collaborator with Pharell Williams, the brand's owner Nigo is a megawatt star. High on style, low on content—while in Tokyo get your hands on a limited edition of at least one T-shirt or jersey at this flagship store.

BAPE KIDS

KIDS

3-29-11 Jingumae, Shibuya-ku, Tokyo
03-5770-4455
www.bape.com/
🕐 11:00–19:00
📅 No holidays
👣 MAP 5-6

¥|¥|¥

Bape Kids is the kid's collection for Bapephile parents. The look remains expectedly Bape, identical to the adult collection with Baby Milo hoodies, ape front star denim non-wash jeans, and lots of T-shirts for kids 2-5. The Bapesta sneakers in bright patent colors are licensed to thrill, and if nothing else it's just fun to visit the shop and its trademark Bape white interiors with a huge rubber banana pool—just as the world's most hip underground ape likes it.

BAPY

WOMEN'S BOUTIQUE

3-8-5 Minami-Aoyama, Minato-ku, Tokyo
03-5766-9177
www.bape.com
🕐 11:00–20:00
📅 No holidays
👣 MAP 1-19

¥|¥|¥

Nigo offers his street cred to women at this store stocked with his Bapy and Apee lines. His female fans—caps pulled down to the eyebrows, eyes covered by gigantic frames—file in here for puffy jackets, bags, mini skirts in denim embroidered with the Bapy logo, bright Ts, pumps with low heels, and other regular Bape separates in smaller sizes. Tough street styles is what makes this shop such fun: think Bond girl meets kiss n'tell girl, with a vinyl bag and tons of chutzpah.

BARNEYS NEW YORK

DEPARTMENT STORE

6–8–7 Ginza, Chuo–ku, Tokyo (Others)
03–3289–1200
www.barneys.co.jp/
⊘ Mon–Wed, Sat, Sun 11:00–20:00/
Thu, Fri 11:00–20:30/Mon–
Sun11:00–20:00
▦ Not fixed
⌶ MAP 4-3   ¥·¥·¥·¥

Hot on the heels of their New York flagship and way ahead in service, Barneys has a selection of women's casuals to please every brand of fashionista: Chloé, Balenciaga, Taverniti So Jeans, Three Dots and Diane von Furstenberg, to name a few. Japanese brands Mint and Green are a must-have to match with a great shoe collection from Manolo Blahnik. Men's businesswear sees offerings from Barneys' own designs and shirts from Barba and Fray. After Five style questions are answered by Dior, Trovata, Lanvin, and Dries van Noten, among others. The first floor is home to fabulous cosmetics and fragrances—imported and Japanese—that are difficult to find elsewhere. With Annick Goutal, Nuxe, Sundari, Kenzoli, Natura Blisses, L'Artisan Parfumeur, Diptyque, the cult Creed and Keiko Mecheri, choosing is definitely tricky. Gear for gents is also as impressive: shoes from John Lobb, C Diem, Edward Green and Alden along with loafers in all colors from Barneys themselves. Cool, posh silver and crystal accessories from Maxi and Phenomenon Beyond Description are the latest It-accessories for men, and for super man skincare there is an entire range of cosmetics from Molton Brown. Barneys offers unparalleled style for every day of the week and their attentive staff easily takes the heat out of shopping.

BASE STATION

VOLUME SELLER MEN'S/
WOMEN'S

6-5-6 Jingumae, Shibuya-ku, Tokyo
03-5778-0412
www.basestation.jp/
⊘ 11:00–20:00
▦ No holidays
⌶ MAP 6-14   ¥·¥·¥

The recently opened Base Station, with its BC label, is giving neighboring Uniqlo a run for its money. With basics for men, women, kids and even dogs in 100% natural fabrics, the shop stocks T-shirts and a wide variety of tanks, free from logos or designs. While white, black and grey are staples all year round, the collections play with three to four trend colors every season. For men the clothes are constructed slightly loose for the Japanese frame, while the women's collection is quite fitted. There's no place smarter for nifty basics shopping.

BBS TOKYO

MEN'S BOUTIQUE/INTERIOR/
MUSIC

GB1F, 5-17-24 Jingumae, Shibuya-ku, Tokyo.
03-5766-3816
www.bbstokyo.com
🕐 12:00–20:00
🗓 No holidays
🔎 MAP 6-15

Ⓨ Ⓨ Ⓨ

A branch of the NYC Break Beats Service shop, this is a great party mix of music, art, arty clothes, and an arty interior. The area just to the right of the entrance always features exciting art or displays of clothes that are veritable works of art. Another step inside, and underfoot is a model of a utopian town specially commissioned from thirty-four artists. Despite the tiny size of the shop, there is always affordable streetwear for men from upcoming Japanese designers, with sweat shirts, T-shirts, a collection of Rag&bone jeans, soft and pliant jackets in the winter, and plenty of other ideas for hip men's casuals in tweed, cotton, and wool. The shop offers a taste of Tokyo youth culture and Cat Street's cool vibes.

BEAMS

MEN'S/WOMEN'S BOUTIQUE

1-15-1 Jinnan, Shibuya-ku, Tokyo (Others)
www.beams.co.jp/
🕐 11:00–20:00 (Sat/Sun/Hol until 20:30)
🗓 No holidays
🔎 MAP 8-9

Ⓨ Ⓨ

Beams has been dressing up wannabe fashionistas for the last thirty years. This is where young males head when they start looking for street fashion essentials. Beams collections feature not just the trends of the moment but generally smart looks, be it military trench coats, jersey tops, sweater vests, lots of jeans (some with exciting colored stripes and zips on the side), and all accessories to pull together a look-cool-live-cool image. Look in their new section for the latest Japanese designers. The summer of 2007 was dedicated to shirts, jeans, and jackets from Japanese designer Factotum. The entire collection in white and grey has a distinct Tokyo street image.

BEAMS HOUSE INTERNATIONAL GALLERY

WOMEN'S BOUTIQUE

3-25-15 Jingumae, Shibuya-ku, Tokyo
03-3470-3948
www.beams.co.jp
🕐 11:00–20:00
🗓 No holidays
🔎 MAP 5-7

Ⓨ Ⓨ Ⓨ-Ⓨ Ⓨ Ⓨ Ⓨ

The shop offers some of the best ways to fast track your fashion ambitions. Dedicated to women's collections, you can find an extensive range of both Japanese and foreign talent. Mosslight, Sacai, Cosmic Wonder, and Junya Watanabe denim are combined with Diane von Furstenberg's wrap staples and bikini selections, along with Maison Martin Margiela, A.F. Vandervost and Phillip

Lim offerings plus intimates from Sally Jones and Mary Green. For temperamental alpha females who abhor brands and want to stand-out on their own in the melee of Tokyo's brand toting public, the shop has rows and rows of stunning bags in the shapes of the season from labels like Aristolasia, Kenji Ikeda, and Elisa Atheniense—the looks without the high price tag. The shoe selection is also exhaustive, with Manolo Blahnik, Stella McCartney, Christian Louboutin, Pierre Hardy, and Rodolphe Menudier. While the women's collection is starry, men are relegated to T-shirts. Head upstairs for Beams Art for Everyday, a retrospective of arty T-shirts from near and far, cleverly displayed on a conveyor belt.

BEAUX-ARTS MELS
WOMEN'S BOUTIQUE/INTERIOR

4-2-15 Ginza, Chuo-ku, Tokyo (Others)
03-3538-1200
www.bluegrass.co.jp/
🕙 11:00–21:00 (Fri/Sat until 22:00)
🗓 No holidays
📍 MAP 3-3   ¥|¥

The shop offers basics for the house and for the wardrobe. The entrance features a range of pretty, simple, and extremely affordable accoutrements for the kitchen, bathroom, and living room, among which the niftiest ideas are: wicker baskets for storage—in chocolate shades that the Balinese are so good at—unfussy table mats for days when you eat in, and lots of flower vases. Further in the shop are reasonably priced touches of luxe for your wardrobe, especially for the winter—little angora cardigans in basic shades, pea coats, dresses, and simple cotton tops.

BELLINROSTON
AROMATHERAPY

20-6 Sarugaku-cho, Shibuya-ku, Tokyo
03-5458-8308
www.roston.jp/
🕙 12:00–19:00 (weekdays)/
   11:00–19:00 (Sat, Sun, Holidays)
🗓 Mondays
📍 MAP 2-12   ¥|¥|¥

Bellinroston is ringing in a new dawn in face washes. Created by the country's top skin specialists, the soaps are completely natural, with no additives or artificial colors. Soaps come in three different varieties for different skin types. Combined with shampoos made from natural ingredients, this is the closest your skin will get to nature. If you have to choose just one thing, let it be the legendary Roston pearl soap; hypoallergenic and without any fragrance, it is said to cure all kinds of skin problems. They also have a series of soaps that can be used for the body and the face at the same time and are so gentle and biodegradable that they protect you and nature too. (Here is some environmental trivia: it takes 800 years for your average shower gel to degrade!). The shop also stocks fragrant eau-de-colognes and bathrobes.

BELT & BELT
MEN'S/WOMEN'S ACCESSORIES

West Bldg. 1F, Tamagawa-Takashimaya,
3-17-1 Tamagawa, Setagaya-ku, Tokyo
03-5717-6330
None
🕐 10:00–21:00
🗓 No holidays
🚻 MAP 15-1　　¥|¥|¥-¥|¥|¥|¥

Tokyo's biggest belt specialty store has more than three hundred versions of this indispensable waist accessory. Over twenty varieties of crocodile, calfskin (available in many colors and emboss patterns), python, suede, and other leathers can be made into belts for men, women, children and even pets. Chose from their in-shop selection of over 50 patterns that the shop resizes according to your specifications. If you have a particular design in mind, they take around a month to stitch it from scratch and then mail it to you wherever you are. While the shop might be off the regular fashion track, it is a great place to stop by when your wardrobe needs a quick jolt of excitement.

BENETTON
MEN'S/WOMEN'S BOUTIQUE

4-3-10 Jingumae, Shibuya-ku,
Tokyo (Others)
03-5474-7155
www.benetton.co.jp/
🕐 11:00–20:00
🗓 No holidays
🚻 MAP 5-8　　¥|¥|-¥|¥|¥

Benetton's contributions to fashion are inexpensive clothes, great knits, a riot of color, and cool advertising campaigns. Benetton's DNA is a range of sweaters in kaleidoscopic colors that they've been producing since the start of the company in the early 60s. Their special process of not dyeing the wool yarn until the very last moment after the sweater has been knitted has resulted in more than fifty colors of knits in their collection, and the same wide color palette is offered in T-shirts for the summer. Added to this is a range of tailored outfits for men, women, mothers-to-be, and kids. Luggage, ski outfits and kitchen accessories too have found a place in the Benetton family.

BERLUTI
MEN'S SHOES

1-1-1 Minami-Aoyama, Minato-ku, Tokyo
03-5775-3451
www.berluti.co.jp/
🕐 11:00–20:00 Sundays/Holidays Until
19:00)
🗓 No holidays
🚻 MAP 16-2　　¥|¥|¥

Set up in 1895, this French brand initially handcrafted only *sur mesure* shoes. Now under the leadership of fourth generation Olga Berluti, and a general love for all things handmade, once a year Berluti's *maitre bottier* takes orders for sur mesure shoes in Tokyo that take one year to make in their French workshop. Famous for its finish, their classic slim fitting shoe comes in many ready-to-wear designs (in different sizes but in just one width)—most famously the *Tatoues* and the *Piercings*, two designs that come with a neat piercing and tattoos at the toes for a duke dandy vile image. Then it's all about Berluti's famed luster and patina. In Paris, Berluti regularly organizes "patina" ceremonies where customers gather around Dom Perignon with linen cloths and polish away for more than an hour to restore the original patina. Although it is the shoes here that have been treading the path to fame, of late the accessories too have been gathering storm, the hottest one being the camel-colored, graffiti strewn briefcase seen hanging from the arms of many a discerning man about town.

BETSEY JOHNSON
WOMEN'S DESIGNER

Shinjuku Isetan 2F., 3-14-1 Shinjuku,
    Shinjuku-ku, Tokyo (Others)
03-3352-1111
www.betseyjohnson.com/
⊘ 10:00–20:00
▦ Not fixed
⌁ MAP 9-4   ¥│¥│¥

Unbelievable that this over-60-year-old New York bombshell is still belting out shimmering accessories that are the heartthrob of every girl in town over ten years old. Fiercely fun, wildly sexy, and with huge impact, Betsey's accessories include pretty evening bags with mirrors, glitter, and sequins, ideally paired with her glam shoes that look best with the corset cocktail dresses with plunging necklines, pretty summer outfits, tiny bright knits, often in red, or cap sleeved shrugs. Her intimate baby-dolls, slips, and camis are bright and beautiful, and her leopard-print, bias-cut lacy swimwear in hot colors has just hit the shelves. Everything in the shop is steamy and stamped with Betsey's philosophy: bad girls have the most fun.

BILLIKEN
TOYS

5-17-6 Minami-Aoyama, Minato-ku,
    Tokyo
03-3400-2214
None
⊘ 12:00–19:00
▦ Mondays/The 2nd Wednesdays
⌁ MAP 1-20   ¥│¥│¥·¥│¥│¥

Previously loved toys have found a wonderful home at this tiny iconic toy store that specializes in nostalgia. Some of these pieces, such as vintage Japanese anime figures, antique cars, dolls, and hand-made Ultraman and Astroboy figures are serious collectibles. But if you are an arctophile (teddy bear collector to the uninitiated), it is the teddies that you will go after. Previously loved hugsters whose prices have sky rocketed elsewhere in the world are still available at a shockingly low price here. And the most wanted among them all, the Steiff bears from the 60s, will put you in an unbeatably warm and fuzzy mood. The shop also holds regular exhibitions of manga-meets-*bande dessinée* illustrations.

BILLIONAIRE

MEN'S BOUTIQUE

4-13 Kioicho, Chiyoda-ku, Tokyo
03-5226-8858
www.bbs-k.com/top.html
🕐 11:00–19:00
📅 No holidays
🚇 MAP 13-1   ¥|¥|¥|¥|¥

Flamboyant is an understatement at this shop where billionaires spend their loose change. Created by Angelo Galasso and F1 Renault's Flavio Briatore, this is for those who can't live without denim with gold thread embroidery, cobra belts in scarlet or purple, and python kicks. The *piece de resistance* however is the *polso orologio* shirt—known as the watch cuff shirt—that allows men to show off their watches without having to lift their cuff.

BIRKENSTOCK

MEN'S/WOMEN'S SHOES

3-23-5 Jingumae, Shibuya-ku,
Tokyo (Others)
03-5413-5248
www.birkenstockjpn.co.jp/
🕐 11:00–21:00
📅 No holidays
🚇 MAP 5-9   ¥|¥-¥|¥|¥

Once just natural and homely, Birkenstock have recently been successfully treading an edgier path with combinations of leathers, prints, and metallic finishes. The simpler slip-ons, sandals, and slippers have universal appeal, and as Birkenstock remain the most comfortable footwear on the planet, summer sees hordes of free-wheeling souls queuing up to get the latest in cork foot beds.

BLUMARINE

WOMEN'S DESIGNER

5-12-6 Minami-Aoyama, Minato-ku,
Tokyo (Others)
03-5467-0717
www.blumarine.com/
🕐 11:00–20:00
📅 No holidays
🚇 MAP 1-21   ¥|¥|¥|¥

Whatever the season, you can be sure that Anna Molinari will always feature girly embroidered dresses and knitwear with floral motifs. Her sophisticated knits—especially cashmere cardigans with fur collars for winter and delicate dresses for summer—have also always been on the must-have list. The clothes feel like heaven, the stars wear it to work and this is as sexy as knitwear gets.

BOBLBEE

MEN'S/WOMEN'S ACCESSORIES

2-8-3 Jiyugaoka, Meguro-ku, Tokyo
03-3725-8169
www.boblbee.co.jp
🕐 12:00–20:00
📅 Wednesdays
🚇 MAP 11-2   ¥|¥|¥-¥|¥|¥|¥

The most fun revolution in bags, Boblbee is synonymous with the arched tortoise shell shaped bags seen on the backs of many a bicycling metrosexual male. In this shop dedicated to all of Boblbee's designs, find not only their entire collections of the voluminous shell series but also laptop-sized cases, smaller holders for music, and even holsters and hip bags. They also sell spare parts for making Boblbee repairs, including all the shells, harnesses, straps—even the nuts and bolts.

BOMB OF THE YEAR
MEN'S BOUTIQUE

GB Bldg. 3F, 5-17-24 Jingumae,
Shibuya-ku, Tokyo
03-3407-2182
www.bomb-of-the-year.com/
🕐 12:00–20:00
📅 No holidays
📍 MAP 6-16   ¥|¥|¥

Bomb of the Year is a shop full of resistance labels by star stylist Tetsuo Kitahara. It essentially stocks, among others, two Japanese labels: Backlash and Back From The Basics. The style is American rock n' roll in a vintage sort of way (think big boots, leather belts, and a lot of motorcycle jackets). Backlash offers denim and deerskin leather pants that combine rock chic with hi tech—deerskin has been fused onto the denim for extra comfort. The long checked flannel shirts too are lined with deerskin and bio-washed for the vintage look. Cowboy shirts are made luxe with details like python collars and sleeves. The shop's prime offerings, however, are the structured, tight-fit biker jackets in colors like white and tomato.

BONPOINT
KIDS

Shinjuku Isetan 6F, 3-14-1 Shinjuku,
Shinjuku-ku, Tokyo
03-3352-1111
www.bonpoint.com
🕐 10:00–20:00
📅 Not fixed
📍 MAP 9-5   ¥|¥|¥-¥|¥|¥

Parents of kids (3-16) love their superb range of shoes, ballerina flats, and pretty party clothes for girls in flowery designs in white and pink. For boys the collection is a bit sturdier, with blazers, linen jackets and cargo pants. While the look is dressy without trying too hard, most parents would think twice before sending their kids to playschool in these fabulous things. Fashionable teenage girls love their collection of jeans, T-shirts and tops.

BOSTON TAILORS
MEN'S BESPOKE

Central Mitake Bldg. B1F, 1-3-1 Shibuya,
Shibuya-ku, Tokyo
03-3498-1129
none
110:00–20:00
📅 No holidays
📍 MAP 8-10   ¥|¥|¥-¥|¥|¥

Boston Tailors is a huge blast from the past; a trip to this mecca of conspiracy theories is unlike any trip to the tailors. Bohemian rather than elegant, the movie-set decor littered with clocks and maps surrounds the tailor, chain-smoking Mr. Yamamoto, the spitting image of George Harrison. Apart from the decor, what distinguishes this place is their total commitment to quality—the entire suit is hand stitched and no part goes through a machine. And what's more, you are offered an extensive choice of 70s and 80s retro swathes of fabric: in colors like olive green and purple. Mr. Yamamoto loves his clients, shares his conspiracy theories, and listens carefully, so if you have special requests such as extra thin lapels or special vents, he is happy to oblige. It takes two months and a minimum of two visits for a suit, but at the end you not only leave with a suit in hand but a head full of scenarios on the current state of the world.

BOTTEGA VENETA
MEN'S/WOMEN'S DESIGNER

4-12-10 Jingumae, Shibuya-ku, Tokyo (Others)
03-5175-0511
www.bottegaveneta.com/
🕐 11:00–21:00
Not fixed
MAP 5-10

¥|¥|¥|¥|¥

Tomas Maier's complete collection is stockpiled over four demi levels here in Asia's biggest Bottega Venetta store. The accessories section has everything imaginable in the world's most adored square leather weaves—bags, baby shoes, travel trunks, cushion covers, and stationery. While Bottega doesn't do cars, if you're in the market for an upgrade in wheels, they are happy to supply you with a made-to-order choice of steering wheel cover in all possible shades of crocodile, python, ostrich, or lamb—style finally hits the roads.

BRAND BANK
MEN'S/WOMEN'S VINTAGE

Shibuya Center Bldg. 4F, 16-8 Udagawa-cho, Shibuya-ku, Tokyo
03-5489-1230
www.brand-bank1.com/
🕐 12:00–19:00
No holidays
MAP 8-11

¥|-|¥|¥

A great place for both men and women for classy previously loved shoes, bags, clothes and accessories in an almost new condition at lovable prices. Also stocks unusual things such as the Prada denim collection, 80s YSL suits, Dolce & Gabbana mules, BAPE's limited edition, Versace, Green, G.V.G.V., etc. As the collections are renewed every week, you need to check out this shop everytime you pass through Shibuya, and while in the building don't miss the previously loved LV bag selection at the shop downstairs.

BREE
MEN'S/WOMEN'S ACCESSORIES

5-27-11 Jiyugaoka, Meguro-ku, Tokyo (Others)
03-3721-1424
www.bree.de/
🕐 11:00–20:00
No holidays
MAP 11-3

¥|¥|¥|¥

Structured and simple bags from Germany that are great for day-to-day use. Based on traditional bag-making techniques, but incorporating the pragmatic touch for modern life as only the Germans do it, Bree's collection is largely made of naturally tanned cowhide leather. While classic styles reign in their handbag collections, the luggage is infused with a bit of glam. Their newest collection is made from caoutchouc, a kind of natural rubber with long-lasting qualities. Bree does a neat take on the German postman's bag, in a series called Punch that comes with shopping bags, travel bags, shoulder bags, children's rolling backpacks and carry-on bags. Dallas is their award winning, reasonably priced suitcase with rollers in super strength, and it comes in washable felt in two sizes. Bree's collections also include wallets, belts, key chains, coin pouches, pen cases, badge holders, and even two sandal designs. The entire collection is wonderfully understated, European-minded and ages gracefully.

BRIONI
MEN'S/WOMEN'S DESIGNER

4–3–13 Ginza, Chuo–ku, Tokyo (Others)
03–5524–2630
www.brioni.it/
🕐 11:00–20:00
📅 No holidays
↑ MAP 3-4   ¥|¥|¥|¥-¥|¥|¥|¥

Established in Rome in 1945, this designer/tailor (well, actually a group of nine-hundred tailors working away in their factory) has been dressing up the likes of Gary Cooper, Kofi Annan, even Pierce Brosnan in his role as James Bond. The brand has suddenly ventured into womenswear with Spanish designer Cristina Ortiz, with voluminous black outfits often with splashes of red, though without many accolades (the women's collection is available only at their store in Takashimaya Ginza), so stick to the men's suits. Because the main parts of the jacket and trousers are made by hand and the finishing touches are made by machine, the results are classic and unrivalled.

BROOKS BROTHERS
MEN'S/WOMEN'S DESIGNER

3-5-6 Kita Aoyama, Minato-Ku, Tokyo (Others)
03-3404-4295
www.brooksbrothers.com/
🕐 11:00–19:30
📅 Not fixed
↑ MAP 5-11   ¥|¥|¥|¥-¥|¥|¥|¥

The original purveyor of the preppy wardrobe, this is America's most gentlemanly export to the world, and Thom Browne, the new menswear, womenswear and accessories designer, promises us a revamped collection. This 200-year-old men's outfitter still makes the world's best button-down collar shirts in cotton, one-pocket classic Ts, corduroys, cargo shorts, boxers and striped ties. Flirting with heroism on 9/11 (having passed down shirts to the New York firemen battling the disaster at the towers next door), Brooks Brothers can also be occasionally innovative: check out the newly designed button-down stretch shirts designed for a perpetual non-iron slim fit.

BROWNIE BEE

WOMEN'S BOUTIQUE

1-35-2 Ebisu-nishi, Shibuya-ku,
Tokyo (Others)
03-5457-1882
www.la-est.com/brownie-bee/brand/
browni_brand.html
⊙ 11:00–20:00
▦ Not fixed
⌐ MAP 2-13   ¥¥-¥¥¥

Cerebral people should stay away; there is nothing in this store that could be vaguely appealing to you. Brownie Bee is only about short-lived trends. Back in the winter when tunics were in fashion, they had more than 50 varieties. In the summer when tailored shorts and jackets were in fashion, they had them in every color. They also do a zillion coats and skirts to match in whatever the new shape, new color, or new mood in town might be. As expected of a place like this, it's all at really cheap prices.

BRUNO MAGLI

MEN'S/WOMENS SHOES

5-8-2 Jingumae, Shibuya-ku,
Tokyo (Others)
03-6418-0700
www.brunomagli.co.jp/
⊙ 11:00–20:00 (Sun–Thu)/11:00–
21:00 (Fri/Sat)
▦ Not fixed
⌐ MAP 6-17   ¥¥¥¥

Bruno Magli remains the preferred shoe shop for men who insist upon great dress shoes. Undoubtedly the best quality that much money can buy, whether it's a great pair of slip-ons, sandals, nubuck mocassins or Maradi dress shoes. The women's collection is also full of superb understated shoes that keep the limelight firmly trained on you. Try the softest ballerinas in gold, grey and tan, or Nanico, a comfortable pair of heels for power-lunching babes. Bruno Magli also makes the softest leather jackets: a great combination of toughness and sophistication, perfect for zipping around town on two wheels.

BURBERRY

MEN'S/WOMEN'S DESIGNER

5-8-2 Jingumae, Shibuya-ku,
Tokyo (Others)
03-5778-7891
www.burberry.com
⊙ 11:00–20:00
▦ No holidays
⌐ MAP 6-18   ¥¥¥¥-¥¥¥¥¥

The slightly frumpy but immensely popular brand for everyday elegance suddenly registered on the style radar after creative designer Christopher Bailey stepped in and catalysed the world's most well-known plaid. Burbery's genius with the trench coat is unrivalled and the shop, apart from stocking an extensive RTW line, offers a fantastic bespoke service with a wide range of fabrics that can go into creating your own one-of-a-kind trench. They also stock quilted jackets in classic Burberry colors like gold, and a range of sportswear. Bailey's genius is particularly visible in the Prorsum collection stocked on the second floor: coat dresses, skirts, tops and shirts, just about all inspired by the trench. Often in very light brocade and other playful fabrics, they are artfully belted, with bell sleeves and a gentle billowing to make the look more playful. The men's collection has a skinny silhouette with dark cropped tuxedo trousers, military coats with epaulettes and big buttons and beautiful knits in jewel tones. The evening looks include silk shirts with tailored pants. An extensive collection of accessories are available on both the floors.

BURBERRY BLACK LABEL

MEN'S/WOMEN'S DESIGNER

6-18-1 Jingumae, Shibuya-ku, Tokyo (Others)
03-5468-3047
www.burberry-blacklabel.com/
🕐 11:00–20:00
📅 No holidays
🚶 MAP 6-19   ¥|¥|¥-¥|¥|¥|¥

Burberry reigns supreme when it comes to easy style, but for those who want to leave behind the trench but keep the plaid, the Black Label serves to make bold statements without showing off. Is that really possible? Created specially for Japan, Black Label keeps the essence of Burberry with little details like lining jackets with plaid patterns in many combinations of black, red and brown and embroidered logos on the sleeves of their knits. Apart from suits and dress shirts there is a collection of casuals including relaxed trousers and coats with toggle zipper fastenings and even jungle prints and denim. Don't forget to check out their bold accessories with low top trainers in jungle print or gold, the trade mark plaid printed discretely on the sole. Women need to be content with smaller sizes of selected clothes from the men's collection.

BURBERRY BLUE LABEL

MEN'S/WOMEN'S DESIGNER

6-18-12 Jingumae, Shibuya-ku, Tokyo (Others)
03-3406-8681
www.burberry-bluelabel.com/
🕐 11:00–20:00
📅 No holidays
🚶 MAP 6-20   ¥|¥|¥-¥|¥|¥|¥

This diffusion line of Burberry reincarnates its trench coats into soft, half canvas coats that retain the Burberry fit but with much younger lines. Round-shouldered and relaxed, they fit like a second skin. Vests, trousers, short coats and shoes also follow the same pattern—essentially Burberry but at cheaper prices. For women there is a range of casual knits, shorts, capris, shirts, and accessories.

CA4LA

MEN'S/WOMEN'S HATS

6-29-4 Jingumae, Shibuya-ku, Tokyo (Others)
03-3406-8271
www.ca4la.com
🕐 11:00–20:00
🗓 Not fixed
✶ MAP 6-21 ¥|¥|¥-¥|¥|¥|¥

Choosing a hat is tricky. CA4LA makes it all the more difficult, with an amazing array on show. Accept help from the staff and, more importantly, immediately put back the hat on the shelf if you're even the slightest bit unsure. But if you want to lead the pack in a hat, head here for names like Phillip Treacy and Misa Harada (both milliners for the Queen), Borsalino (who makes the finest fedoras in Belgian rabbit fur), and Mulbauer, Austrian specialists of hats with style and originality such as peaked, flat skull caps and cloches. And with the great collections of Jacques Le Corre, Christophe Coppens, Richard Plank, Collection Privee, Rodkenan, and Stephen Jones, and CA4LA'S own designs of beanies, baseballs styles, berets, and toques, there will be no hesitation when it is time to pay.

CABANE DE ZUCCA

MEN'S/WOMEN'S DESIGNER

3-13-14 Minami Aoyama, Minato-ku, Tokyo (Others)
03-3470-7488
www.a-net.com/
🕐 11:00–20:00
🗓 Not fixed
✶ MAP 1-22 ¥|¥|¥-¥|¥|¥|¥

Another offering from the Issey Miyake studio, designer Akira Onozuka's brand of clothes are more about noble French fashion pieces: unisex, androgynous and with a dedicated fan following. In natural fabrics like cotton, silhouettes are sometimes oversized, sometimes fitted, and sometimes come in a tiny flower print. Most of the items are naturally washed out for comfort, and the trousers are cut wide. Cabane de Zucca also has a cult following with its watches. Produced in collaboration with Seiko and made of silicone, they are collector's items as new models are released every year. This wall-to-wall concrete-and-glass store that stocks the entire collection also has a beautiful Japanese garden make this place a great alternative to the city's ubiquitous multi-brand boutiques.

CABOURG

VINTAGE

Grandmaison Daikanyama 1F, 3-7-10 Ebisu Minami, Shibuya-ku, Tokyo
03-5722-3741
none
🕐 11:00–20:00
🗓 No holidays
✶ MAP 2-14 ¥-¥|¥|¥

Cabourg is one secret that no Tokyo fashionista in her right mind would ever divulge. Miu Miu, Prada, Chloé, YSL, Gucci and loads of other previously loved but still desirable clothes sit side by side in dry-cleaned splendor inviting you to splurge. The accessories are the best bargain with Chanel sunglasses, Chloé necklaces, Pucci scarves and almost always an extensive range of YSL bags. For the best deals stop by at least once a month when you can peddle your stuff, too. (Cabourg pays you sixty percent if they manage to sell your designer stuff.) At such rock bottom prices, we can't think of a better way to spend the weekend.

CAILAN'S
MEN'S/WOMEN'S BOUTIQUE

2-9-15 Jiyugaoka, Meguro-ku, Tokyo
03-3725-4153
www.cailans.com
⊘ 11:00–20:00
▦ No holidays
⌾ MAP 11-4   ¥|¥|-¥|¥|¥|¥

Cailan is the little secret that makes a lot of freak flags fly in a grungy, cool, street kind of way. Cutting edge and a little aggressive casual items litter the place. What you get in terms of clothes are primarily jeans and military jackets embellished with rivets, chains, and zips with a leaning towards imports from Italy including Ai, Replace, and G-star. It wouldn't be advisable to dress head-to-toe in what they sell, so be sure of what you want before heading to this store. The customers are slightly aggressive types and the service too tends to be in that direction.

CALVIN KLEIN
DESIGNER

Ebisu Mitsukoshi Dept. Store 4-20-7
  Ebisu, Shibuya-ku, Tokyo
03-5423-1111
None
⊘ 10:00–20:30
▦ Not fixed
⌾ MAP 10-2   ¥|¥|¥|-¥|¥|¥|¥

The Calvin Klein brand is back with a vengeance through its ultimately talented Brazilian designer Francisco Costa. He has been coloring the brand with his own personal likes and dislikes, such as his love of architecture and the color black. Simplicity reigns with clean, modern, contemporary lines, a lot of exposable lingerie and languid style slip dresses for the day, as well as evening dresses and coats.

CALVIN KLEIN UNDERWEAR
MEN'S/WOMEN'S UNDERWEAR

1-35-17 Ebisu-Nishi, Shibuya-ku, Tokyo
03-5784-3120
None
⊘ 11:00–20:00
▦ No holidays
⌾ MAP 2-15   ¥|¥|-¥|¥|¥

Offering freedom from frills and lace, CK underwear excels in comfort and formfitting definition. It looks best under clothes, of course, but not so bad either when peeping out from beneath. Basic, confident, cool, and really comfortable, women love the cotton and silk underwear and camisoles sets. For guys, boxers, briefs, and muscle shirts should do the trick.

CALZALONE

MEN'S/WOMEN'S LEG WEAR

Roppongi Hills West Walk 4F, 6-10-3
Roppongi, Minato-ku, Tokyo
03-5770-6911
www.fukusuke.com
⊘ 11:00–20:00
▦ No holidays
⌐ MAP 12-7   ¥|¥-¥|¥|¥

A neat little shop that stocks lacy women's stockings from La Perla and Fermazione in all sizes up to large, along with leg warmers and long cotton and cashmere socks for the snowy months. Men's business socks come in various shades of grey and black, with an award-winning design that adds pressure to the ankle and calf to relax the feet and legs. They also have styles for the weekend that range from thick knits for a sporty look to finer knits in many different colors for any formal occasion. As the entire collection remains quite conservative, it is almost impossible to go wrong here.

CAMPER

MEN'S/WOMEN'S/KIDS' SHOES

6-3-9 Jingumae, Shibuya-ku,
Tokyo (Others)
03-5778-2880
www.camper.com
⊘ 11:00–20:00
▦ No holidays
⌐ MAP 6-22   ¥|¥-¥|¥|¥

It's Spanish, it's comfortable and it's very cool. Camper has been making this delightfully colorful and fairly fashion-friendly stuff for your soles since 1975. The secret is in the design of the light rubber under the shoe that fits like a sock around your feet. The designs remain really simple, but if its colors and quirkiness you are looking for, Camper does yellows, reds, whites, oranges, blacks, and beiges, very often in slightly mismatched styles, such as a dove pattern on the right foot and an olive branch on the left, or a leaf and a flower. Shoes for kids come in sizes 14.5–22 cms Recently launched Camper For Hands provides matching twisted ideas for handbags.

CANALI

MEN'S BOUTIQUE

6-7-9 Ginza, Chuo-ku, Tokyo (Others)
03-5568-4300
www.canali.it/
⊘ 11:00–19:30 (Sun/holidays until
18:30)
▦ No holidays
⌐ MAP 4-4   ¥|¥|¥|¥

Launched in 1934 in Italy, Canali offers solutions to any man's sartorial quandaries. Impeccably tailored bespoke suits, shirts, belts, and other necessities ensure every gent remains debonair. Younger clients choose Canali for chinos, shoes and assorted sports wear. Undoubtedly, Canali's appeal is that it adds aplomb to the man whose style is ahead of the game.

CANNABIS

MEN'S/WOMEN'S BOUTIQUE

5-17-24 Jingumae, Shibuya-ku, Tokyo
03-5766-3014
www.hpfrance.com/Shop/Brand/
 CANNABIS.html
⊙ 12:00–20:00
▦ No holidays
⌁ MAP 6-23   ¥|¥|¥-¥|¥|¥|¥

Cannabis is the king of underground designers and a world away from those ubiquitous fashion emporiums. Occupying two top floors of the GVGV building, it has long been the breeding ground for young Japanese fashion talent. The purple floor is a mecca of casual wear straight from the rock world. Diet Butcher Slim Skin, a new star in the Japanese fashion scene, takes tailored garments, stresses them and crushes them to give them a rock edge. John Lawrence Sullivan takes shirts and sweaters and plays around, adding pleats, plunging necklines, and a lot of extracurricular fashion ideas. This floor also stocks Junya Watanabe's patterner Nozomi Ishiguro's exclusive collection for Cannabis. Climb up the stairs and discover suits with a difference, that range from Marka's tailored pants and blazers sold separately, to Digital Diverse's take on the tailored track suits, and a range of military style jackets that could be paired with stressed or patent leather derbies or bright red lace-ups from Czech shoemaker Cebo. Everything here, including the service, is served up with a little dash of vanity and why not? They are, after all, the hottest bed of budding Japanese talent in town.

CARAMEL BABY & CHILD

KIDS'

Hillside Terrace C, 29-10 Sarugaku-cho,
 Shibuya-ku, Tokyo
03-5159-3193 (Press Contact)
www.caramel-shop.co.uk/
⊙ ▦ Shop hours and holidays unavailable at press time
⌁ MAP 2-16   ¥|¥|¥-¥|¥|¥|¥

Fashion loving mommies and daddies needn't ever compromise again on the lack of fashion options for their darling babies. Designer Eva Karayiannis trained to be a lawyer before deciding to set up an ultimately beautiful children's label that would be luxurious, understated, and without silly logos. Heading to Peru to find fine knitwear and looking around to source soft fabrics in the UK, she created Caramel—a range of clothes from 0-12 that are great for play or school. Caramel's collections have only recently arrived in Tokyo, and consist of sweet and brilliantly colored tops, shirts, trousers, sweaters, jackets, hats, and accessories inspirationally embroidered and decorated with pom-poms or tassels, with faint tribal designs. At last a collection that is neither too sharp nor too precious, or given to overly colorful theatrics.

CARLIFE

WOMEN'S BOUTIQUE

Shibuya Parco Part3 1F, 14-5 Udagawa-
cho, Shibuya-ku, Tokyo (Others)
03-3496-2205
www.carlife.cc
🕐 10:00–20:00
📅 Not fixed
🗺 MAP 8-12

¥|¥|¥

Carlife stations itself in a cute little corner of Parco and comes up with basics where no two pieces are the same—knits with gold bead trimming, cardigans, skirts, and casual jackets. But most people stopping here leave either with designer Ahkah's dainty little 18K gold bracelets and necklaces or Carlife's extensive range of sweet smelling cosmetics from L'Artisan Parfumeur, Dr. Hauschka, and Weleda.

CASSINA IXC

INTERIOR

Cocoti Bldg. 1F/B1F, 1-23-16 Shibuya,
Shibuya-ku, Tokyo (Others)
03-5464-7060
www.cassina-ixc.jp/
🕐 11:00–19:30
📅 No holidays
🗺 MAP 8-13

¥|¥|¥|¥

Thanks to Cassina, we get to adorn our interiors with remakes of the LC series of Corbusier, the Hill House chair from Mackintosh, the red and blue chair from Rietveld and the Taliesin table and Imperial Tokyo sets from Corbusier. But it is not just these remakes that identify this company. Cassina has some innovative and fabulously modern design to its credit. Their Cab dining chair, entirely in leather (including the legs), has spun off numerous copies in the market, their Veranda sofas can be folded in many ways for added comfort, and their beds and sofa sets are built to last forever. If it is shelves you are after, Cassina does some mean and really lean ones. While the furniture takes up the upper floors, the ground floor is dedicated to interior articles to please every taste. Exquisite porcelain, tableware, home fragrances, vases, cushions, stemware, and candles are laid out in a very distinguished manner to please every mood.

CATHERINE MEMMI

INTERIOR

5-3-22 Minami-Aoyama, Minato-ku,
Tokyo
03-5468-5625
www.catherinememmi.com/
🕐 11:00–19:30
📅 No holidays
🗺 MAP 1-23

¥|¥|¥|¥

Catherine Memmi's collections are stocked on two huge floors. Just as you enter you will be mesmerised by her near-Japanese minimalist designs of sofas, tables, chairs and shelves in chocolate and white all waiting to decorate your interior magazine style apartment. Step down for her decadent accessories collections of nightwear and bathrobes in ice cream pastels in the softest of colors and her fragrant linen waters, soaps and bath oils. Combine this with her furniture and you will wish every day was a Sunday.

CELINE

WOMEN'S DESIGNER

3-5-29 Kita-Aoyama, Minato-ku,
Tokyo (Others)
03-5771-4801
www.celine.com/
🕐 11:00–20:00
📅 No holidays
📍 MAP 5-12

¥|¥|¥|¥|¥

Celine started out as a children's shoemaker and is now the preferred shopping destination for megawatt celebrities. With its new collection taken over by designer Ivana Omazic, you'll see trench coats, knee-length flared skirts in fabrics like cotton silk gabardine, and silk organza tops, all quiet but exquisitely beautiful. Styling is simple but the looks are luxe with super fine fabrics. The key item—the skirt, with perfect length and flare—looks perfect on demure yet killer legs. Even the polo shirt becomes an item of refinement with just the logo on the pocket. In line with its origins, the best things here are still the shoes, handmade with perfect finishing. The bags compete closely, with the Boogie being a perennial favourite, the luxe leather hobos and totes too are great and the lovely series of belts and other accessories embossed discreetly with Celine's blazon. Celine never conforms to passing trends, so put all this in your wardrobe and pull it out five years later and it will still feel fresh.

CHACOTT

DANCE WEAR

1-20-8 Jinnan, Shibuya-ku,
Tokyo (Others)
03-3476-1311
www.chacott-jp.com/
🕐 11:00–20:00
📅 No holidays
📍 MAP 8-14

¥|¥-¥|¥|¥|¥

Chacott is a home-grown, one-stop shopping destination for all jazz, ballet, and ball room dancers. The upper floor stocks ballet staples like tutus, practice clothes, and underwear , and also superb knit and velvet leotards for both boys and girls. The second floor is dedicated to toe shoes, leg warmers, and dancing shoes of all kinds, plus ballet shoes up to size 24.5 cm from Fred, Repetto, Capezio, and Gambia. The ground floor has the less glamorous but serious stuff, like Beau-Rex tights for both men and women which support the body and are famed to greatly assist *fouéttes* and *saut de chats*. The Goopo slippers are quite a sight, but make pointe work a breeze. There is a whole corner of professional make-up, foundations, glitters, and extra fast colors. They also stock books and DVDs on dancing, and if you are lost in translation ask help from the wiry sales people who are all professional dancers and keen to help you put your best foot forward.

CHANDELIER

WOMEN'S BOUTIQUE

3-1 Sarugaku-cho, Shibuya-ku, Tokyo
03-3461-0556
www.world.co.jp/brand/chandelier.html
🕐 12:00–20:00
📅 No holidays
📍 MAP 2-17   ¥¥¥-¥¥¥¥

Unfussy easy styles reign supreme at Chandelier with jeans, shorts, and clothes from Christy Turlington's Nuala line for lounging around, Diane von Furstenberg's dresses for lazy summer vibes, and Sass & Bide casuals from down under for a cocktail-by-the-pool ambience. This chill-out wardrobe makes the Tokyo girl's perfect "must-have" list. If you're in for more luxury pieces, though, head instead to the superb Aquagirl collection just across the street.

CHANEL

WOMEN'S DESIGNER

3-5-3 Ginza, Chuo-ku, Tokyo
03-5159-5555
www.chanel-ginza.com
🕐 11:00–20:00
📅 No holidays
📍 MAP 3-5   ¥¥¥¥¥

You don't get a discount buying Chanel in Japan, but you *do* get extra special attention—plus the added incentive of shopping in Peter Marino's architectural winner that is stocked only as Karl Lagerfeld could have done it—modern remakes of Chanel tweed jackets, nudy chiffon black banded dresses, tweed jumpers, stretch satin skinny pants, crimson quilted bags and black patent pumps. When the cloud in front of your eyes clears, you may also notice the Chanel chains, earrings and belts. And if all the tweed has left you famished, head to the Alain Ducasse restaraunt upstairs to dine, also upholstered in Coco's favorite beige tweed. After dinner, step out and look back as the building's tweed inspired façade sparkles in the evening lights.

CHA NO GINZA
TEA

5-5-6 Ginza, Chuo-ku, Tokyo
03-3571-1211
www.uogashi-meicha.co.jp
🕐 11:00–19:00
📅 Mondays
📍 MAP 4-5   ¥¥

Green tea reigns supreme in every discerning person's kitchen cupboard, and there isn't a more fashionable place than Cha no Ginza, the ultimate minimal experience in tea shopping. Exquisitely wrapped Gyokuro, Sencha, Kukicha, Houjicha and Genmaicha come in both powder and bag varieties, and the attentive service in English guides you through a tasting. If you have a bit more time on your hands head upstairs to their tearoom where you can experience some of these teas with exquisitely prepared Japanese sweets.

CHARLES JOURDAN

WOMEN'S DESIGNER

2-1-1 Marunouchi, Chiyoda-ku, Tokyo (Others)
03-5220-3530
www.charles-jourdan-bis.jp/
⏱ 11:00–21:00 (Sun/Holidays until 20:00)
🗓 Not fixed
🚶 MAP 7-4   ¥|¥|¥|¥-¥|¥|¥|¥

Amidst a boudoir-like decor, Charles Jourdan shows his pink, beige, and gold leather pumps below rows of pretty tweed suits that can be effortlessly combined with a whole range of soft knitted camisoles and pretty lacy tops.

CHLOÉ

WOMEN'S DESIGNER

5-3-2 Minami-Aoyama, Minato-ku, Tokyo (Others)
03-4335-1750
www.chloe.com
⏱ 11:00–20:00
🗓 No holidays
🚶 MAP 1-24   ¥|¥|¥|¥-¥|¥|¥|¥

Chloé was a darling of Tokyo's gorgeous long before it recently opened its first stand-alone store on chichi Miyuki Street. The Chloé design team's latest collection stars here with soft easy vintage-inspired shapes, buttons that are either miniscule or mammoth, and Chloé's signature style, combined with mini-skirted earthy, military chic. As Swedish designer Paolo Melim Andersson, the new designer from Marni takes over, Chloé retains its girlishness but seems to be getting tougher. While Chloé find its voice in the next few seasons fans will still remain in love with their foxy accessories and shoes in silver, gold and beautiful shades of brown. The complex is also home to boutiques for Omega watches and Cartier and there's a nearby restaurant run by Michelin three-star chef Pierre Gagnaire.

CHRISTIAN LACROIX

WOMEN'S DESIGNER

3-3-1 Ginza, Chuo-ku, Tokyo (Others)
03-5524-3365
www.christian-lacroix.fr/
⏱ 11:00–20:00
🗓 No holidays
🚶 MAP 3-6   ¥|¥|¥|¥

If you see something really red and very crazy walking down the street, it could quite possibly be a Christian Lacroix creation. His wit, provincial taste for flashy colors, and unquestioning loyalty to his buoyant silhouettes at a time when the world was going Japanese minimal, make him a brave man in the fashion world. His clothes for women are all about color, decoration, and hyper femininity. Tokyo loves this man and why not? In this cute flagship store there is a lot of eyepopping gear, including red velvet jeans for men combined with navy pea coats and military greatcoats in a sartorial style that belongs only to him. His recent comeback makes this shop a great visit.

CHRISTOPHE COPPENS

MEN'S/WOMEN'S HATS

3-7-6 Kita-Aoyama, Minato-ku, Tokyo
03-5774-5426
🕐 11:00—20:00
📅 No Holidays
🚶 MAP 6-24   ¥|¥|¥|¥

The only sign outside of the decorative plumes waiting for you inside is a huge empty white aviary. Step through the aviary to be immediately transported into Christophe Coppen's 1940s boudoir, full of his precious hats: inspired classic haute couture pieces, head dresses with plumes and tiny triangles, and his famous toques with ruffles that come in silk in summer and tweed and wool in the winter. Christophe aspires to quench women's thirst for accessories with scarves in tulle, lace and silk, leather brooches in the shape of a duck, and slim gloves. The men's section rocks like an 80s discotheque: straw hats with a hand sculpted on the head, a mask modeled again on the top of the hat, caskets in tweed or edelweiss flower prints, herringbone and dotted silk hunting caps, and a tie collection with sequins and embroidery that can be a great accessory for women too. This is Coppen's only boutique outside Brussels and because he takes such personal care of each corner here, you will also find his own toy collection on sale, along with his sculptures and baby face candles. A superb destination to head to when you are itching to spend your bonus.

CHROME HEARTS

MEN'S/WOMEN'S ACCESSORIES

6-3-14 Minami-Aoyama, Minato-ku,
  Tokyo (Others)
03-5766-1081
www.united-arrows.co.jp/ch/
🕐 weekdays/12:00—20:00.Holidays/11:00—20:00
📅 second Wednesdays
🚶 MAP 1-25   ¥|¥|¥|¥

Badass rock-chic celebrity shop, a favourite haunt of Santana, Lenny Kravitz, Mischa Barton, Karl Lagerfeld et al. Everything here is handmade luxury but comes with tons of attitude. Some of the stuff comes with a "fuck you" label and most of the rings, pendants, and sunglasses come with the trademark dagger or fleur-de-lys symbol. The second floor stocks leather jackets and boots, all with a metallic dagger symbol. You don't have to be badass or a rocker to wear this, but if you want people to look at you differently, this is one quick way to do it.

CIAOPANIC

MEN'S/WOMEN'S BOUTIQUE

6-12-22 Jingumae, Shibuya-ku,
  Tokyo (Others)
03-5774-7941
ciaopanic.com/index.html
🕐 11:00—20:00
📅 Not fixed
🚶 MAP 6-25   ¥|¥

Enter this spacious complex decorated in wood and you will find that Ciaopanic sells clothes, not fashion. Clothes, that is, that you would never wear anywhere but on the weekend: scarily cheap bomber jackets, biker jackets, trousers, cotton shirts, skirts, tops, dresses, and loads of duffle bags and backpacks. There is not much reason to shop here for clothes, but the casual bags do make it worth the trip. Besides you never know what you'll find. How about some handmade totem dolls, perfect for your mobile phone?

CIBONE
INTERIOR

Aoyama Bell–Commons B1F, 2–14–6 Kita–Aoyama, Minato–ku, Tokyo (Others)
03–3475–8017
www.cibone.com/
🕐 11:00–21:00
📅 Not fixed
📍 MAP 16-3

¥|¥|¥|¥

Cibone offers bright ideas for compiling the overall look for your house. This remains the only shop in town that dares to make business sense out of really extravagant product design—case in point, the Moooi horse lamp, a life-size horse sculpture with a lamp on its head that costs close to a month's salary. The shop remains loyal to this design collaborative and also stocks a great collection of their furniture. Those looking for the wow factor, but less loaded with cash will be delighted with the extensive collection of fabrics for the house, rugs, duvets, and curtains, knives from Global, and coffee makers and mixers with a retro cool vibe. The sporty will love the Saya Form dumbbells and the Speedo Comme des garçons bathing suits. To go for glamor for the house while ignoring yourself would, of course, be unacceptable, so Cibone also sells dead-stock Pucci dresses and tops.

CLASSICS THE SMALL LUXURY
HANDKERCHIEFS

Roppongi Hills West Walk 4F, 6-10-3 Roppongi, Minato-ku, Tokyo
03-5786-9790
www.classics-the-small-luxury.com
🕐 11:00–21:00
📅 No holidays
📍 MAP 12-8

¥|-|¥|¥

This shop dedicated to handkerchiefs celebrates the great come-back of these indispensable little cloth accessories. An initialed or monogrammed handkerchief in one of the many beautiful colors available in cotton, silk, or the most coveted linen, can add unique style to any outfit. Personalise them, as the shop offers an impressively thick album of motif designs at a very reasonable cost. Men who love to sport pocket squares can mooch about to find the perfect casual round puff, the right angle, or the diagonal.

COACH

MEN'S WOMEN'S ACCESSORIES

20-11 Udagawa-cho, Shibuya-ku,
Tokyo (Others)
03-6415-7711
www.coach.com
🕐 11:00–20:00 (Sun–Thu)/11:00–
21:00 (Fri/Sat)
📋 Not fixed
🚇 MAP 8-15   ¥¥¥-¥¥¥¥

Coach is definitely the hottest favorite of all preppy Tokyo women—especially since designer Reed Krakoff added some much-needed pizzazz with his powder blue, apple green, and ruby red take on previously frumpy Coach bags. This shop features total Coach coordinates, including cell-phone cases, pouches in all shapes, sizes, colors, ever popular hats, sunglasses, notebooks and, of course, bags, bags and more bags. For flying in style, their luggage could definitely be an option. And check out the Tokyo-only, limited-edition collection created specially for this city's truly-loyal women.

COCCINELLE

WOMEN'S ACCESSORIES

Shin-Kokusai Bldg.1F, 3-4-1 Marunouchi,
Chiyoda-ku, Tokyo
03-5224-6222
www.coccinelle.it/
🕐 11:00–20:00
📋 Not fixed
🚇 MAP 7-5   ¥¥¥-¥¥¥¥

Another Milanese leather accessories maker to make you drool, with an extensive bag collection that caters to budgets large and small. Beetle-inspired shapes in many different sizes, leathers, colors and unfussy styles.

COLE HAAN

MEN'S/WOMEN'S SHOES

Roppongi Hills Hill Side B1F, 6-10-2
Roppongi, Minato-ku, Tokyo (Others)
03-5771-2801
www.colehaan.com
🕐 11:00–20:00
📋 No holidays
🚇 MAP 12-9   ¥¥¥

Cole Haan's sporty, casual, and formal bags and shoes come with great style and at great prices. While the women's collection sees winning pumps in suede and calf leather, the men's collection is loved for the range of semi casual sporty styles in leather. But if you love Cole Haan, the essential item for both men and women is the collaboration with Nike Air. NBA and white-soled trainers some to mind? Look again. Cole Haan does its usual elegant lasts in patent leather and suede, and Nike lends its air soles. The result is platform heels that are tall, glamorous and very comfortable. For men the result is round-toed, sharp-looking comfort shoes in dark leather with fine velcro straps.

COLLEX LIVING
INTERIOR

1-1-4 Aobadai, Meguro-ku, Tokyo
03-5784-5612
www.collex.jp/
⊘ 11:00–20:00
▦ Not fixed
⌐ MAP 2-18   ¥|¥|¥|¥

Yet another shop to help you accessorize your Tokyo pad. Rolls of fabric, cushion covers, curtains, bags, blankets, place mats, napkins, lighting, tableware, flower vases and all other accoutrements for living in style. The shop also offers graphic design posters and the best of Emilio Pucci-designed vintage ceramics absolutely impossible to find elsewhere.

COLOUR BY NUMBERS
MEN'S/WOMEN'S BOUTIQUE

20-23 Daikanyamacho, Shibuya-ku,
  Tokyo
03-3770-1991
none
⊘ 12:00–20:00
▦ Not fixed
⌐ MAP 2-19   ¥|¥|¥-¥|¥|¥|¥

An offshoot of the cult shop Loveless, the collections at Colour By Numbers read like the latest trend report from the catwalk. While the foreign brands are undoubtedly the best names, if you are a Japanese fashionophile, the collections here are a have-to-have with Green, Green man, Mastermind Japan, John Lawrence Sullivan, Foundation Addict, Mosslight, Education From Young Machines, Kolor, Yoshio Kubo, Ensor Civet, Nozomi Ishiguro and Nom de Guerre. Attentive service and bright arty interiors add to the shopping experience.

COMME DES GARÇONS
MEN'S/WOMEN'S DESIGNER

5-2-1 Minami-Aoyama, Minato-ku,
  Tokyo (Others)
03-3406-3951
none
⊘ 11:00–20:00
▦ Not fixed
⌐ MAP 1-26   ¥|¥|¥|¥-¥|¥|¥|¥

Trail blazer and *enfant terrible* Rei Kawakubo's avant garde clothes are not for the faint hearted. For her fans, this superb Future Systems designed shop is a shrine to anticonservatism and extreme personal style, with her entire collections of Comme des Garçons, Comme des Garçons Comme des Garçons and her men's collection. You will often find androgynous clothes in black, dark gray, and white, with flashes of her favorite color, red, and trimmings with velvet or stripes. Not all is extreme, though; there are black umbrella-cut dresses to be paired with beautiful patent ballerinas in shocking red and black—and the most superbly tailored dark suits for men to be worn with military boots. Japanese fans of Rei Kawakubo are known to sport the same hairstyle as the donna herself, with heavy bangs and shoulder-length hair. Once they acquire a taste for her clothes, few ever buy anything else. You will also find collections from Azzedine Aläia and for Homme, Homme Deux, Tao and Tricot head to the nearby 10 Corso Como Comme des Garçons store.

COMPTOIR DES COTONNIERS
WOMEN'S BOUTIQUE

5-5-2 Minami Aoyama, Minato-ku, Tokyo (Others)
03-5766-2891
www.comptoirdescotonniers.co.jp
🕐 11:00–20:00
📅 Not fixed
📍 MAP 1-27   ¥|¥-¥|¥|¥

It's true that no one waxes lyrical about their separates, but the good quality 100% cotton and wool, in shapes that are basic enough to take you through trend after trend, are just some of the reasons why all the hotties discreetly keep on coming back for more. Their clothes in white, black, grey, and bordeaux, with shirts, cable-knit sweaters, pea coats, pants, and skirts, for mere and fille, are clean, wise, and fuss free.

CONCENTO H.P. FRANCE
WOMEN'S BOUTIQUE

Ginza Komatsu Store 2F, 6-9-5 Ginza, Chuo-ku, Tokyo
03-3573-0390
www.hpfrance.com/concentoweb/
🕐 11:00–20:00
📅 No holidays
📍 MAP 4-6   ¥|¥|¥-¥|¥|¥|¥

A great place for style swapping or easing into new looks, be it preppy, sporty chic or boho splendor. Cozy knits in beautiful yarns sometimes with a bit of eccentric lace, pencil skirts in gabardine, low boots, high boots, metallic sandals, embroidered tunic caftans, avant-garde T-shirts, and the occasional Stephen Jones hat, Concento's prolific buyers stock it all from boyish to beautiful.

CONCIERGE GRAND
INTERIOR/ACCESSORIES

12-8 Sarugaku-cho, Shibuya-ku, Tokyo (Others)
03-5728-5794
www.concierge-net.com/
🕐 12:00–20:00
📅 No holidays
📍 MAP 2-20   ¥|¥-¥|¥|¥

Bonjour! Que desirez-vous? Concierge is for everyday knickknacks *à la française*, from Hermès-inspired luggage to an entire series of Repetto shoes, plus aromatherapy goods, linen totes, organic soaps, handmade paper notebooks and little pieces of luxury that hark back to a slower southern French way of life. There's a number of shops around town, each with a different collection.

CONRAN SHOP

INTERIOR

Shinjuku Park Tower 3/4F, 3-7-1 Nishi-
Shinjuku, Shinjuku-ku, Tokyo (Others)
03-5322-6600
www.conran.ne.jp/
🕐 Mon/Tue/Thu 10:30–19:00 Fri/Sat/
Sun 10:00–19:30
📅 closed on Wed and the 1st and 3rd
Tues of the month
📍 MAP 9-6   ¥/¥-¥/¥/¥/¥

When you buy gifts from the Conran shop you secretly want to
keep them for yourself. Quality kitchen equipment such as Mukka
Express for a good cappuccino experience, Conran cups, saucers,
dishes, and bowls, body care items made of yoghurt and white tea,
trikes and toy registers for kids, fashion storage solutions, vases,
lamps (including the Taliesin lamp from Frank Lloyd Wright), a
beautiful array of candles come Christmas, Alessi watches, trendy
CD compilations including the neighboring Park Hyatt compilation
and 10 Corso Como and state-of-the-art mini gymnasiums for the
house. While the shop in Tokyo is more scaled down than its over-
seas counterparts, there is still enough going on here to give your
Tokyo apartment a great pedigree.

COPO

WOMEN'S LEGWEAR

2-30-4 Dogenzaka, Shibuya-ku, Tokyo
03-3461-0620
www.miyama-tex.co.jp/copo/copo_
02.html
🕐 10:00–21:30
📅 No holidays
📍 MAP 8-16   ¥

Witness the climax of Japan's wildest and weirdest leg fashions
here—from five toed socks, lacy nothings tied around the calf, and
fluoro pink bands tied high on the thigh, to more than a hundred
styles of the humble ankle-length sock. While socks with stilettos
still upset the establishment, every self-respecting 00s girl should
own at least a dozen. There is no place better in the world to fully
indulge your foot fetish.

CORIOLIS

WOMEN'S BOUTIQUE

6-2-9 Minami-Aoyama, Minato-ku, Tokyo
03-5469-8080
www.coriolis.jp/
🕐 11:00–20:00
📅 No holidays
📍 MAP 1-28   ¥/¥/¥/¥-¥/¥/¥/¥

Coriolis does not seem like a diehard fashionista haunt but its collection of neatly laid-out Hermès, Chanel, and Bottega Veneta
delectables are bound to make any fashionista quiver. Coriolis
sells new and secondhand versions of these most wanted bags and
very often in colors that are impossible to find elsewhere. The best
thing, however, is that there is no wait for any of these winners and
you could leave with a Kelly or a Birkin swinging from your arm as
soon as you are ready to splash the cash.

CORNELIANI

MEN'S BOUTIQUE

3-1-1 Marunouchi, Chiyoda-ku, Tokyo
03-3214-2500
www.corneliani.com
🕐 11:00–19:00
📅 Wednesdays
♪ MAP 7-6

¥|¥|¥|¥

The elegance of Corneliani strikes you immediately as you step into the shop. For the best head to the rows of *su misura* custom made suits that line the wall. With two buttons, three buttons and double breasted six button jackets they can be remade to perfectly fit you. The suits go to Italy, along with your measurements and take a minimum of 45 days to re-size until they are delivered to you. Apart from the suits, you can buy almost any article of men's clothing here. They also do single-breasted and double-breasted ready made suits, shirts, ties, and accessories plus weekend casuals such as neat jackets that are favored by young convertible-driving CEO types.

COSME KITCHEN

COSMETICS

19-4 Daikanyama, Shibuya-ku, Tokyo
03-5428-2733
gw.tv/fw/shop/pc/cosme/
🕐 11:00–20:00
📅 No holidays
♪ MAP 2-21

¥|¥

Commuters who pass through Daikanyama station, where this store is conveniently located, get off to replenish, resource, recharge and go back to the basics with the best entirely organic collections in town. Agronatura's essentials, Weleda products both for parents and baby, Borba skin balance crystals, Lavera/Bloom natural cosmetics, a superb collection of the natural cosmetics collection from Ren, the Burt's Bees range made from natural beeswax, and many other old and beauty favorites. If the shopping proves exhausting, replenish with their natural juices and Vitamin C shakes available at the juice bar in the corner.

COSTUME NATIONAL

MEN'S/WOMEN'S DESIGNER

5-9-6 Minami-Aoyama, Minato-ku,
  Tokyo (Others)
03-3499-4004
www.costumenational.com/
🕐 11:30–20:00
📅 No holidays
♪ MAP 1-29

¥|¥|¥|¥

Designer Ennio Capasa trained under none other than Yohji Yamamoto. Hence, the severely sleek sharp lines, lots of brooding black, and luxe textures. The look is street inspired, constantly edgy and razor sharp with a strong tailored look. Even the leather jackets for men feel light and sharp. The women's collection is about super tight jackets with no room for anything underneath and lots of trouser-suit and skirt-suit combinations. Costume National Homme is favored by those men who like their trousers sharp and tapered and their jackets and shirts to make a chic underground style statement.

COURRÈGES

WOMEN'S DESIGNER

4F Tokyu Shibuya, 2-24-1 Dogenzaka, Shibuya-ku, Tokyo (Others)
03-3477-3815
www.courreges.com/
🕐 11:00–19:00
🗓 Not fixed
MAP 8-17

¥│¥│¥

Trends come and go but Courrèges will always be about A-line silhouettes in jackets, skirts and dresses combined with white boots and accessories for what Courrèges calls a "moon girl" look. Andre Courrèges was the father of the mini and the brand cuts away all the unnecessary for a stark, minimal look The pants have a unisex appeal and the only accessories that match well with them are the flat, shiny white mid-shin high PVC boots first created in 1964 and matching golf gloves.

CP COMPANY

MEN'S/WOMEN'S BOUTIQUE

6-4-6 Minami-Aoyama, Minato-ku, Tokyo (Others)
03-5766-8358
www.cpcompany.com
🕐 11:00–20:00
🗓 No holidays
MAP 1-30

¥│¥│¥

If you think haute couture is a pain, and preppy style is a bit twee, you are a CP Company kind of guy. This Italian company's quality and function always strikes a chord with freewheeling liberal types. Inspired by camping, CP Company is most famous in Japan for its windproof and rainproof, ultra sturdy, double layered nylon mesh coat that you can stuff with newspapers to keep warm in case of an earthquake or on a run through the jungle at night. Highly designed, practical and definitely strange; CP Company or Stone Island's stuff is more product design than catwalk style.

CRADLE

EYEWEAR

5-11-5 Minami-Aoyama, Minato-ku, Tokyo
03-6418-0577
www.cradle.ne.jp
🕐 11:00–20:00
🗓 Tuesdays
MAP 1-31

¥│¥│¥-¥│¥│¥│¥

Cradle's beautifully designed wooden interiors offer a made-to-order service for eyewear, where you can design a perfect pair of frames for yourself, or select one of their many ready-made models which are then reworked to suit your face. If you prefer ready-made, Cradle offers a superb selection from the world's greats such as Alain Mikli, the extravagant ic! Berlin, retro Selima Optique, sporty Oakley, classic Theo, and many others. The collections here are slightly different from Globe Specs but chosen with as much discretion, so visiting both these shops gives you an uparalleled view through the world's best frames.

CROON A SONG

WOMEN'S BOUTIQUE

6–11–8 Minami–Aoyama, Minato–ku, Tokyo (Others)
03–3797–4003
www.croon-a-song.com/
🕐 11:00–20:00
📅 Wednesdays
↟ MAP 1-32   ¥|¥|¥

A quick-fix shop for all your fashion blues. Croon A Song has a collection of men's and women's urban casual chic separates from the trendiest of Japanese and foreign brands. For men there are a lot of cardigans, coats, pants, shirts, and suits, all fit for a modern day poet. For women the typical style would be a shirt from Biba paired with a 60s inspired A-line woven skirt and Nathalie Costes accessories in beautiful rounded shapes of wood in bright colors. While the look is that of high luxe, the prices remain reasonable.

CYNTHIA ROWLEY

WOMEN'S DESIGNER

5-9-9 Minami-Aoyama, Minato-ku, Tokyo (Others)
03-6419-8355
www.cynthiarowley.com
🕐 11:00–20:00
📅 Not fixed
↟ MAP 1-33   ¥|¥|¥

Another New Yorker loved by Tokyoites, Cynthia Rowley is the perfect destination for dresses with a buzz. They come in almost all colors under the sun, from red, electric blue, and emerald green, to brown, black and fuschia. Rowley takes a miniskirt and adds trimmings and frills, gives tops layered sleeves and wide necks, and embroiders and beads cardigans to create looks that are oh-so-cute. She also does tops and coats all inspired by her dress philosophy, and her bags, shoes, and supporting accessories conjure up images of chillin' with the likes of Eva Longoria and Hillary Duff. Her shop is decorated both inside and out in pretty swirls, and also stocks colorful eyewear and her book of stories called *Slim*.

CZ LABO

SPA

Omotesando Square Bldg. 4F, 4-3-2 Jingumae, Shibuya-ku, Tokyo (Others)
03-5772-4200
www.ci-z.com/salon/index.html
🕐 11:00–20:00
📅 Not fixed
↟ MAP 5-13

The most hedonistic spa indulgence available on the planet. Try the celeb champagne gold course, where you bathe in a jacuzzi filled with 22 bottles of champagne, followed by a body peel with diamond dust guaranteed to leave you dazzling. With the hefty price tag, there have been only five people who have been able to justify this expense. For the rest of us, the extensive range of very professional problem skin rejuvenation and body care therapies leave the skin sparkling and the wallet in excellent shape.

DANIEL CREMIEUX

MEN'S BOUTIQUE

6-3-11 Minami-Aoyama, Minato-ku, Tokyo (Others)
03-3486-8933
www.danielcremieux.com/
🕐 11:00–20:00
🗓 Not fixed
🚇 MAP 1-34

¥│¥│¥-¥│¥│¥│¥

If you happen to approach a Parisien type of well-dressed gentleman in an al fresco café on the weekend, there is a 60 percent chance that he's dressed in Daniel Cremieux—the brand for sartorial French chic. For years he's been outfitting the French Open staff, and recently he's been celebrating thirty years with two great jackets: Dandy Parisien, a one button loose fitting pinstripe blazer ideally paired with a white shirt, and the khaki Titi Parisien. The latter is a great take on the traditional safari suit with large pockets, great for the urban crusader of all ages. This shop also stocks his dress shirts, shoes, bags, fragrance, and lots of French toiletries and other things that traditionally rule men's wardrobes. While the shop looks nondescript, rumors have it that very soon Tokyo will be home to the biggest collection of Daniel Cremieux in the world

DARJEELING DAYS

MEN'S BOUTIQUE

1-9-4 Yurakucho, Chiyoda-ku, Tokyo (Others)
03-5293-4900
www.darjeelingdays.jp/
🕐 11:00–20:00
🗓 Not fixed
🚇 MAP 7-7

¥│¥│¥

Darjeeling Days has chic casuals for weekends when action is limited to cafes, movies, and candlelight dinners. Chinos, slacks, shirts, cotton vests, knit sweaters, scarves, and berets form the greater part of this classic yet youthful collection aimed almost exclusively at dandies.

DECADE

MEN'S/WOMEN'S BOUTIQUE

5-12-4 Minami Aoyama, Minato-ku, Tokyo
03-5468-3755
www.atelier-h.co.jp/
🕐 11:30–20:30
🗓 Wednesdays
🚇 MAP 1-35

¥│¥│¥

One of Japan's claims to fame in the fashion world is hi-tech fibers. At this cozy store, you are privy to some of the best home grown knit labels like Kiit—a brand that weaves ultra fine knits with super stretch cotton yarn into comfortable and reasonably priced men's casuals. T-shirts, jerseys, tanks, and button-downs that can all be paired with each other. The favorites among the city's fashion pack are the cotton coats in black, and olive green trousers in a self-argyle weave. Perfect finishing means that most clothes can almost be worn in reverse. Decade also stocks some German designers in the same tone, and casual staples from Stephan Schneider.

DELFONICS

STATIONERY

Omotesando Hills Main Bldg. B3F, 4-12-10
Jingumae, Shibuya-ku, Tokyo (Others)
03-5410-0590
www.delfonics.com/
🕐 11:00–21:00
📅 Not fixed
📍 MAP 5-14   ¥|¥|¥

Delfonics consider themselves purveyors of culture so they fuse style with stationery. Head here if you need a dramatic writing instrument, a show-stopping diary, or a theatrical leather pen case. Write history on their myriad note books in fruity colors. Their sculptural holder transforms a humble roll of cellophane tape into an item exuding power and confidence on your bureau. Find also calendars to help you plan your next date and if nothing else you will fall for their simple wooden ball-point pens, Japanese cloth diaries, file covers or little knick knacks that always find a place in your briefcase or purse.

DESIGN COLLECTION

INTERIOR

Matsuya Dept. Store 3-6-1 Ginza,
Chuo-ku, Tokyo
03-3567-1211
www.matsuya.com
🕐 10:00–20:00 (Mon/Tue. until 19:30)
📅 Not Fixed
📍 MAP 3-7   ¥-¥|¥|¥

In 1955, just as theories of modern design were starting to grip Europe, visionaries at Matsuya created a shop dedicated to "good design." Half a decade later, this still remains one of the most interesting product design shops in town. The shop has its very own Design Committee (that includes luminaries like architect Kengo Kuma and Kiyonoro Kikutake) that handpicks products on sale here. Among other hot favorites are the one-of-a-kind Reidel sake tasting glass, beautiful and reasonable Dbros plastic foldable flower vases, Eschenbac binoculars and the latest furoshiki cloth, traditionally used for wrapping gifts and lunchboxes in Japan. While collections change often there is always a range of winning cutlery, glassware and stationery, handpicked by the shops star design committee that leaves even the most difficult design diva gasping for more.

DESIGNWORKS CONCEPT STORE

MEN'S/WOMEN'S BOUTIQUE

B1F–2F, 4-21-26 Minami Aoyama,
Minato-ku, Tokyo (Others)
03-5772-1115
www.abahouse.co.jp/
🕐 11:00–20:00
📅 Holidays
📍 MAP 1-36   ¥|¥|¥-¥|¥|¥|¥

Luxury for gents at a price that doesn't break the bank is hard to come by in this town. This store offers just that with high quality traditional and stylish clothes. Heavy on shirts and accessories from Etro and Alessandro Dell'Acqua, the shops own labels include shirts, trousers and suits in casual fabric with formal styling. Nothing is super expensive here, but depending on how you coordinate, you could make it look that way. Great accessories such as alligator, ostrich and lizard skin belts, Vinci loafers and a good collection of bags for men completes the wardrobe. The women's collection is classic, with Mulberry bags, Louboutin shoes and clothes from Givenchy, Chloé and Cividini.

DESTINATION TOKYO
MEN'S/WOMEN'S BOUTIQUE

Lumine est B2F, 3-38-1 Shinjuku, Shinjuku-ku, Tokyo (Others)
03-3350-5027
www.destinationtokyo.net
◷ 10:30–21:30
▦ No holidays
⌁ MAP 9-7   ¥¥¥-¥¥¥¥

A small shot of contemporary art and fashion to heal the culturally deprived, this space is charged with creativity. Ex-pilot-turned-lighting designer Ante Vojnovic often does the window displays using things he finds in Akihabara, and the entrance features installations created by artists like Nozomi Ishiguro. The shop stocks a huge collection of Jacques Le Corre's unstructured hats and bowler bags in many colors and combinations. Argentinian star Tramando's collections of silky, hand-dyed polyester clothes line the racks alongside Brazilian Alexandre Herchcovitch, and for feet that crave variety, Francesca Giobbi's jewel-like shoes and sandals in the softest of precious leathers and myriad colors are an all-round winner.

DES PRÉS
WOMEN'S BOUTIQUE

Marunouchi Bldg. 1F, 2–4–1 Marunouchi, Chiyoda–ku, Tokyo (Others)
03-5220-4485
www.despres.jp/
◷ 11:00–21:00 (Sundays until 21:00)
▦ No holidays
⌁ MAP 7-8   ¥¥¥

Des Prés' best offerings are their knit lines, especially pieces in wool and silk, that include sexy wraparound dresses, sweaters and skirts. While shopping here is most fun in the winter, summer sees linen jackets, tailored shorts, and cotton shirts all better for the office than the weekend. But be it summer or winter, Des Prés always stocks some nice little cocktail dresses with short hemlines, full skirts and pretty colors and textures to be elegantly complemented by shoes from Christian Louboutin and Manolo Blahnik.

DEUXIEME CLASSE
WOMEN'S BOUTIQUE

5–3–25 Minami Aoyama, Minato–ku, Tokyo (Others)
03–5469–8868
www.baycrews.co.jp/deuxiemeclasse/
🕐 11:00–20:00
🗓 Not fixed
♪ MAP 1-37 ¥¥¥

In fashion speak this shop is oxymoronically described as "young French traditional." But you could call it another version of Drawer, with the same shoes and accessories (but much cheaper) and coats, blouses, skirts and dresses of great quality. There are also a lot of original vintage-inspired dresses and formal gear to impress at wedding parties. With a lot of designs from near and far, the store offers luxury at a pretty decent price.

DEVICE TOKYO
MEN'S/WOMEN'S BOUTIQUE

6-16-2 Jingumae, Shibuya-ku, Tokyo
03-5774-5107
None
🕐 12:00–20:00
🗓 No holidays
♪ MAP 6-26 ¥¥¥

Device Tokyo's exploration of street clothing is done to a turn. T-shirts are stretch cotton, but come in black and white leopard prints and reach almost to mid-thigh. Suits are given a kick with classic lapels that are extended to go around the waist. Trousers have attached skirts; vests come with extra long turtlenecks; and there are many other such ideas guaranteed to turn curious heads.

DIABRO
WOMEN'S BOUTIQUE

3F, 4-2-16 Shinjuku, Shinjuku-ku, Tokyo
03-5367-0203
www.diabro.jp
🕐 11:00–20:00 (Sat/Sun/Holidays until 21:00)
🗓 No holidays
♪ MAP 9-8 ¥¥¥

Diabro is tiny, hidden, and very humble looking. Importing the latest it-bags, shirts and T-shirts, what it lacks in ambiance it makes up for with great prices. Currently the rage is for Marni shirts, Pucci and Dsquared T-shirts, and a great range of Miu Miu and extensive Balenciaga—Twiggy, Motorcycle and City bags. Diabro manages to get new stuff everyday, and an excellent web page in English helps minimize your shopping time.

DIANE VON FURSTENBERG

WOMEN'S DESIGNER

6–1–3 Minami–Aoyama, Minato–ku, Tokyo
03–3498–4301
www.dvf.com
🕐 11:00–20:00
📅 No holidays
📍 MAP 1-38

¥|¥|¥-¥|¥|¥|¥

This is all about the wrap dress, Diane's signature dresses (that she made a comeback with in the late 90s after having closed shop for almost two decades) in many different colors and patterns, unleashed faster than the seasons and keeping you constantly in touch but still above trends. Easy to wash, wear, and keep, girls are known to have armies of these in their wardrobe because they walk you through the day at work and off to any dinner or event with an equal amount of charm. If you have too many dresses already, then get the jersey skirts and matching silk shirts; they fit well and last through many seasons.

DIESEL

MEN'S/WOMEN'S DENIM

2-32-5 Jingumae, Shibuya-ku, Tokyo (Others)
03-5786-0291
www.diesel.co.jp
🕐 11:00–20:00
📅 No holidays
📍 MAP 5-15

¥|¥|-¥|¥|¥

Under creative and financial overlord Renzo Rosso, Diesel has elbowed its way from ultra casual to hottest on the high street. Since 1985 Diesel has been spinning regular winners, with the American Indian T-shirt, superbly beaten oh-so-hot jeans, equally stressed bags, shoes and chunky silver jewelry that could equip even the biggest preppy with the tools to hit the most underground night club. This shop has a zone dedicated to denim freaks—plus great women's wear and men's wear in tech fabrics and graphic design prints. If you're looking for the perfect fit, you can be sure Diesel has it, in more than one style.

DIESEL DENIM GALLERY

MEN'S/WOMEN'S DENIM

20-13 Sarugakucho, Shibuya-ku, Tokyo (Others)
03-5784-3812
www.diesel.com/
🕐 11:30–20:00
📅 No holidays
📍 MAP 2-22

¥|¥|-¥|¥|¥

In case you didn't know already, Diesel Style Lab is Diesel gear straight from the sizzling catwalks. This is where Diesel stocks all the testosterone. The collections are limited edition jeans, denim jackets, shirts, cashmere sweaters, and a range of buttery T-shirts that come with quintessential Diesel edge but at higher prices.

DIOR

WOMEN'S DESIGNER

5-9-11 Jingumae, Shibuya-ku,
Tokyo (Others)
03-5464-6260/6261
fashion.dior.com
⊘ 11:00–20:00
🗓 Not fixed
↲ MAP 6-27

¥|¥|¥|¥

The entire Dior collection of clothes, bags, shoes, accessories and cosmetics takes center stage here in this architectural gem by Japanese architects Sanaa. The latest slouchy Gaucho bags are a hot favorite, along with the all-time favorite hourglass Dior jackets available in spy lace, sexy silk and casual chic denim. The second floor is also home to inspiringly romantic knee-length and floor length dresses. Go backstage at the show collections upstairs and experience complete Dior makeovers along with manicures and pedicures with Dior logo nail art.

DIOR HOMME

MEN'S DESIGNER

5–9–11 Jingumae, Shibuya–ku,
Tokyo (Others)
03–5464–6260/6261
fashion.dior.com
⊘ 11:00–20:00
🗓 Not fixed
↲ MAP 6-28

¥|¥|¥|¥

Today's man's man must have at least one Hedi Slimane suit in his wardrobe. His looks are luxurious and sharply tailored but exude an energy found only in underground street labels. Sexy and lean, his razor cut pieces are great at work and beyond. Drainpipe trousers, stick suits, clingy sweaters, long dress shirts and just about slim everything for those with the wallet and the waist. The result made even Karl Lagerfeld shed pounds to get into the smallest size of Dior Homme.

DIPTYQUE

AROMATHERAPY

Ginza Komatsu 3F, 6-9-5 Ginza,
Chuo-ku, Tokyo
03-3571-4655
www.diptyque.tm.fr/
⊘ 11:00–20:00
🗓 No holidays
↲ MAP 4-7

¥-|¥|¥

The cult home parfumeur from Paris has finally breezed into Tokyo with a tiny corner in the plush Ginza Komatsu boutique. Their exquisite collection is exactly the same as in Paris—50 fragrances in candles, upliftingly sweet and sharp home perfumes, Eau de Toilette, hair- and body-wash in their richest and most lavish bouquets.

DISTRICT UNITED ARROWS

MEN'S/WOMEN'S BOUTIQUE

5-17-9 Jingumae, Shibuya-ku, Tokyo
(Other)
03-5464-2715
www.district.jp
🕐 12:00–20:00 (Sat/Sun/Holidays
11:00–20:00)
📅 No holidays
📍 MAP 6-29　　　¥|¥|¥|¥

For a wardrobe with a healthy collection of things that stand out, shop here for Kris van Assche, Dries Van Notten, Raf Simons, and Japanese designers Sae, Mandou, and Kolor. The stress is on "core dressing"—a favorite phrase among stylists meaning basics that get you noticed. They are also fond of tailoring, and since no one does men's pret-a-porter better than Heidi Slimane, you'll find some beautifully tailored jackets and slim pants.

DKNY

MEN'S/WOMEN'S DESIGNER

5-17-4 Jingumae, Shibuya-ku,
Tokyo (Others)
03-6418-8185
www.dkny.com/
🕐 11:00–20:00
📅 No holidays
📍 MAP 6-30　　　¥|¥|¥-¥|¥|¥|¥

DKNY brings Donna's school of cool to sporty casuals—"all American" tops, skirts, jeans, Ts, sweats, sweaters, and even a range of party clothes. For women, all the clothes strive to keep bits and pieces of feminine details like frills, lace or animal prints, and the look is best when it's hastily put together. The men's look is funkier, with body-hugging jerseys with V- and crew-necks, merino sweaters, and motorcycle jackets. Try also the DKNY jeans in skinny black for men, a new style that has recently come out in classic low-rise and is now climbing up the popularity charts.

DOLCE & GABBANA

MEN'S/WOMEN'S DESIGNER

Omotesando Hills, 4-12-10 Jingumae,
Shibuya-ku, Tokyo (Others)
03-5785-0853
www.dolcegabbana.it
🕐 11:00–21:00
📅 Not fixed
📍 MAP 5-16　　　¥|¥|¥|¥-¥|¥|¥|¥|¥

Extravagant, nonchalant, in-your face, and sexed-up. Headline makers and rule breakers swamp this black-lacquer, metal-curtained flagship store, which comes equipped with a martini and champagne bar. It is the men's casual collection that takes honors with leather, velvet and old school jackets in colors and stripes, providing a bitter and saucy tone. The must-have Dolce Gabbana item is the grey pinstriped, one button, three-piece suit that always looks great no matter what the occasion. Their drainpipe trousers are also a must-have regardless of season along with the boys' fab jeans that are best worn with a shirt and blazer. Women have their regular collection of snappy accessories in lizard and croc, T-shirts and mini dresses with flowers.

DONNA KARAN

MEN'S/WOMEN'S DESIGNER

3-5-29 Kita-Aoyama, Minato-ku, Tokyo (Others)
03-5414-5500
www.donnakaran.com/
🕐 11:00–20:00
📅 Not fixed
🚇 MAP 5-17

¥|¥|¥|¥

Donna Karan means exquisitely draped dresses in shades of navy and black for elegant women. The way to shop here is to get her basic pieces- the dress, the top, the wraparound skirt, and the jacket that can all be mixed and matched. Her evening looks are often long, draped and in hues of gold and black. Nothing radical; just a great way of dressing for the power woman, which lasts over seasons and years.

DORMEUIL

MEN'S BOUTIQUE

1-1-1 Minami-Aoyama, Minato-ku, Tokyo
03-3470-0251
www.dormeuil.jp/
🕐 11:00–20:00 (Sat/Sun until 19:00)
📅 Not fixed
🚇 MAP 16-4

¥|¥|¥|¥

Dormeuil suits are made from fine fabric woven by Dormeuil. Pure wool woven into a super 180 means that you will be enjoying the warmth of a really thick cable-knit sweater in a feather-light weave—music to the ears for those who hate a lot of winter bulk. Dormeuil's mohair, cashmere, and merino too, are the finest in the world, so you can chuck all your previous woolies for a sleeker, smart all-day look, yet remain toasty warm.

DOUBLE STANDARD CLOTHING

WOMEN'S BOUTIQUE

2F, 4-9-29 Minami-Aoyama, Minato-ku, Tokyo (Others)
03-3401-3770
www.doublestandard.jp/
🕐 11:00–20:00
📅 Not fixed
🚇 MAP 1-39

¥|¥-¥|¥|¥

This shop, with its striking red mannequins and bright walls, is quite a sight for the first-time visitor. They were well known for selling tuxedo jackets long before they became a runway hit. There is a range of masculine and feminine influences, and a combination of many different styles including street, reggae, party, and business. The label has also long been providing quality clothes for older women, successfully combining aspects of tailoring with trends of the moment—such as volume, skinny silhouettes, and a lot of light-weight dresses in summer and day-to-night dress ideas in winter. The good quality also means that the clothes can comfortably survive a few seasons.

DOVER STREET MARKET

MEN'S/WOMEN'S BOUTIQUE/
COSMETICS/INTERIOR

5-12-3 Minami Aoyama, Minato-ku, Tokyo
www.doverstreetmarket.com
03–5468–8301
🕐 11:00–20:00
📅 No holidays
📍 MAP 1-40

¥|¥|¥|¥

Visiting style junkies tend to make a beeline for this guerrilla store decorated like a wooden shack with temporary displays. Collections change often and at the time of printing the store was supposed to be open right though 07. This is the venue of assignation for things like Dover Street original Mickey Mouse merchandise, Tshirts, the Unique series from Top Shop, Junya Watanabe, and Comme des Garçons shirts. Temporary collaborations with many designers and labels are also featured, like their special edition polos with Lacoste, a range of swimwear with Speedo, and jackets from Mon Cler.

DRAWER

WOMEN'S BOUTIQUE

5-12-4 Minami Aoyama, Minato-ku, Tokyo (Others)
03-5464-0226
www.united-arrows.jp/drawer/
🕐 12:00–20:00
📅 Not fixed
📍 MAP 1-41

¥|¥|¥-¥|¥|¥|¥

Expect to see a crowd of Manolo wearers shopping at Drawer for luxurious clothes with the finest detailing. They're looking for the sheerest of frilly tops with draped skirts, iconic black coats in the softest of cashmere, fine woolen dresses that swirl around the knees and lots of extremely smart tailored shorts with jackets. All this can be teamed up with their selection of great imported shoes from Jimmy Choo, Louboutin and YSL, along with the much-talked-about black spider accessories from Lanvin.

DRESSCAMP

MEN'S/WOMEN'S DESIGNER

5-5-1 Minami-Aoyama, Minato-ku, Tokyo
03-5778-3717
www.dresscamp.org/
🕐 12:00–21:00
📅 Not fixed
📍 MAP 1-42

¥|¥|¥-¥|¥|¥|¥

Starting from a humble textile design company a few years ago, Dresscamp's sexy, flamboyant, in-your-face style has taken the fashion world by storm. Multitalented designer Toshikazu Iwaya offers a much welcome deviation from the usually intellectual and deconstructed repertoire of major Japanese designers. Animal print dresses in fabulous colors, baroque print underwear for men, sexy, tight and plunging dresses for the girls and glam casual with big gold buttons for the boys. Iwaya is also the king of collaborations, including a diamond and metal cone watchstrap for Piaget, some Swarovski studded sports wear for Champion, and other hot items that are snapped up as soon as they hit the glam shelves of this flagship store.

DROGA

INTERIOR

20-20 Daikanyama-cho, Shibuya-ku, Tokyo
03-5728-3135
www.droga.jp
🕐 11:00–22:00
📅 No holidays
📍 MAP 2-23

¥¥-¥¥¥

Tokyo just doesn't seem to get enough of interior shops—and this one too tries hard to give a sense of adventure to lifestyle matters. Cactus, soft towels, elegant soap dishes, Eva Solo crockery, folding umbrellas, onion paper note pads, sofas, dog collars, Authentics dustbins, and Le Creuset cookware are part of an extraordinary array of things that the shop insists you absolutely need for your house.

DUAL

WOMEN'S BOUTIQUE

5-12-14 Jingumae, Shibuya-ku, Tokyo
03-5468-3635
www.dualtokyo.com/
🕐 11:00–20:00
📅 Not fixed
📍 MAP 6-31

¥¥¥

Dual will soon have you obsessing about everything from Brazil. First, you'll focus on the great collections from Brazilian designers, both high and low. Comfortable cotton pieces, balloon skirts, great sexy evening looks in a lot of colors, some cover up and some reveal. Since nothing Brazilian could be complete without the bikinis—you'll soon swoon over a range of really brightly colored ones. Once you're satiated with clothes, you'll find other treasured souvenirs—like feather earrings, coco shell accessories, and thread wish bracelets, plus to-die-for Maria Bonita platforms in patent leather.

DUNHILL

MEN'S BOUTIQUE

Daini Iwatsuki Bldg., 6-7-15 Ginza, Chuo-ku, Tokyo (Others)
03-3289-0511
www.dunhill.com
🕐 11:00–20:00
📅 No holidays
📍 MAP 4-8

¥¥¥¥

No longer selling tobacco, this Jermyn Street luxury goods house has transformed itself into a luxury men's lifestyle brand; one, in fact, that outfits the Japan national soccer squad. From fashionable double breasted coats for motoring (*motorities*) in the 20s, to all the stuff a guy needs to board a plane today (*avorities*), the Dunhill family has done a great job with their tradition of reincarnation. Expensive jackets and casual bomber-style blousons in grey, pin stripes, and checks combined with T-shirts and formal shirts line the wood-paneled interiors. The best things are the accessories—croc leather lighters, silver tiger cuff-links, classic leather belts, and a row of leather bags for conservative business elegance.

EDDIE BAUER
MEN'S/WOMEN'S BOUTIQUE

Mosaic Ginza 4F, 5-2-1 Ginza, Chuo-ku,
    Tokyo (Others)
03-3289-2316
www.eddiebauer.co.jp
🕐 10:30–21:00
📅 No holidays
ℹ MAP 4-9   ¥|¥|¥

This popular casual brand was originally a supplier of clothes to White House guards, the navy, and the police. In its high street reincarnation, it was only expected that they launch into military casual looks for the public. Wrinkle resistant Ts, flat fronted chinos, the "must" military jacket, swimwear, shirts, blouses, knit-tops and hoodies for men and women, plus loads of outerwear and gear for life on the road.

EDIFICE et IÉNA
MEN'S/WOMEN'S BOUTIQUE

2-5-2 Marunouchi, Chiyoda-ku,
    Tokyo (Others)
03.6212.2460
edifice.baycrews.co.jp
🕐 11:00–20:00
📅 No holidays
ℹ MAP 7-9   ¥|¥|¥

Edifice et Iéna is a boutique for both men's and women's outfits, but for sartorial elegance at the office, it's the menswear that pulls in the biggest crowd. Suits in luxe fabrics, cotton shirts, leather shoes, handkerchiefs, cashmere scarves, and colorful leather accessories plus Orobianco bags in embossed leather, all make for a great work wardrobe with a sharp impact at a small price.

EDIT FOR LULU
WOMEN'S BOUTIQUE

4-2-14 Jingumae, Shibuya-ku,
    Tokyo (Others)
03-5772-3266
editforlulu.baycrews.co.jp/
🕐 11:00–20:00
📅 No holidays
ℹ MAP 5-18   ¥|¥-¥|¥|¥

The skirt, the shirt, the craft, the lace, and the dress. Introducing Edit for Lulu, a charm school that beckons ladies looking for key items in their closet every season. Day dresses come in soft feminine jersey, evening dresses would be halterneck, and you will always find sensible denim jackets and ballet flats or moccasins. For the weekends get the back-to-college T-shirts or plaid shirts. And just as things were getting to sound a wee bit predictable, their ever-optimistic stylist rushes in and saves the day with a vintage Hermès scarf or a great pair of Manolo pumps.

EDWIN

MEN'S/WOMEN'S DENIM

6-30-6 Jingumae, Shibuya-ku,
 Tokyo (Others)
03-5466-9361
www.edwin.co.jp/index.html
🕙 11:00–21:00
📅 No holidays
🚉 MAP 6-32

¥|¥

Edwin, the cult Japanese denim brand which invented, among other things, distressed jeans and the stonewashing process, has gone hybrid. Their collection has expanded to include plaid shirts in perfect red, blue and orange colors, and the seasons must-have: burgundy herringbone sweaters. Head here for denimwear cult classics.

EGOIST

WOMEN'S BOUTIQUE

Shibuya 109 4F, 2-29-1 Dogenzaka,
 Shibuya-ku, Tokyo (Others)
03-3477-5143
www.egoist-inc.com/
🕙 10:00–21:00
📅 Not fixed
🚉 MAP 8-18

¥|¥

Egoist has the reputation of being for really bad girls who shop here for saucy pieces designed to ensnare sugar daddies. The label has dictated the lives of a whole generation of women who dress up in its super low, second-skin jeans, plunging V-neck knit dresses, thigh-high denim shorts, and indecently tight tops with lots of long fake pearl and gold chains. Every New Year sees thousands of girls waiting outside to grab the first sales items and—with their looks—not all of them could be wrong. But, for most of us, the sexy nymphet style is better in small doses, so the best thing would be to shop here for individual items.

E.MARINELLA NAPOLI

MEN'S TIES

Tokyo Midtown 9-7-1 Akasaka,
 Minato-ku, Tokyo (Others)
03-5413-7651
www.marinellanapoli.it/
🕙 11:00–21:00
📅 Sun/Holidays
🚉 MAP 12-10

¥|¥-¥|¥|¥

There is a new wave of ties in town and it is called E. Marinelli Napoli. His jetsetting ties and chic essentials are some of the few things that can leave men gasping for more. Painstakingly hand-made hundred percent silk ties in a mind-blowing color palette, and cashmere and silk scarves (however conservative), make you feel like you're among the best dressed in town.

EM DESIGNS
MEN'S/WOMEN'S ACCESSORIES

Omotesando Hills Main Bldg. B1F, 4-12-10 Jingumae, Shibuya-ku, Tokyo
03-5785-0760
www.em-grp.com
⏰ 11:00–21:00
🗓 No holidays
♪ MAP 5-19   ¥|¥|¥

EM Designs are the hottest accessories in town. Elegant, refined, and small, e.m. plays with disorganization, fun, asymmetry, broken lines, and a damaged look set with cubic zirconium, water pearls, natural stones like coral and chrysoprase, and sometimes brilliant precious stones. The trendiest item here are the rings, the designer's signature piece, among which the three-ring set and the seven-ring set are the most popular pieces. If you are in for something quirky, nothing beats the small figure with a Kalashnikov set on a precious stone. While they do wedding rings too, it is the matching mother and baby rings with animals mounted on the top that scream to be bought. The key holders in fine silver and a myriad of charms also provide endless accessorizing possibilities.

EMILIO PUCCI
WOMEN'S DESIGNER

4-3-9 Ginza, Chuo-ku, Tokyo (Others)
03-5524-1266
www.emiliopucci.com
⏰ 11:30–20:30
🗓 No holidays
♪ MAP 3-8   ¥|¥|¥-¥|¥|¥|¥

Who could ever design Pucci better than Christian Lacroix, the king of color and joy? Or so we thought, until the brand took a U-turn under British designer Matthew Williamson. With Christian Lacroix, Pucci saw its colors take on even brighter swirls as seen in his little black dresses with trademark Pucci prints in trimmings, shoes and bags. But for Matthew, it is a totally different story: he wanted to completely escape the swirls, and is now doing mono-chrome frocks. But, of course, Pucci without swirls is not Pucci, so while the designers battle it out to find a new face for this turn-of-the-century Tuscan design house, 21st century grownups should stick to the basics—shawls, scarves, shoes, and bags with infinitely colorful swirls and curves.

EMMA HOPE
WOMEN'S SHOES

Roppongi Hills Keyakizaka Street, 6-9-1 Roppongi, Minato-ku, Tokyo
03-5772-7800
www.emmahope.co.uk
⏰ 11:00–20:00
🗓 No holidays
♪ MAP 12-11   ¥|¥|¥-¥|¥|¥|¥

British Emma Hope does sensible shoes with a lot of style. Loved by business women for pumps that walk through the changing fash-ion seasons with ease, she works wonders with nappa, suedes, silk velvet, brocade, and grosgrain. If the day styles are too conserva-tive, try her evening shoes that offer the same comfort with a lot more drama. Her collection—inspired by Cleopatra—uses beads, sequins, and silk, and comes in red-green, turquoise-orange, and gold and silver combinations.

EMPORIO ARMANI

MEN'S/WOMEN'S DESIGNER

5-2-29 Jingumae, Shibuya-ku, Tokyo (Others)
03-5778-1631
www.emporioarmani.com
🕐 11:00–20:00
📅 No holidays
🚇 MAP 6-33
¥|¥|¥|¥

While Armani is now seen as a real estate king in Milano, those who still believe that he is an arbiter of good taste are usually delighted by this collection—it's all about his suits and jackets for both men and women, marked with his genius touch of minimalism at an affordable price. Of late, however, the label has strayed off the less-is-more path and has been churning out a lot of frills, accordion pleats, and skinny jackets for women in a riot of colors. Whatever the king does, to his fans he is always right. But some still prefer to stick to his classic original collections of sporty suits in luxe Italian fabrics. The jeans line, too, has a fan following among die-hard Armani lovers, who crave for these weaves that—though not the latest trendy thing—offer a feeling of luxury like none other.

ENCHAINEMENT UNI

WOMEN'S BOUTIQUE

2-1 Sarugakucho, Shibuya-ku, Tokyo (Others)
03-5456-0569
www.biscayeholdings.co.jp/
🕐 12:00–20:00
📅 Not fixed
🚇 MAP 2-24
¥|¥|¥

Southern French farm style with turn of the century silhouettes, Provencal prints, and lots of cotton clothes. One of the few shops in town that stocks clothes from organic fabric, the ones here are from Japanese designer Evam Eva. Also stocks beautiful basics made of linen and lace and simple leather riding boots. Clothes refreshingly free of theatrics for when you want to be cute and comfortable, sip a Perrier on a slow Sunday summer afternoon, or visit a gallery.

EPOCA THE SHOP

WOMEN'S BOUTIQUE

5-5-13 Ginza, Chuo-ku, Tokyo (Others)
03-3573-3417
www.epoca-the-shop.com/
🕐 12:00–20:00 (Sun/Holidays until 19:00)
📅 No holidays
🚇 MAP 4-10
¥|¥|¥

If you like elegant suits, Epoca stocks them in many different patterns, all of them equally elegant and desirable. You'll also find a lot of jersey dresses and shirtdresses from Diane von Furstenberg, plus pretty frocks for the evening from Nina Ricci, Japanese designer Tadashi, and Vera Wang's Lavender Label. For the plucky, there is a great collection of Corto Moltedo bags that make a chunky but nevertheless superb statement. This is the just the kind of place a style shrink might send you to sort out your wardrobe blues.

ESCADA

WOMEN'S BOUTIQUE

Roppongi Hills Keyakizaka, 6–12–1 Roppongi, Minato–ku, Tokyo (Others)
03–5772–2071
www.escada.com/
11:00–20:00
No holidays
MAP 12-12 ¥¥¥¥¥

German label Escada does electric looks head to toe in blue, green, red, yellow, orange and other colors that would even put a butterfly to shame. Add frills and heavy embroidery and you get dollar dripping looks. Mature ladies love their classic suits. And their embellished sweaters and tops—whether paired with either a formal skirt or jeans—will win you admiring glances on the street.

ESTNATION

MEN'S/WOMEN'S BOUTIQUE

Roppongi Hills Keyakizaka 1/2F, 6-10-2 Roppongi, Minato-ku, Tokyo (Others)
03-5220-0205
www.estnation.co.jp/
11:00–21:00
No holidays
MAP 12-13 ¥¥¥-¥¥¥¥

Fling open your wardrobe and dream of a perfect selection of outfits: Givenchy blouses, Miu Miu skirts, Diane von Furstenberg wraparound dresses, jeans from seventeen different brands, and lacy intimates from Dolce and Gabbana. Estnation provides an entire huge floor of just this combined with matching shoes collected from all over the world, as well as accessories from the most sought after brands, including the extremely unique Superneedle's hand embroidered necklaces from India. The basement is dedicated to men, with an endless range of preppy to casual outfits from Ralph Lauren and Dolce & Gabbana, and tons of shoes and other gear.

ETRO

MEN'S/WOMEN'S DESIGNER

Ginza Namiki Street, 6-6-1, Ginza, Chiyoda-ku, Tokyo (Others)
03-5537-3443
www.etro.it
11:00–20:00 (Sun/Holidays until 19:00)
No holidays
MAP 4-11 ¥¥¥¥-¥¥¥¥¥

While Etro has started to make noises in the clothes department, it is their paisley trademark accessories that remain beloved to people of a certain age. Inspired by the traditional Jamawar shawls woven in Kashmir, Etro manages to print these intricate patterns on leather. All their creations remain very colorful and eclectic with hand bags, totes and wallets in paisley, some with interiors in precious leather dyed in a vibrant, orange, magenta, and turquoise—all at the same time.

EUGENIE

MEN'S/WOMEN'S BOUTIQUE

4-21-26 Minami Aoyama, Minato-ku, Tokyo
03-5414-5801
www.sannfreres.co.jp/shop/index.html
🕐 11:00–20:00
📅 Not fixed
✦ MAP 1-43

¥ ¥ ¥ ¥

Eugenie feels like a club for princesses from everywhere and beyond. Catherine Malandrino's gypsy tops in lacy beige for the feminine boho types. Just Cavalli's denims and roaring prints on body hugging clothing for the party girl. Juicy Couture for lounging around and Vera Wang for special occasions. Eugenie also stocks the sexiest, form-fitting down jackets in town from Ermano Scervino and, for ultra luxury bags at fairly reasonable rates, there is none other than Brazilian Nancy Rodriguez, who makes handmade croc and python bags in many colors and shapes on her own farm. There's also a small collection of nice clothes for men from Neil Barrett, Just Cavalli and the softest bomber to biker jackets from Ermano Scervino.

EVISU

MEN'S/WOMEN'S DENIM

1-1-5 Kamimeguro, Meguro-ku, Tokyo (Others)
03-3710-1999
www.evisu.com/
🕐 12:00–20:00
📅 No holidays
✦ MAP 2-25

¥ ¥ - ¥ ¥ ¥

This Japanese cult label, best known for its streetwear, dresses you up in shirts, track tops, and all kinds of jeans. The firm uses turn of the century spinning and weaving looms, so most items are still handmade and come only in limited editions, making them collector's items. Remember the collections here favor small sizes, so you might have to take the Karl Lagerfeld route to vanity, while being ready to shed a bit of weight from your wallet, as they are the most expensive jeans in business.

EXR

MEN'S/WOMEN'S BOUTIQUE

6-25-10 Jingumae, Shibuya-ku, Tokyo
03-5469-0550
www.exrjapan.com/
🕐 11:00–20:00
📅 No holidays
✦ MAP 6-34

¥ ¥ - ¥ ¥ ¥

A long time favorite of Korean stars, EXR's casual sporty style has become the uniform for many stars in this part of the globe. A combination of sports and denims gives them this unusual style. Sexy and racy fashion combined with accessories such as sneakers with heels—while the looks might not be for everyone they are certainly a hit with the city's fashion addicted teens.

FABER-CASTELL

STATIONERY

Tokyo Midtown, 9-7-4 Akasaka,
Minato-ku, Tokyo (Others)
03-5464-2305
www.faber-castell.com/
⊘ 11:00–20:00
No holidays
MAP 12-14   ¥-¥¥¥

Faber Castell is one of the bevy of stationery brands that are today considered absolutely essential to make a fashion statement while getting your work done. While others are known for their pens, Faber Castell's pencils have long sketched the world in style. The colored ones are smooth (it's like writing with silk!), but the one need-right-now item is called the Perfect Pencil. This is a lead pencil that comes in brown and green fitted at the back with an eraser and a smart aluminum cap that serves as a sharpener. The Perfect Pencil also comes in sterling silver and is the niftiest little instrument that should find its way into your jacket pocket.

FACIAL INDEX

EYE WEAR

2-2-3 Marunouchi, Chiyoda-ku, Tokyo
03-5288-8220
www.facial-index.com/
⊘ 11:00–20:00
Not fixed
MAP 7-10   ¥¥¥

Facial Index is the most cutting edge optical shop in town, with a sister branch in New York and a dedicated following among the more intellectual red carpet denizens—like Kirsty Hume, Samuel L. Jackson and Janeane Garofalo. They do only handmade Japanese eyewear in acetate, titanium, and 14K gold. The most popular range here is the Spivvy frames—architectural and bold in red and black. While they do have superb shapes in sunglasses too, it is the black bold and big frames that they do best. All are handmade in the ateliers of traditional Japanese eyewear makers, and some of them are affordable museum pieces, like the ones in black lacquer with traditional Japanese gold leaf art on the temples made by designer Isshu. The FG series is a luxury series in 18 K gold that is trendy but distinguished. Serious post-modernist looks mostly favored by serious boys.

FACTORY

MEN'S/WOMEN'S BOUTIQUE

Eyes Bldg B1F, 6-8-4 Jingumae,
Shibuya-ku, Tokyo
03-5466-7371
www.hpfrance.com/Shop/Brand/
FACTRY.htma
⊘ 12:00–20:00
No holidays
MAP 6-35   ¥¥-¥¥¥

Created by a group of fashion elite, the men's and women's collections here strive to be free from trends, use quality fabrics and keep styles minimalist. That's the reason why visiting designers consider this a must stop to discover the latest in Japanese and foreign talent. Colors rarely stray beyond whites, beiges, blacks, and greys. The collections include Bruno Pieter's blacks for a brooding tailored presence, Brazilian Alexandre Herchcovitch's post-modern designs, Japanese Sladky's cute but tailored creations, Itazura's range of clothes that are at once naughty and thoughtful, and Public Image, an upcoming Japanese label that is fast gaining a great reputation for its fine finish and elegant knits. Shoes from Sladky could be sexy rainboots one year and pumps the next, while Japanese label Yuks never strays beyond filmy and feminine ideas for your feet. Those in the know make a beeline for this store every season, as this outpost is where many new designers get their first break, so they offer the freshest looks at unbeatable prices.

FAT
MEN'S BOUTIQUE

3-20-1 Jingumae, Shibuya-ku, Tokyo
03-5775-3877
www.fatyo.com
🕐 11:00—20:00
📅 No holidays
MAP 5-20

¥¥-¥¥¥

Pronounced "ef-ay-tee," the shop features collections inspired by black culture, evidenced by the music and videos playing in the shop. American casuals inspired by the best of military and worker's clothes with a healthy mix of Japanese ideas is what Fat is most proud of. Fans flock here for their low-rise jeans and thick logo T-shirts. Weatherbeaters, overalls, jerseys with leather epaulets, baseball hats, and belts in materials like wool, knit, and velvet make it a wildly popular streetwear shopping destination. The shop also boasts superb sales staff who are all stylists in their own right and come highly recommended for those taking their first steps in street fashion.

FENDI
MEN'S/WOMEN'S DESIGNER

3-5-29 Kita-Aoyama, Minato-ku,
  Tokyo (Others)
03-5771-4541
www.fendi.com/
🕐 11:00—20:00
📅 Not fixed
MAP 5-21

¥¥¥¥

Karl Lagerfeld and the Fendi sisters created a unique identity with the double F logos, and since the 60s have revolutionized luxury furs and leather goods. At the upscale Omotesando outpost you will find A-plus accessories, like the unmistakable Baguette, Spy, and B bags. A must-have from Tinseltown to Cannes, one of these status symbols is worth the investment. In sequined blacks, leopard prints, beige embroidery and mirrored clasps, Fendi stands out in this brand-conscious milieu.

(SALVATORE) FERRAGAMO

MEN'S/WOMEN'S SHOES

2-5-1 Yurakucho, Chiyoda-ku, Tokyo (Others)
03-3575-2213
www.ferragamo.com/
🕙 10:30–20:30
🗓 No holidays
MAP 3-9
¥|¥|¥|¥-¥|¥|¥|¥

Ferragamo does not discriminate: male or female, mature or youthful, this Fiorentino legend never fails when it comes to topnotch accessories and superb leather goods. Old school tradionalists rely on classic loafers, scarves, neckties, belts, and an assortment of practical essentials. Ideal for the boardroom or an exhibition, Ferragamo's range of ready-to-wear, fragrances, and gift items keeps you in style without overkill.

FIFI & ROMEO

PETS

2-8-2 Jiyugaoka, Meguro-ku, Tokyo (Others)
03-3725-8006
www.fifiandromeo.jp
🕙 10:00–20:00
🗓 Wednesdays
MAP 11-5
¥|¥-¥|¥|¥

Fifi and Romeo is a small, crazy world decorated in baby blue for capricious ladies and their precious dogs. Now you can shop for yourself *and* your dog at the same time, and even buy the same clothes! Collections are casual chic for women, such as cardigans with emblem brooches, turtleneck sweaters, and cargo pants that can be matched with a sweater for your dog with an emblem too. Printed silk flower dresses can be matched with a military style cape for the dog, and down jackets for the colder weather come in master and pooch versions. Of course, almost every ensemble comes with a matching canine carrier bag in leather or polka dots.

FILO DI SETA

WOMEN'S BOUTIQUE

5-11-8 Minami-Aoyama, Minato-ku, Tokyo
03-5467-9124
www.world.co.jp/brand/filofiseta.html/
🕙 11:00–20:00
🗓 No holidays
MAP 1-44
¥|¥|¥|¥

After working with Jean Paul Gaultier, designer Ichiro Seta decided to return, and combine his international experience with the femininity that his country is well known for. He makes all his clothes with fabrics sourced in Japan, so he is best at luxurious formal style outfits in colors like beige, pink, and gold. Suits in beige are classic and timeless, combined with shirts with trimming around the collars or neat little ruffles on the front. Coats with short or quarter sleeves appear frequently, and evening dresses are often in tunic styles. Seta's style is fun, chic, and works well any time of the day.

FLAIR

WOMEN'S BOUTIQUE

3-14-4 Kita-Aoyama, Minato-ku, Tokyo
03-3400-5708
www.flair-j.com
⊘ 11:00–20:00
🗓 No holidays
🚶 MAP 6-36   ¥|¥|¥

Flair takes pieces of cloth in natural shades of off-white gray and beige, and turns them into something really simple and wearable (yet trendy in an off-beat way). To sell such an idea in this town demands delicacy and tact, both of which the shop's collections have in spades. The pants therefore might be in linen, but are crushed and really loose with a kind of Jane Birkin charm; the tops come in the same range of fabrics and fit like tunics just as Charlotte Gainsbourg would have done it; the shoes are sensible and flat in worn leather or felt, just as Sienna would like it; and the matching bags are either in stressed leather or fabric. The look is about revelling in chic boho styles without trying too hard.

FLOAT

MEN'S/WOMEN'S BOUTIQUE

1-36-6 Ebisu-nishi, Shibuya-ku, Tokyo
03-3780-0480
www.float-float.com
⊘ 12:00–20:00
🗓 Not fixed
🚶 MAP 2-26   ¥|¥|¥

At this warm and friendly boutique, Californian brand Trovata takes center stage, providing wardrobe maintenance for weekend informality. Men's and women's knit tops, tees, shorts, outerwear, and jeans in the classic Trovata sophisticated urban casual style, and in colors that never stray beyond dusty, silhouettes that never try too hard to get noticed, and a fit so comfortable that you could take in a film and a night club visit in the same leg.

FOUNDFLES

WOMEN'S BOUTIQUE

3–7 Sarugakucho, Shibuya–ku, Tokyo
03–5784–2681
www.world.co.jp/brand/foundfles.html
⊘ 11:00–20:00
🗓 No holidays
🚶 MAP 2-27   ¥|¥|¥

This Southern Mediterranean cocoon offers a great respite from fluff carpet posh and offers real clothes that are wearable and very smart. Loads of knits, because they are so good at them, puff-sleeved tops, plunging V-necks, striped dresses paired with woolen skirts on the right side of vintage in moss and aquamarine blue, and cocoon styles with raglan sleeves and voluminous backs for great looks whether at office or out about town.

FOXEY
WOMEN'S BOUTIQUE

6-8-1 Ginza, Chuo-ku, Tokyo (Others)
03-3573-6008
www.foxey.co.jp/
🕐 11:00–19:30 (Sun/Holidays 12:00–18:00)
🗓 the 3rd Monday
𝄖 MAP 4-12 ¥¥¥-¥¥¥

Foxey is where extremely well-heeled, finishing school-educated mothers and daughters shop when they feel like splurging on Russian sable coats for which the shop is well known, or on cashmere dresses and fine polo knits, conservative pumps in beige and chocolate suede and boots, flat sandals, and rows of cocktail dresses. The shop is also well known for dressing Japanese celebrities for parties in frocks with plunging backs and balloon skirts, and they can be ordered to your size from their extensive collection of dress patterns. The second floor is reserved for cruise collection viewings and trunk shows.

FRANC FRANC
INTERIOR

Shibuya Parco Part 2 B1F/2F/3F, 3-7 Udagawa-cho, Shibuya-ku, Tokyo (Others)
03-3477-8848
www.francfranc.com/
🕐 10:00–21:00
🗓 No holidays
𝄖 MAP 8-19 ¥¥-¥¥¥

The top shop for interior design selects young designers from all over the world—known and unknown—and commissions items specifically suited to Japan. You'll find shelves that could fit in even in the most miniscule of Tokyo pads, compact speakers, folding sofa beds and loads of other reasonable things, including a great series of iconic lamps from sculptor Isamu Noguchi. Bright colorful shapes, maximum choice and reasonable prices make this a great haunt for all Japanese shoppers, from high school students to society dames.

FRENCH CONNECTION
MEN'S/WOMEN'S BOUTIQUE

4-3-3 Jingumae, Shibuya-ku, Tokyo (Others)
03-5786-0555
www.fcuk.com/
🕐 11:00–20:00
🗓 No holidays
𝄖 MAP 5-22 ¥¥

Hot blazing styles greet you at this fashionable high street brand where catwalk fashions make it to the floor before you've closed the style-mags. Trendy and absolutely affordable, FCUK's slim pants, pretty skirts, fitted jackets, and beautiful summer clothes are absolutely perfect for when there are no dress codes.

GABRIELLE PECO

LINGERIE

6-32-5 Jingumae, Shibuya-ku, Tokyo
03-3498-7315
www.g-peco.com/
🕙 11:00–20:00
📅 No holidays
👠 MAP 6-37   ¥|¥-¥|¥

A hidden secret, this shop could be the answer to your lingerie worries in Tokyo. Shoppers are greeted by two tiny terriers and walls of steamy underwear: lacy nothings, silk bras, black panties with red lace, almost-there thongs, snappy G-strings, and a whole range of baby dolls in innumerable prints, not to mention lacy nightwear in hot pink, red, and black combinations. A winning mix of imported and domestic brands ensures that all sizes are on-hand (if not on display, one of the two sales staff will dish it out from the lower drawers). They also stock corsets in red and black lace for naughty evenings, net Oroblu stockings and everything else needed to unveil your sensual side.

GALLARDA GALANTE

WOMEN'S BOUTIQUE

5-2-2 Jingumae, Shibuya-ku,
    Tokyo (Others)
03-5766-1855
www.palgroup.co.jp/galante/
🕙 11:00–20:00
📅 No holidays
👠 MAP 6-38   ¥|¥-¥|¥|¥

Vena Cava silk empire line dresses, wraparounds, pretty purses, vintage clutches, and a wide range of accessories and shoes, including a small but smart collection of Allessandro Dell'Aqua's shoes plus an excellent collection of fitted Moncler jackets in winter, all go into making Gallarda Galante one woman's fashionable eclectic and another woman's pretty clutter.

GAP

MEN'S/WOMEN'S BOUTIQUE

4-30-3 Jingumae, Shibuya-ku,
    Tokyo (Others)
03-5414-2441
gap.co.jp/
🕙 10:00–21:00
📅 No holidays
👠 MAP 5-23   ¥|-¥|¥

With Madonna, Macy Gray, and Missy Elliott staring down from massive billboards in their Gap clothes, this label tries to up its ante, but still remains committed to staples—especially T-shirts, ribbed tank tops, sweatshirts, khakis, down jackets, car coats, cardigans, and an extensive and ever-growing collection of denim. Despite its star ambassadors, Gap remains the most coveted shopping destination for teenagers who can really play around with these looks of layering, lengths, and lots of color. The service is high-spirited and friendly, and the entire family can stack up on basics for summer and winter at fairly reasonable prices.

GAP KIDS
KIDS'

4-30-3 Jingumae, Shibuya-ku, Tokyo (Others)
03-5414-2441
gap.co.jp/
🕙 10:00–21:00
📅 No holidays
📍 MAP 5-24   ¥

Gap Kids offers the most down-to-earth collections of kids wear at reasonable prices. Cute T-shirts, rugby shirts, jackets, sweaters, shoes, bags, caps, and a lot of accessorizing. Sizes fit slim kids better and trousers come with an adjustable waistband to counter the growth curves. The T-shirts in particular are so cute that some (very slim) Japanese women are known to pick up the entire color palette.

GARCIA MARQUEZ GAUCHE
WOMEN'S ACCESSORIES

4-11-15 Jingumae, Shibuya-ku, Tokyo (Others)
03-5413-0873
www.garcia-style.com/
🕙 12:00–20:00 (Sun/Holidays until19:00)
📅 Not fixed
📍 MAP 5-25   ¥/¥

Brilliantly colorful bags with a high fun quotient, a brand whose potency is evident in the fact that almost every Tokyo girl worth being called *kawaii* has at least one of these. Their lines include the St. Germain tote, the Cafe Lip pouch, the Kroner duffel, the Transit messenger, the Studio briefcase, the Champs Elysees shopping bag, the Deauville weekender, and also wallets and baguettes in so many colors.

GARNI
MEN'S/WOMEN'S ACCESSORIES

Silk Road Daikanyama B1F, 1-22-5 Ebisu-nishi, Shibuya-ku, Tokyo
03-3770-4554
www.garni.co.jp/
🕙 12:00–20:00
📅 No holidays
📍 MAP 2-28   ¥/¥/¥

A tunnel from a nameless exterior welcomes you into this unisex jewelry salon of homegrown designer Eiji Yoshitani. Those men who believe men's jewelry doesn't fit with the finer threads in their wardrobe will find a superb collection of sculptural pieces—link chains, medallions, and thick bands that hold attention by themselves. Women too will love the designs for the lack of the superfluous and the many possibilities of layering the fun items. They have recently branched into casual clothes and a denim line too. While lacking the hype of fellow countryman e.m., Garni manages to hold its own with a style that is great for the office as well as After Five occasions.

GAS JEANS

MEN'S/WOMEN'S BOUTIQUE

6-28-9 Jingumae, Shibuya-ku,
Tokyo (Others)
03-5766-6088
www.gasjeans.com/
🕐 11:00–20:00
📅 No holidays
🚶 MAP 6-39   ¥|¥

Tokyo's fashion clutter beckons simplicity and that is where Gas jeans comes in. Now the city's youth, including thirtysomethings, flock here to stock up on minimal but trendy total dressing. Great edgy basics with a complete line of tops, sweaters, jackets, jeans, leather trousers, and even trilbys for men. The women's collection is all about skinny pants with flirty chiffon blouses, and leather jackets with zips. Shoes for both men and women come in large European sizes. Yes, Gas is perfect for those who like it simple, basic, and on the right side of trendy.

GEM KAWANO

MEN'S/WOMEN'S BOUTIQUE

3-28-11 Shinjuku, Shinjuku-ku,
Tokyo (Others)
03-3354-5207
www.kawano-gem.co.jp/
🕐 11:30–20:30
📅 Not fixed
🚶 MAP 9-9   ¥|¥|¥-¥|¥|¥|¥

This is one of the largest import shops in Japan, with a wide selection of major brands: Hermès, Louis Vuitton, Chanel, Prada, the much loved Coach and, more recently, Pucci and Pucci-inspired prints, all at surprisingly low prices. Don't be irritated by the lack of posh surroundings; none of Tokyo's chi-chi crowd who regularly shop here seem bothered. Dresses by Emilio Pucci are in particular demand, along with logo T-shirts from See by Chloé, denim from DSquared, and the much-loved T-shirts and underwear from *Dorugaba* (as locals lovingly call D & G). Nothing conservative, all strikingly personal, and of course at great prices.

GEOX

MEN'S/WOMEN'S/KIDS' SHOES

Ginza Nakaya Bldg. 1F., 5-8-16 Ginza,
Chuo-ku, Tokyo
03-5537-7077
www.geox.com
🕐 10:30–20:00
📅 No holidays
🚶 MAP 4-13   ¥|¥

Geox keeps feet dry through a patented sole that breathes (the sole releases moisture through tiny holes). In this tiny flagship they are doing all of Tokyo's humid summer walkers a great favor selling their fairly stylish collections that work better for kids and men than women. Office shoes, smart sneakers in beige and brown, and loafers for men, and cute little baby and junior collections for kids. The women's collection is being overhauled from round toe flat styles to pretty little ballerinas and smart pumps in metal and white.

GENTEN
WOMEN'S ACCESSORIES

4-6-1 Ginza, Chuo-ku, Tokyo (Others)
03-3561-0115
www.kuipo.co.jp/genten/
🕐 11:00–20:00
📅 the 3rd Wednesdays
🚇 MAP 3-10   ¥ ¥ - ¥ ¥ ¥

Go green with Genten and Ecomaco; two brands that are doing a great job of bringing fashion closer to the environment. Using natural tannin leathers, Genten makes mostly totes and wallets in a masculine style, with earthy natural colors revolving around brown and Hermès orange, burnt sienna and black, whereas Ecomaco is more light and flirty, with sunny yellow, baby pink, powdery blue and leafy green. Ecomaco also has a series of clothes in organic cotton that includes light tops, scarves, and skirts all in the same shades and deviates from Genten's stark minimalism by offering pretty bits of embroidery on the cover flap or handle of the totes.

GEORG JENSEN
MEN'S/WOMEN'S ACCESSORIES/
INTERIOR

3-4-1 Marunouchi, Chiyoda-ku,
   Tokyo (Others)
03-5220-3053
www.georgjensen.com
🕐 11:00–19:00
📅 No holidays
🚇 MAP 7-11   ¥ ¥ ¥ ¥

This Danish silversmith is revered for his lack of ornamentation. He went on the market at a time when the rest of the world was still obsessed with decorative forms. Now, one hundred years later, Georg Jensen's cutlery—and thermoses, watches, hollowware and superb jewelry—is not only still on wedding wish lists but, more importantly, is still respected as the finest in product design. Designed by Jensen himself, the namesake main line carries the original early 20th-century designs of cutlery, jewelry and table ideas. While this pricey collection comes in silver, Georg Jensen Living provides reasonable ideas with cutting edge design in stainless steel. This shop stocks almost the entire collection. The 2007 lapis lazuli pendant, for example, has been specially designed with the Asian woman in mind, and is sold only in Asia.

GERARD DAREL
WOMEN'S BOUTIQUE

Shinjuku Takashimaya 6F, 5-24-2
   Sendagaya, Shibuya-ku, Tokyo (Others)
03-5361-1620
www.gerarddarel.com/
🕐 10:00–20:30
📅 Not fixed
🚇 MAP 9-10   ¥ ¥ ¥ ¥

In France, Gerard Darel is trying hard to convey an ultra trendy appearance by using Charlotte Gainsbourg as their model, but in Japan it looks like it may take a while for this new exuberance to have an effect. Still, Gerard Darel's sweaters are a worthwhile panacea if you require retail therapy. The craftsmanship is reflected in the cut, quality, and finish, and is usually more elegant than other knitwear brands. Also popular among career women are the office-appropriate suits, and pretty feminine dresses.

GIANFRANCO FERRE

MEN'S/WOMEN'S BOUTIQUE

3-1-1 Marunouchi, Chiyoda-ku, Tokyo (Others)
www.gianfrancoferre.com
🕙 10:00–20:00
📅 No holidays
📍 MAP 7-12

¥¥¥¥

Another man, made in Milano, whose dramatic stylings are at a level only architects like him can get away with. Exaggerated sleeves with tight cuffs, and fitted bodices with dramatic collars that you can wear with skinny trousers or a blown taffeta skirt, for example. Lately, he, too, has been buffeted by the sartorial winds of our times, so his shirts come in slim silhouettes, while skirts gather proportions and lose length. With brisk business in Asia, Ferre's kimono leanings are always fun, and though he always provides drama he never lets his clothes get out of hand.

GIEVES AND HAWKES

MEN'S BESPOKE

Omotesando Hills Main Bldg 2F, 4-12-10 Jingumae, Shibuya-ku, Tokyo (Others)
03-5785-2216
www.gievesandhawkes.com/
🕙 11:00–21:00
📅 Not fixed
📍 MAP 5-26

¥¥¥-¥¥¥¥

Savile Row descends into town with Gieves and Hawkes, one of Tokyo's largest branded tailoring service for shirts and suits. It takes them four weeks to rustle up something perfectly suited to your size, in your choice of fabric and with your monograms if desired. They offer both made-to-measure and bespoke. Great service comes at a reasonable cost, especially for lightweight suits. A qualified tailor is always around to dispense advice with tape in hand. If suits are not your thing, the shop also offers the best quality lightweight jerseys and the softest T-shirts in town.

GINZA KOMATSU BOUTIQUE

WOMEN'S BOUTIQUE

Ginza Komatsu 3F, 6-9-5 Ginza, Chuo-ku, Tokyo
03-3572-8793
www.ginza-komatsu.co.jp
🕙 11:00–20:00
📅 No holidays
📍 MAP 4-14

¥¥¥¥

One of the oldest boutiques in town that specialize in selected imported fine labels, Ginza Komatsu is superb with formal looks. Sharp pant and skirt suits in beautiful fabrics with trend-of-the-moment silhouettes such as the drainpipe trousers and just-at-the-knee pencil skirts, all of which can be paired with ultra feminine lace and silk separates for the summer, or fine wool and cashmere knits in the winter. The store tends to be partial to collections from Pollini, Rochas, Alessandro Dell'Aqua, Jasmin Shokrian, Lanvin, Cividini, Menichetti, Andrew Gn, and hLam, among others.

GIORGIO ARMANI

MEN'S/WOMEN'S DESIGNER

4-5 Kioi-cho, Chiyoda-ku, Tokyo (Others)
03-3221-2571
www.giorgioarmani.com
🕚 11:00–19:00/11:00–21:00 (Thursdays)
📅 No holidays
🚩 MAP 13-2   ¥|¥|¥|¥

His creations have undoubtedly been the most singular of our times, and equally essential in the reconstruction of suits for the man and the woman. Armani suits take years off a man, giving maximum comfort in the smartest livery possible—famously unstructured suits that are comfortable due to their lack of lining. Women, too, can be completely at ease yet sexy, in or out of the office. The visionary now dabbles in everything from suits to real estates. For a piece of hot property head to this flagship store.

GIRLS END KIWA

WOMEN'S ACCESSORIES

Omotesando Hills B1F, 4-12-10 Jingumae,
  Shibuya-ku, Tokyo
03-5410-0830
www.girlsend.com/index2.html
🕚 11:00–21:00
📅 Not fixed
🚩 MAP 5-27   ¥|¥|¥

Tokyo's top Swarovski man went retail and asked jewelry designers to create bling moments. The result is necklaces, brooches, bracelets, and bags in all colors, shapes, prices, and emotions of Swarowski crystals all set in an opulent artsy interior. If you're wondering about the panda heads on the wall, they were created by artist Nagi Noda, the darling of Tokyo's art world. The concept behind this glorious splendor? Lolita meets La Dolce Vita.

GISÈLE PARKER

WOMEN'S BOUTIQUE

5-2-14 Jingumae, Shibuya-ku, Tokyo
03-5778-3350
www.giseleparker.com/
🕚 11:30–21:00 (Sun/Holidays 11:00–20:00)
📅 No holidays
🚩 MAP 6-40   ¥|¥|¥

Ever wondered why some Japanese girls look perfectly turned out day and night, always with the right tone between classic and contemporary? The secret is shops such as this, offering a careful collection with a necessary blend of Japanese and foreign designers for formals, denim and luxurious casuals—a superb harmony of mix and match. Try Akiko Ogawa's skirts and tops, beautifully cut and draped, that will last you through seasons of fluctuating trends. Taverniti So jeans and vintage denim from True Religion offer a heady mix and match with haute couture-style shirts from Coast, pants and jackets from Weber, and knits and sewn tops from Ahaus. Verdict: cathartic possibilities for the stylist in you.

GIULIANO FUJIWARA
MEN'S BOUTIQUE

6-8-18 Minami-Aoyama, Minato-ku, Tokyo
03-5469-5558
www.giulianofujiwara.com/
🕐 11:00–20:00
📅 No holidays
📍 MAP 1-45

¥|¥|¥|¥

Giuliano Fujiwara's Italo-Japanese aesthetic is clearly visible in his superbly tailored minimalist collection made from fabrics like Loro Piana. While Fujiwara himself tragically died in an accident a few years ago, designer Matsumura Masataka keeps his label alive. The best here are the suits that are literally stitched on you at the workshop on the second floor. These suits are sharp and sometimes with great trimmings such as leather piping or patches, and never too skinny but well-shaped, fastened with one or two buttons in the front and adorned with peaked lapels. Despite the leaning towards sartorial elegance, Fujiwara experiments with fun too, with close-fitting velvet suits, high quality slim-fitting knits, skinny ties and gabardine down jackets all arranged gallery-like on the first floor. Everything here shows a good masculine body off to best advantage.

GIVENCHY
WOMEN'S DESIGNER

Aoyama Twin Tower 1F, 1-1-1 Minami-Aoyama, Minato-ku, Tokyo (Others)
03-5785-3431
www.givenchy.fr
🕐 11:00–20:00 (Sun/Holidays until19:00)
📅 No holidays
📍 MAP 16-5

¥|¥|¥|¥|¥

Through the years, Givenchy has maintained its elegance in black (and, occasionally, with brilliant shades like scarlets and fuschias). While creative director Ricardo Tisci keeps this DNA he brings in his own vision of contemporary fashion that uses heavy dark fabrics for extremely elegant skirts, suits, and coats. His knit lines are equally unique with handstitched details, drapes and gathers in undeniable elegance. His couture lines (that can be ordered via the press office) follow the same themes but his techniques, like smocking, cutwork, embroidery, and bending ensure the look is always modern yet handcrafted. Givenchy Men, under Ozwald Boateng, is strict, sharp, and handsome with dark colors and heavy fabrics that give the clothes a strong silhouette for a bold statement.

GLOBE
INTERIOR

2-7-8 Ikejiri, Setagaya-ku, Tokyo
03-5430-3550
www.globe-antiques.com/
🕐 11:00–20:00
📅 No holidays
📍 MAP 18-1

¥|¥|¥-¥|¥|¥

Enter a time machine and be transported to country homes back in the United Kingdom of the 1920s and 30s, where spacious manors set in sprawling gardens were decorated with wooden bureaus,

Windsor chairs, mahogany and walnut armoires, mouton arm-chairs, walnut settees, and coffee tables. Despite its three floor spacious surface area, the shop is bursting at the seams with its collections. It is proud of its reproduction and original lamp collection that dates back to the same period, but the best here is, perhaps, the huge array of mirrors—Louis Philippe gold leaf reproductions, rare nineteenth-century Venetian mirrors, and lots of tiny plain beveled mirrors with unusual contours that would be hard to find at such amazing prices anywhere else in the antique loving world.

GLOBE SPECS
MEN'S/WOMEN'S EYEWEAR

Daikanyama Address 3F, 17-6
  Daikanyama-cho, Shibuya-ku,
  Tokyo (Others)
03-5459-3645
www.globespecs.co.jp/
🕐 10:00–20:00
📅 Not fixed
↳ MAP 2-29   ¥|¥|¥-¥|¥|¥|¥

This is a breeding ground for the hottest in eyewear design. You'll find authentic American eyewear in 40s and 50s styles with cat-eye shapes and aviator rims, including The Spectacle—made famous by Whoopi Goldberg, Tom Cruise and Harrison Ford. For something bigger, go for Hamptons-inspired Robert Marc—big glasses that cover the face, oval shapes, and a lot going on over the temples: shagreen detailing, for example. Sama—supplier to Badgley Mishka and Loree Rodkin—make risque eyewear in one-of-a-kind shades in black polka dots, and blush or ivory colored frames with purple lenses. Globe Specs also stocks Selima, Blindo, Penguin, and Volte Face—brands that adorn the noses of every major celeb in Tinseltown. But the neatest pair of sunglasses, which none of these celebs have, and are sold right here, are Globe Specs' own great collaboration with United Arrows: a series of metal frame shades in aviator styles in black, blue, and pink, with supermodel results and skinny prices.

GLOBETROTTER
MEN'S/WOMEN'S ACCESSORIES

5-12-2 Minami-Aoyama, Minato-ku,
  Tokyo
03-5464-5255
www.globe-trotterltd.com/
🕐 11:00–20:00
📅 Not fixed
↳ MAP 1-46   ¥|¥|¥|¥

They've been handcrafting the world's most loved suitcases in classic British tradition since 1897. The Tokyo flagship stores the entire range in all colors and sizes. Particular favorites are the reasonably priced, bright orange airplane hand luggage trunks. Pairing it with a 16-inch mini-trunk of the same size makes it fit for a travelista to lug around. Prices at the flagship are the same as anywhere else in the world; for duty-free service head to their in-store location at Shinjuku's Isetan Department Store (the men's department).

GOLDIE H.P. FRANCE

WOMEN'S BOUTIQUE

Shibuya Parco Part 1 1F, 13-1 Udagawa-cho, Shibuya-ku, Tokyo (Others)
03-5456-5017
www.hpfrance.com/goldie/
🕙 10:00–21:00
🗓 Not fixed
✦ MAP 8-20

¥|¥|¥

Collection Privee's collections (the best thing at Goldie H.P. France) ensure that your presence always registers over and above their slouchy, calf-leather It-bag collections—a wonderful feeling in a world where clothes and accessories tend to be more recognizable than the wearer. This shop stocks their largest collection of Bostons, and while the shop also has accessories which the parent company HP France is understandably proud of, look around at the unstructured buckets from Aristolasia and superstructured colorful ones from De Couture. The shop also sells ultra glam Bruno Frissoni and Rupert Sanderson pumps for women, Collection Privee shoes for both men and women, Jacques Le Corre hunting caps, and Coppens's famous toques.

GOYARD

MEN'S/WOMEN'S ACCESSORIES

3-17-11 Minami Aoyama, Minato-ku, Tokyo
03-3401-2301
www.goyard.fr/goyard.html
🕙 12:00–21:00
🗓 Not fixed
✦ MAP 1-47

¥|¥|¥|¥

When many presidents and royals plan trips, this shop is at the top of their pre-departure agenda. Goyard's matching pieces in Chevron canvas (linen and hemp with a waterproof coating) have long been a symbol of really elegant travel, as they are exquisitely beautiful, sturdy, and functional. But as no suitcase is safe from a lashing at the baggage belt, you might choose to limit yourself to the exquisite smaller pieces. While the totes are popular with women and the briefcases with initials are often bought by subtle male style crusaders, everyone loves the option of being able to add on hand-painted retro stripes and personal initials. Even the smallest article, like wallets, can be personalised. Head upstairs (and to the basement) to visit Loveless for a sneak peek at the hottest labels coming out of Japan.

GRAPEVINE BY K3

WOMEN'S BOUTIQUE

4-9-1 Jingumae, Shibuya-ku, Tokyo
03-5772-8099
none
🕙 12:00–20:00
🗓 Not fixed
✦ MAP 5-28

¥|¥|¥

Among the many different collections in this beautiful space you'll find one of the finest homegrown talents— G.V.G.V. This one label makes collectible romantic classics with just the right amount of frills. Off-shoulder dresses with heart motifs, clean and simple pant suits with straight lines, velvet jackets and high on the must

must-have list bell-shaped skirts. G.V.G.V also does short puff-sleeved jackets combined with shorts and other elegant neooffice looks in steel gray. The shop's easy breezy merchandiser also stocks NY label Vena Cava who are best at offbeat, vintage-inspired, flirty dresses, tops and skirts.

GREEN
MEN'S/WOMEN'S DESIGNER

2-9-8 Ebisu-Nishi, Shibuya-ku, Tokyo
03-3780-1302
none
⊙ 12:00–20:00
▦ Mondays
⌐ MAP 2-30   ¥|¥|¥-¥|¥|¥|¥

Green is the hottest new Japanese kid on the block. They are particularly good at Chesterfield coats, tuxedos, and very manly silhouettes that look super stylish when worn. They might play around a lot with lengths and volumes, but tailoring remains strict and classic, clean and monotoned. If you are looking for lace and frills this is not the place to go. But if you are the power bomb, you can absolutely level with Green's no-nonsense, deadly feminine trouser glam just as our age wants it, a combination of Edwardian ruffles and urban chic.

GUCCI
MEN'S/WOMEN'S DESIGNER

3-6-7 Kita-Aoyama, Minato-ku,
  Tokyo (Others)
03-5469-1911
www.gucci.com
⊙ 11:00–20:00
▦ No holidays
⌐ MAP 6-41   ¥|¥|¥|¥|¥

Tom Ford was replaced by Alessandra Facchinetti, who immediately went and dug up a bit of Gucci history in the cursive script and splashed it over the bags. Then came designer Frida Giannini who dug up another bit of Gucci history, with the Flora print bags that announced the arrival of not just spring but a final departure from Tom Ford's hyper-sexed looks. Die-hard Gucci fans will not be disappointed, as the essential hardness of Gucci is still present—especially in men's suits and women's pants (albeit laced with a bit of Victoriana and ethnic chic).

GUILD JACOMO
WOMEN'S SHOES

Atre Ebisu 4F, 1-5-5 Ebisu-Minami,
  Shibuya-ku, Tokyo (Others)
03-5475-8445
www.mej.co.jp/
⊙ 10:00–21:30
▦ Not fixed
⌐ MAP 10-3   ¥|¥

Fashionable students and young office ladies love these shoes for their high street take on luxury brands and nonchalant copies of the latest trends. Ballet shoes with heels, a zillion patent leather ideas, suede pumps, stilettos, Mary Janes, and many matching bags, all at prices that will keep you coming back.

GUMPS

WOMEN'S ACCESSORIES

18-12 Sarugakucho, Shibuya-ku, Tokyo (Others)
03-3462-1250
www.gump.co.jp
🕐 11:00–19:30
📅 No holidays
🎞 MAP 2-31　　¥¥¥-¥¥¥¥

A centuries-old American purveyor of fine things, Gumps was known as the Tiffany of the west. In minimalist Tokyo, the shop might have an overdecorated, stuffy kitsch quality to it, but those in the know head here for an assortment of things like photo frames in pewter, towel sets, Reidel's sommelier series of wine glasses, and Lalique candlesticks. Come Christmas, the whole shop turns into a wonderland waiting for Santa with brocade stockings, decorated trees, and wooden reindeers. The section of the shop on the other side of the building stocks dainty evening bags, small leather accessories, Annick Goutal perfumes, diamonds, and silver jewelry for all ages.

HANAE MORI

WOMEN'S DESIGNER

3-6-1 Kita-Aoyama, Minato-ku, Tokyo (Others)
03-3406-1021
www.hanae-mori.com/
🕐 10:30–19:00
📅 No holidays
🎞 MAP 6-42　　¥¥-¥¥¥¥

The first lady of Japanese fashion undeniably put Japan on the global fashion map. Also known as Madame Butterfly (due to her constant use of butterfly motifs), her label has been about East truly meeting West, with kimono dresses using printed fabrics inspired by Japan, and classic tailoring. Despite her retirement a couple of years ago, this shop carries on with a few of her selected items. Alma en Rose, a casual-plus label with rose motifs on T-shirts, dresses and spring coats, and Hanae Mori, a label with reasonably priced silk suits perfect for a formal evening occasion. If none of this pleases you but you would like to leave with a souvenir, the shop has a neat selection of Hanae Mori's accessories—handbags, wallets, make-up pouches and scarves that are timeless and ageless.

HAN AHN SOON

WOMEN'S DESIGNER

Omotesando Hills Main Bldg B1F, 4-12 Jingumae, Shibuya-ku, Tokyo (Others)
03-3746-2130
www.hanahnsoon.com/
🕐 11:00–21:00
📅 Not fixed
🎞 MAP 5-29　　¥¥-¥¥¥

Korean Han Ahn Soon designs mainly dresses; these include beautiful handmade lace layers over a fitted dress, dresses with fringes zigzagging over the front, dresses that accentuate the hips, off-shouldered dresses in bright red—the list would go on were it not for the equally beautiful trousers cut with a knife and tops which have the same devil woman in them as the dresses. All this romanticism is justified, as Han Ahn Soon explains, "Because I am a girl."

HANJIRO

VINTAGE

YM square Harajuku 3/4F, 4-31-10
Jingumae, Shibuya-ku, Tokyo
03-3796-7303
www.hanjiro.co.jp
🕐 11:00–20:00
📅 Not fixed
📍 MAP 5-30   ¥-¥¥

This huge shop offers casual vintage at rock bottom prices. All the stuff is arranged neatly in great rows of similar articles, such as a hundred slouchy boots, a few dozen 1970s baseball hats, metal chain wallets, clutches, shirts, skirts, slippers, pumps, and even jewelry. Great place to stock up on skinny tank tops and plaid shirts for both men and women. The interior, complete with a huge birdcage, is typical of the surprises around every corner. Regular check-ins are a must to find the best deals.

HANWAY

UMBRELLAS

Roppongi Hills West Walk 4F, 6-10-3
Roppongi, Minato-ku, Tokyo
03-5786-9600
www.hanway.jp/
🕐 11:00–20:00
📅 No holidays
📍 MAP 12-15   ¥¥-¥¥¥

Tokyo has its share of rain, so it's understandable that the population has a thing for umbrellas. Not just any umbrella, but umbrellas that can be flourished with great style. If you're looking for Briggs, this is not the shop for you. But if you like a bit of color on your canopy, and patterns and shapes, they offer more than a few dozen varieties. Their bespoke collection lets you chose the canopy, the notches, and the runner and, most importantly, the natural wood stick shafts finished with silver- or ivory-colored tips. If you love the traditional Japanese *wagasa*, the shop makes a most practical version, with a silky polyester, extra-large canopy, where the many rivetless ribs feel like original bamboo. The shop also stocks Mary Poppins'-style sun umbrellas with frills, and their large pret-a-porter collection is designed to please every wallet and style.

HARNESS DOG

PETS

3-9 Sarugakucho, Shibuya-ku, Tokyo
03-3477-2445
www.creativeyoko.co.jp/
🕐 11:00–20:00
📅 No holidays
📍 MAP 2-32   ¥¥

If you are the kind of person who prefers your dog not at your feet but hanging from your arm as an accessory, look no further. You can order a collar with your beloved pet's name embroidered in Swarovski crystals and also revamp its wardrobe with T-shirts, dresses, and sunglasses. There are dog cosmetics such as shampoo, conditioner, and toothpaste, plus bags, bags, and more bags for pets and owners of every size. But the must-haves are the made-to-order Fiorucci wedding outfits for your dog and its loved one. Nowhere in town will a dog find such careful attention, the reason why every pillar from the Tokyo showbiz pantheon stops by, pooch in hand, to stock up on the season's latest dog couture.

HARRODS
MEN'S BOUTIQUE

6-12-4 Roppongi, Minato-ku,
  Tokyo (Others)
03-5770-3590
none
🕐 11:00–21:00
📅 No holidays
🚶 MAP 12-16   ¥|¥-¥|¥|¥

Dandy British tailored classics for men in the best of fabrics. You will find fine cashmere sweaters, cotton and linen shirts, very traditional cufflinks, handkerchiefs, as well as scarves in silk and linen in block colors. You'll also find Loro Piana cashmere sweaters in the winter, Chesterfield coats, and the most perfect double-breasted coats paired with dress shoes, all at prices that include meticulous service. The bespoke section is upstairs, with a selection of the finest Scottish cashmere and other traditional British favorites. Harrods here might be miniscule compared to the original Knightsbridge mecca but if you are looking for dauntingly traditional and exceptionally well-made men's gear, look no further. The Ginza branch stocks equally conservative staples for women.

HEDDIE LOVU
MEN'S/WOMEN'S DENIM

Omotesando Hills West 1F, 4-12-10
  Jingumae, Shibuya-ku, Tokyo
03-3746-3328
www.heddielovu.p
🕐 11:00–21:00
📅 Not fixed
🚶 MAP 5-31   ¥|¥|¥-¥|¥|¥

Another Japanese gem in the denim fashion industry. Dyed fourteen times in pure indigo from India, this haute denim wear uses 100 percent denim cloth. Combining technology with hand stitching, the brand offers four lines: the regular straight "mahogany," regular bootcut "Alder," high cut straight "maple," and the regular fit boot cut "rose wood." Obsessive attention has been paid to details, such as cushioning around the ankles and legs cut high on the side to make them look a mile long. This is haute denimwear with an haute price tag, but then this *is* unquestionably one of the world's finest denim brands, after all.

HELIOPOLE
WOMEN'S BOUTIQUE

Mode Cosmos Building 1F, 28-10
  Sarugakucho, Shibuya-ku,
  Tokyo (Others)
03-3770-6438
www.interbridge.co.jp/heliopole.html
🕐 11:00–20:00
📅 Not fixed
🚶 MAP 2-33   ¥|¥|¥

A warm ambience in hazelnut brown and sandy beige with wooden floors and soft music greets you as you step into Heliopole. The demographic here ranges from beautiful young things in their twenties to sharp career dames in their forties. The collections are quite varied with fabric garments, knitwear, and smart outerwear for the chilly season. The most popular items are the formal dresses in 100 percent silk that can be matched with one of the many coats—the favorite being the perennial houndstooth double breasted coat dress with mini metal buttons with a Chanel-inspired gold chain belt. Knit tailored jackets with Milano ribbing go well with any of the skirts and every person should equip themselves with the basics to beat the fiercest wind: a Macintosh or a Moncler down jacket. Heliopole also has a great range of kitten-heeled pumps and boots (albeit in small and medium sizes).

HELMUT LANG
MEN'S/WOMEN'S DESIGNER

5-13-2 Minami-Aoyama, Minato-ku, Tokyo
03-6419-8144
www.helmutlang.com/
🕐 11:00–20:00
🗓 Not fixed
⌘ MAP 1-48   ¥¥¥¥-¥¥¥¥¥

After a two-year hiatus following Helmut Lang's disappearance in 2005, along comes designer couple Michael and Nicole Colovos, formerly of the jeans label Habitual. Now, while Lang is sunning himself in Long Island, this creative couple have taken it upon themselves to give the label a new image. Gone is Lang's formalism; but his love for tech fabrics and minimal expressions remain. While he used sporty mostly as a metaphor, the current collection is more about a casual sporty glam—think unlined jackets and comfy bottoms, beautifully cut casual day clothes like hoodie jackets in tech fabrics, cotton T-shirts and nostalgic dark denim jackets, luxe sweaters and shorts and trousers in cotton twill.

HERMAPHRODITE
WOMEN'S BOUTIQUE

5-6-18 Minami-Aoyama, Minato-ku, Tokyo
03-3486-6488
none
🕐 12:00–20:00
🗓 Not fixed
⌘ MAP 1-49   ¥¥¥

Tokyo is having an organic cotton moment (feigned stress is the excuse, but perhaps it's just another reason to indulge). Come here for relaxed silhouettes in organic cotton, wool, and linen for men and women, and a unisex line of basics that are becoming the latest find for novelty chasing fashion adventurers.

HERMÈS

MEN'S/WOMEN'S DESIGNER

5-4-1 Ginza, Chuo-ku, Tokyo (Others)
03-3289-6811
www.hermes.com/
🕐 11:0–19:00
📅 No holidays
📍 MAP 4-15   ¥|¥|¥|¥

While this Renzo Piano-designed star boutique is status in itself, its precious contents sell more in a month here than a year in Europe. All the leather accessories, ties, jewelry, scarves, cashmere wraps, and beautiful tableware that you can stand to admire, wait to be gifted with, watch or buy, all in the midst of luxurious Hermès-clad attentive staff. A Birkin on your arm comes much faster here than anywhere else in the world and at a slightly higher price. But, hey, after crossing the million yen threshold, who's counting?

HH STYLE

INTERIOR

6–14–2 Jingumae, Shibuya–ku, Tokyo (Others)
03–3400–3434
www.hhstyle.com
🕐 12:00–20:00
📅 No holidays
📍 MAP 6-43   ¥|¥|¥

Star architect Kazuyo Sejima's museum-like construction houses the largest designer chair collection in town, which is a highly respected, if slightly inert affair with Eames, Panton, Jasper Morrison, and Philippe Starck. But move away from these perennial attention grabbers and discover a great range of lights from Isamu Noguchi, along with such beautiful stuff as the classic Sori Yanagi butterfly stool. There are also some great designers from around the world, such as Erwan and Ronan Bouroullec so keep coming back if only to keep abreast of the global design trends.

HIROFU

MEN'S/WOMEN'S ACCESSORIES

Roppongi Hills Keyaki Street 1F, 6–15–1 Roppongi, Minato–ku, Tokyo (Others)
03–5775–0162
www.hirofu.co.jp
🕐 11:00–20:00
📅 No holidays
📍 MAP 12-17   ¥|¥|¥|¥-¥|¥|¥|¥

Hirofu is Japan's finest leathercrafts label—one that makes basics of everything from simple shoes and bags to rippling leather accoutrements for the house. While the shoes and the bags use the simplest forms, Hirofu's best work is seen in the accessories—fine leather key chains, wallets and soft calf skin toilette cases. The home accessories section has leather cushions in many different sizes in camel, caramel, mahogany and black. Hirofu is justifiably proud of its croc selection with boots, totes, shoes and a humongous shopping bag that might cost you as much as a Kelly, but be comforted as it is ten times in size. Hirofu is logo-free and well appreciated by Tokyoites as Bottega Veneta-style but for less.

HIROKO HAYASHI

MEN'S/WOMEN'S ACCESSORIES

5-13-1 Minami-Aoyama, Minato-ku,
  Tokyo
03-3499-7364
www.world.co.jp/brand/hirokohayashi.
  html
🕐 11:00–20:00
🗓 No holidays
🔲 MAP 1-50

¥|¥|¥

If you really like your bags and wallets to be something apart from those of the madding crowd, Hiroko Hayashi's quiet little arty boutique is a good place to go. Every season she takes new ideas in leather (like laminated buttons fused on leather), and then incorporates them into wallets, clutches, messengers, and Bostons. Every season sees exactly the same shapes, so the choice is simplified. If you are looking for something for the evening go for the series in gold: the clutch has a lot of volume, and as it opens on the reverse side with a concealed zip, it looks perfect unmarred by closings or zippers. You will also love the label for its freedom from logos, unisex approach and affordable prices.

HIROMICHI NAKANO

MEN'S/WOMEN'S DESIGNER

6-27-8 Jingumae, Shibuya-ku,
  Tokyo (Others)
03-5778-3024
www.hiromichinakano.com/
🕐 11:00–20:00
🗓 No holidays
🔲 MAP 6-44

¥|¥|¥

This ace Japanese designer, now firmly established in the Paris collections, has been costuming movies, stage, and celebrities for a long time. He might have lost his steam of late, but continues to roll out extremely reasonable collections for both men and women. Usually layered in brilliant colors with his miniature floral prints and ultra feminine silhouettes, flowy, frilly, and long, paired with sailor striped T-shirts or shorts. For men there is the never-ending collection of T-shirts in all colors, plaid shirts, and trousers. Loads of casual bags perfect for the gym in acrylic pile, enamel quilting, and metallic nylon and a very thoughtful DJ bag for those who rock the town.

HISHIYA CALEN BLOSSO

MEN'S/WOMEN'S ACCESSORIES

1-9-8 Jiyugaoka, Meguro-ku,
  Tokyo (Others)
03-5726-1540
www.calenblosso.jp/
🕐 11:00–20:30
🗓 Not fixed
🔲 MAP 11-6

¥|¥|-¥|¥|¥

Hishiya Calen Blosso weaves Japanese tradition into ultra modern creations. Their mission is to fuse timeless Japanese crafts into contemporary creations. For example, they use traditional Japanese block printing with indigo dyes to make briefcases and wallets. Each article uses recurrent animal motifs from Japanese art: the carp, the dragon and their logo—the zebra. But it is the Japanese wooden elevated slippers called *zori* that people love here. In patent leather, cloth, and traditional velvet, they rock when worn with jeans. Come summer and the city's fashion guerrillas head here to spend their yen for perfect summer feet.

HITMAN
MEN'S/WOMEN'S SHOES

2-6-1 Marunouchi, Chiyoda-ku, Tokyo (Others)
03-5222-5288
www.hitman.co.jp/
🕐 11:00–20:00
📅 No holidays
📍 MAP 7-13   ¥|¥|¥-¥|¥|¥

Hitman brings hand made shoes from Italy to your doorstep. They stock men's and women's collections that are whimsical and artsy and take you on a trip down memory lane. For example, Rue de la Pompe is inspired by 1960s downtown London and creates mannish but pretty looks in rust in platform heels, brogue pumps, and cashmere suede slip-ons. Shoe designer Chie Mihara's experiences in Brazil, Japan, New York, Paris, and Spain have given her an unrivalled sensibility for shoes. Inspired from such sources as 1930s and 1940s fashions and military uniform shoes, she creates crafted heels, co-respondents and button-embellished long boots for women. Her favorite colors are olive green and stewardess navy blue, and all her shoes are wonderfully comfortable. Tempo Pretty, Italy Made Park Mansion, and Eva Turner are three other brands that suggest old movie dramas and romance epics. To finish the look, the store also stocks umbrellas with colorful trimmings and a small selection of men's handmade shoes.

HOPE CHEST
WOMEN'S VINTAGE

5-17-25 Jingumae, Shibuya-ku, Tokyo
03-3797-3228
none
🕐 12:00–20:00
📅 No holidays
📍 MAP 6-45   ¥

This is the kind of treasure you suddenly stumble across when you are on Cat Street. What the shop lacks with its dour service it makes up with its great vintage blouses, bags and shoes from Dior, Christian Louboutin, Miu Miu, Gucci, and Prada. The coats are a special surprise with occasional items from Marc Jacob's first collection. Prices vary, so visit often for the best deals.

HP DECO
INTERIOR

5-2-11 Jingumae, Shibuya-ku, Tokyo
03-3406-0313
www.hpdeco.com
⊘ 11:00–20:00
▦ Not fixed
⌐ MAP 6-46   ¥|¥|¥-¥|¥|¥|¥

HP Deco offers bohemian chic for your house with eclectic arty pieces collected from all over the world, but—reflecting the owner's love of France—especially from that country. From previously loved furniture to objets d'art cutlery, and some really funky lighting and chandeliers, HP Deco offers something for every budget. Visit frequently to find reasonably priced 1960s Japanese wooden furniture. Climb up into the neighboring room for a great collection of lamps, cutlery, jewelry, and everyday objects turned into surrealist decorations for the house from designers near and far.

HP FRANCE BOUTIQUE
WOMEN'S ACCESSORIES

La Foret Harajuku 1F, Jingumae, Shibuya-ku, Tokyo
03-5411-2704
www.hpfrance.com/Shop/Brand/Boutique.html
⊘ 11:00–20:00
▦ Not fixed
⌐ MAP 5-32   ¥|¥|¥

A showcase of European jewelry, the shop sizzles with goods such as Serge Thoraval's pocket rocket accessories, Stefano Poletti's ice breakers, like the reindeer series, and for those who love a bit of theater, estate antique-inspired jewelry such as beaded peacock brooches and necklaces with fist-sized pendants from Wouters&Hendrix. If you manage to tear your eyes from the display, look up to discover proof of why bags are icons today. The shop offers a great collection of almost-collector-item bags, such as beaded swan bags for the evening, gold and turquoise minaudieres, and special editions from Collection Privée and Jacques le Corre—all with suitably sparkling shoes to match, and sunglasses in a riot of colors from Theo and Histoire de Voir.

HP FRANCE WINDOW GALLERY
WOMEN'S ACCESSORIES

Lumine est B2F, 3-38-1 Shinjuku, Shinjuku-ku, Tokyo
03-3350-5027
www.hpfrance.com/Art/
⊘ 10:30–21:30
▦ Not fixed
⌐ MAP 9-11   ¥|¥|¥-¥|¥|¥|¥

Stylist and arbiter of taste Yumiko Takemoto dreamed up this tiny gallery space where, for two months, lucky artists get to bedazzle passing commuters with their art, at no cost for the artist or the viewer. Hidden behind this tiny gallery space is a huge space that dazzles, with trinkets of every possible variety meticulously displayed in gold cases. Designers Iosselini, Serge Thoraval, Sonya

Boyajian, and the Gem Kingdom are just a few of the alchemists who cast jewelry with a strong contemporary flavour, in 18K gold, wood, feather, coral, silver, turquoise, and diamonds. Every trinket-loving person should put this address high on their must-visit list.

HPH

MEN'S BOUTIQUE/ACCESSORIES

hpgrp 2F, 6-9-16 Ginza, Chuo-ku, Tokyo
03-5537-2740
www.hph.jp/
12:00–20:00
the 3rd Tuesday
MAP 4-16 ¥¥¥-¥¥¥¥

This men's shop is a heady combination of the excitement of discovery, ideas in leather, unique accessories, shoes with a difference, and bags that women would love too. The clothes selection is ruled by collections from Dresscamp, with sleeveless fur jackets in the winter and barely-there T-shirts in the summer. The Izree Duvetica collaboration resulted in icons such as down jackets with sleeves in python skin. The more classic would walk tall in their beautiful, stark-white tailored jackets, and for a risqué night, one should try the leopard print series. Immensely popular among women are the leather-and-silver butterfly brooches, and a great collection of Japanese designer Yuichi Wakatsuki's delicate unisex silver accessories. This is the shop that also introduced designer Mastermind to the fashion scene, so the shop always stocks some classic pieces from their clothes and shoes collection. If you want to leave with just one accessory, let it be the silver necklace with an antique-look key locket. You could take it to the local locksmith and have your own set made making it the most fashion friendly house keys in town.

HP FRANCE BIJOUX

WOMEN'S ACCESSORIES

Omotesando Hills B1F, 4-12-10 Jingumae, Shibuya-ku, Tokyo (Others)
03-5410-0361
www.hpfrance.com/bijoux/
11:00-21:00
Not fixed
MAP 5-33 ¥¥¥

Undoubtedly a paradise for those searching for the wickedest and the most unique jewelry from all over the world, HP France started as one man's love affair with France. Londoner Scott Stephen's quirky take on accessories that combine unusual materials with tweed, crystal, chain, and vintage elements leaves you well dressed enough to star in a boardroom drama, shine on a TV chat show or host a cocktail party at home. Roses are everywhere this year, and those in the know have fallen in love with corals all over again. Home-grown designer Dragon Rose's precious creations in pearl and translucent coral earrings and bracelets, and Scot Carol Mather's obsession with handsome hunting dogs create jewelry that is guaranteed to be the ice breaker wherever you go.

HUGO BOSS
MEN'S/WOMEN'S BOUTIQUE

5-8-5 Minami-Aoyama, Minato-ku,
 Tokyo (Others)
03-5485-6624
www.hugoboss.com/
🕐 11:00–20:00
▦ No holidays
↧ MAP 1-51   ¥|¥|¥-¥|¥|¥|¥

Classic and crisp silhouettes, especially in black and white, have been a great favorite among successful men and women execs in the last two decades. So how did a German brand get that famous? Well, men love Hugo Boss's trousers for their slim cut that looks superb with or without a jacket while women love his deal-making, two-piece pant suits. Hugo Boss might have lost some of its late-nineties appeal but die-hard Hugo Boss fans love shopping in this flagship that stores all their collections (but for the Red Label). Boss Black labels for both men and women provide flawlessly elegant day and night looks. The more expensive Selection line, with hand stitched details, has a bespoke feel to it and, for the weekend, Boss Green looks great while putting or lazing around at the golf hut, while Boss Orange appeals to those with more urban pastimes. The service here is flawless, but for the occasional disappointment: sizes for certain pieces might be quite limited.

HUGO HUGO BOSS
MEN'S/WOMEN'S BOUTIQUE

6-15-1 Roppongi Keyakizaka-dori,
 Roppongi, Minato-ku, Tokyo (Others)
03-5485-6624
www.hugoboss.com/
🕐 11:00–20:00
▦ No holidays
↧ MAP 12-18   ¥|¥|¥-¥|¥|¥|¥

Hugo Boss's diffusion line takes center stage here with fun separates and suits in the latest trends and colors. But come here for the Hugo shoes that are not available anywhere else in town. They are comfortable, reasonable (for a designer label), and in superb quality leather. While others do sexier bottines and pumps, Hugo's stand out for their look of handfinished luxe. The men's biker boots with side buckles, leather sneakers with suede lining, and dark dress shoes all offer modern styling and hints of a perfect work/life balance.

HUNTING WORLD
MEN'S/WOMEN'S ACCESSORIES

5-17-2 Minami-Aoyama, Minato-ku,
 Tokyo (Others)
03-3486-8818
www.huntingworld.com
🕐 11:00–20:00
▦ No holidays
↧ MAP 1-52   ¥|¥|¥|¥

A certain young Bob Lee made a trip to Africa in 1955. Amazed by the beauty of the country and its wildlife he returned there to set up his own safari organization. His friends started arriving with luggage and camera bags completely ill-suited for the bush and the rest, as they say, is history. Not much here is suited any more for the bush but the handbags, duffle bags and luggage are all about urban adventure with inspiration from the jungle. The most classic thing here is the Battue series, in urethane with a foam lining in khaki and olive green, front pockets, thick handles, metal fittings, zippers, and curving leather insets that make them shock absorbent. For the fashion-conscious Hunting World lovers there is a series of crocodile handbags in dark brown with croco flaps and calf leather bodies with white accents.

HYSTERIC GLAMOUR

MEN'S/WOMEN'S/KIDS' DESIGNER

Roppongi Hills M/H 2F, 6-4-1 Roppongi, Minato-ku, Tokyo (Others)
03-5785-2153
www.hystericglamour.jp
🕐 11:00–20:00
No holidays
MAP 12-19
¥|¥-¥|¥

This is a real pop funk label that marries rock n' roll and art to street chic. Designer Kitamura Nobuhiko's high quality, luxurious casuals caused the explosion of the skinny T, hip hugging jean and killer legs in vintage denim a couple of years back. Inspired by Andy Warhol and Moriyama Daigo he has been delivering a great mix of class and fake, fine large baubles as accessories and terribly waspish styles. Great military coats, trench coats, superbly graphic T-shirts and rows and rows of jeans are housed in this beautifully decorated shop inspired by *The Last Supper*. For rock royalty kids who learn the attitude at a very young age, Hysteric Glamour offers the perfect get-up. Start with hip-hugging jeans with studded pockets for a one year old. Combine this with T-shirts with crystals and jungle down jackets with fur for the slightly older. And come summer there is always a heady range of denim mini skirts, ripped shorts, corduroy collections and T-shirts that scream rock n' roll.

ICB

WOMEN'S BOUTIQUE

Shinjuku Isetan Main Dept 4F, 3-14-1 Shinjuku, Shinjuku-ku, Tokyo (Others)
03-3225-1890
www.icb-brand.com/
🕐 11:00–20:00
No holidays
MAP 9-12
¥|¥

This is the homeland of the International Concept Brand, a comfortably uncerebral Japanese brand that makes simple clothes in cotton, wool, linen and other comfy fabrics. Casual chic looks for daytime are undoubtedly the best things here. Fine wool-knit dresses paired with the season's obsession with leggings (not a must-have look for the office), cashmere skirts and knits, stretch pants and skirts, accessories in calf and fine leather, as well as fine trousers in wool and volume knits paired with high leather boots and elegantly cut down jackets. In summer too the breezy look retains elegance. And for those of us who stand tall, this is one of the few Japanese brands that make chic things for those used to a view from above.

IKEA

INTERIOR

201-1 Orimoto-Cho, Tsuzukui-ku, Yokohama, Kanagawa (Others)
045-470-7500
www.ikea.com/ms/en_JP/
10:00–21:00
No holidays
MAP 20-1 ¥-¥¥

As the company famously says, this is for people with "more taste than money." The largest furniture chain in the world has only recently set foot in Japan, bringing its affordable solutions for home, kitchen, living room, bedroom, and (famously) children's rooms to the outskirts of Tokyo. Ikea in Japan is also very good at wardrobe solutions that can fit in those enormous closets without shelves that are often part of homes in Japan. If you have no space for any more furniture, Ikea is also the place for lamps, home fabrics, and a neat collection of Swedish food that includes vodka and crispbreads. Ikea flaunts everything—the hidden design store pop camp, the furniture retailers basics collection, and loads of Scandinavian ideas that quench the thirst for affordable design classics.

IL BISONTE

MEN'S/WOMEN'S ACCESSORIES

5-8-7 Jingumae, Shibuya-ku, Tokyo (Others)
03-5774-0651
www.ilbisonte.jp/
11:30–20:00
No holidays
MAP 6-47 ¥¥-¥¥¥

Design in vachetta leather marries function with Florentino Wanny di Filippo's handbags, wallets, luggage, and other beautiful leather accessories. The smell of cured leather pervades the entire store. Though not cheap, due to strict import regulations, the vegetable-dyed tan leather pieces come of age seductively over many years. Hobos, totes, weekenders, washbags, shopping bags, wallets, card cases and diaries all come in natural soft grey, brown and black tones all stamped with the trademark bison logo. The men's briefcases are cleverly structured, offering room and a sharp silhouette, and there are plenty of top quality gift ideas: small leather accessories, belts, bracelets, scarves, hats and key chains.

ILLUMS

INTERIOR

2-1-1 Marunouchi, Chiyoda-ku, Tokyo (Others)
03-5223-8366
www.illums.co.jp
11:00–20:00
Not fixed
MAP 7-14 ¥¥-¥¥¥

Illums is a huge but discreet shop, straight from Copenhagen, well appointed with all things Scandinavian, leaning heavily on the simple and natural. Kitchenware, lighting, interior accents, lifestyle goods, Hans J. Wagner and Alvar Alto designed chairs, and a huge collection of Ittala and Kosta Boda tableware. As for home textiles, there is nothing bolder than Marimekko for your table and bed, and the simple but iconic Kinnasand rugs. Royal Copenhagen fans can also find an extensive collection of porcelain and faience flatware, and a range of mugs made specially for this shop.

IMMUDYNE
DIET

Roppongi Hills Westwalk 4F, 6-10-1
   Roppongi, Minato-ku, Tokyo (Others)
03-5414-7200
www.immudyne.co.jp/
🕑 11:00–21:00
📅 No holidays
MAP 12-20   ¥|¥

An unexpected perspective of beauty by this don of eyeshadow and eyelashes, Shu Uemura's latest shop is dedicated to inner beauty in a digestive way. The shop stocks cosmetics for the insides sold through its "Fasten Club," a system of fasting to lose weight. Products sold here include the Fasten Club Speed Diet fruit juice with orange, apple, grape, pineapple, apricot, peach, and lemon that you drink four times a day for spectacular results in just two days. There is a host of other beautifully packaged supplements on sale, such as fish collagen, aloe, and black plum vinegar to make you beautiful inside out.

IN THE ROOM
INTERIOR

3-1-13 Shinjuku, Shinjuku-ku, Tokyo
03-3354-0101
www.intheroom.jp/
🕑 11:00–20:00
📅 Not fixed
MAP 9-13   ¥|¥|¥-¥|¥|¥|¥

Eight floors of stuff for the house. They offer total coordination advice for people who need a quick fix, but the nicest thing here is perhaps the great range of designer electronics, such as flat panel display TVs and the latest cutting-edge noise canceling Bose headphones, to match your haute interiors. There are also loads of iPod paraphernalia to suit all your iPod needs. A good place to stock up on everything you need to dress your house up in a discreet individualism that is neither slapdash nor too crafted.

INTERMIX TOKYO
WOMEN'S BOUTIQUE

11-1 Sarugakucho, Shibuya-ku,
   Tokyo (Others)
03-3770-4600
www.intermix-ny.com
🕑 11:00–20:00
📅 No holidays
MAP 2-34   ¥|¥|¥-¥|¥|¥|¥

Girl-next-door style clothes with the right amount of Chloé and Balenciaga thrown in with T-shirts, tank tops, and denim. Well known among Tokyo's women for their great collection of jackets from Development. While lacking the pizzazz or the collections of the other shops, this place is a favorite among a wide range of girls from the chavvy types to posh totties.

IPHIL

MEN'S BOUTIQUE

Tokyu Dept. Store 2-24-1 Dogenzaka,
Shibuya-ku, Tokyo (Others)
03-3477-3360
www.i-phil.jp
⊘ 11:00–20:00
▦ Not fixed
⌐ MAP 8-21   ¥¥¥-¥¥¥¥

Imagine Jean Reno, Alain Delon, James Bond and all swaggering
sugar daddies and uncles around town. Iphil offers Italian city smart
casuals with trousers, top quality shirts, T shirts, open cable sweaters,
sailor caps and mile long scarves and mufflers. Comfy chic for
a barbecue on the weekend, an art gallery or a roadside cafe.

IRIÉ

WOMEN'S BOUTIQUE

5-8-10 Minami-Aoyama, Minato-ku,
Tokyo
03-3498-9901
none
⊘ 11:00–20:00
▦ No holidays
⌐ MAP 1-53   ¥¥¥

Irie-san was once the Comme des Garçons of Tokyo's glitterati.
His penchant for the latest fabrics was legendary, while his designs
remained classic. While the Paris shop is where the jazz is, this
quiet little shop stocks a superb collection of both the classic Irie
and the Irie Wash—their patented fabric in polyester and nylon that
is all washable at home and mostly iron-free. Great for the office,
get sharp jackets, wide or slim trousers, dresses and even short
trenches, plus knits of all kinds, featherweight skirts and loads of
shirts. Save trips to the local drycleaner.

ISABELA CAPETO

WOMEN'S DESIGNER

Omotesando Hills, 4-12-10 Jingumae,
Shibuya-ku, Tokyo
03-5785-0351
www.isabelacapeto.com.br/
⊘ 11:00–21:00
▦ Not fixed
⌐ MAP 5-34   ¥¥¥-¥¥¥¥

Brazillian born Isabela Capeto embroiders fairy tales into her
clothes. Her line of colorful tunics, slip on dresses, tops, and skirts
might be simple in structure, but are fun and playful. They come
in a riot of pastel color combinations with beautifully embroidered
shells, buttons, beads, sequins, eyelets, mirrors, and flowers, and
offer more romance in happier color combinations than any love
story.

ISABURO

MEN'S/WOMEN'S ACCESSORIES

5-5-24 Minami-Aoyama, Minato-ku, Tokyo
03-3406-1326
www.isaburo.com/
🕐 12:00–20:00
📅 Wednesdays
📍 MAP 1-54   ¥|¥|¥-¥|¥|¥|¥

Isaburo Matsuzaki was the first purveyor of modern bags in Tokyo way back in 1889 when Japan was first opening up to Western fashions, and their first hit collection of luggage came out in the nineteenth century. Known as the Matsuzaki suitcases, they became legendary among foreigners traveling to Japan at that time for their good quality. The current Isaburo 1889 series is derived from this original concept of luggage, and the design is inspired by the sea turtle, a creature that spends its life continuously traveling. Besides this, there is a made-to-order system that lets you chose from among a wide variety of leathers and colors. The ready-made collections put you on the go with the City 123 series, made of hard resin with waterproof zippers and a nylon hard shell. It can accommodate everything from PDAs to mobile phones, laptops, and iPods. Isaburo's handbags and accessories are never discreet, so walking with one of their orange turtle-shaped bags in hand means you are well on your way to changing the cityscape.

ISETAN

DEPARTMENT STORE

3-14-1 Shinjuku, Shinjuku-ku, Tokyo (Others)
03-3352-1111
www.isetan.co.jp/
🕐 10:00–20:00
📅 Not fixed
📍 MAP 9-14   ¥|¥-¥|¥|¥|¥

With so many flagships scattered around, coupled with the elusive boutique culture that makes shopping for a simple article a whole day trip, stores like Isetan make shopping a pleasure, with their super collections efficiently stacked one after the other. Prada, Chanel, Hermès, D&G, Zadig & Voltaire, Diesel, Trovata, See by Chloé, Paula and Joe Sister, Juicy Couture and all the hottest of Japanese designers, even tableware, children's wear—in short, the best of the best at duty-free prices (for non-residents). And if you are a Tokyo resident, Isetan's free "iclub" membership offers you super special privileges that include services such as finding you an apartment and booking your holidays. The show stopping men's collection is in the neighbouring building.

ISETAN MEN'S

MEN'S DEPARTMENT STORE

3-14-1 Shinjuku, Shinjuku-ku, Tokyo
03-3352-1111
www.isetan.co.jp/
🕐 10:00–20:00
📅 Not fixed
📍 MAP 9-15   ¥|¥-¥|¥|¥|¥

Isetan Men's is a huge boy's cache with the best luxury goods and service on the planet. If you want to do bespoke, there is Zegna,

Dunhill, Ferragamo, Burberry, Kiton, Brioni and Aquascutum. For a taste of great Japanese menswear try Number Nine's noir creations and skull accessories, Cabane de Zucca, Ys for men, Junya Watanabe, and Yohji Yamamoto. You'll also find BWL accessories from Malibu, an extensive collection of briefcases, socks, shoes, and umbrellas, and a connoisseur's selection of fragrances and beautiful products from Penhaligon's, The Art of Shaving, Aqua di Parma, and the cult Santa Maria Novella. Loads of gear with which to unleash your inner playboy.

ISETAN SHINJUKU RE-STYLE
WOMEN'S BOUTIQUE

Isetan Shinjuku 4F, 3-14-1 Shinjuku,
Shinjuku-ku, Tokyo
03-3352-1111
www.isetan.co.jp/
🕙 10:00–20:00
📅 Not fixed
📍 MAP 9-16   ¥ ¥ ¥ ¥

Made-for-Tokyo fashions straight from the catwalk. Recently the emphasis has been on futurism, retro, sporty, ballet shoes, salopettes, mini skirts, bloomers and short pants. Sacai is one of the great designers here who does pretty confections that are at once street friendly and office friendly too. Lanvin, Derek Lam and Phillip Lim have found a stage here too and for accessories there is a range of metallic and sparkling items. The collections sizzle without going over the top and shopping at Isetan, where this store is located, means that all this could come at duty-free prices too.

J.
INTERIOR

5-26-4 Okusawa, Setagaya-ku,
Tokyo (Others)
03-5731-6421
www.j-period.com/
🕙 11:00–20:00
📅 Not fixed
📍 MAP 11-7   ¥ ¥ ¥ - ¥ ¥ ¥ ¥

Synchronising panache with minimalism as the Japanese do it best, this shop sells handmade furniture and all kinds of interior goods with a distinctive *wa* flavor. Definitely the best minimalist shop in the world featuring natural materials. White, black, red, simple symmetrical shapes of tableware, and other interior items—and everything here is handmade by skilled Japanese craftsmen. To top it off, it is greatly wallet-pleasing as well. The furniture too is a simplistic modern take on traditional Japanese beds, chests, and dressing tables. If you love great taste and have time for only one shop while in Tokyo, this should be your top choice.

JAEGER

MEN'S/WOMEN'S BOUTIQUE

5-1-27 Minami-Aoyama, Minato-ku,
Tokyo (Others)
03-5485-5705
www.jaeger.co.uk/
🕐 11:00–20:00
📅 No holidays
🗺 MAP 1-55　　¥|¥|¥-¥|¥|¥

The brand might lack the necessary thrills and frills for men and women in the fast lane, but it makes up for that with an excellent range of super classic modern suits for the office—tweed, knit, and woolen in the winter and silk cotton in the summer. Jaeger is favored by clients whose parents also shopped here for their simple good taste and superb quality.

JAMIN PUECH

WOMEN'S ACCESSORIES

5-2-11 Jingumae, Shibuya-ku, Tokyo
03-5464-2780
www.jamin-puech.com/
🕐 11:00–20:00
📅 Not fixed
🗺 MAP 6-48　　¥|¥|¥-¥|¥|¥

There is an instant je ne sais quoi starry quality about Benoit Jamin and Isabelle Puech's bags. Great patches of leather and raffia in a heady mosaic of colorful silks, beads, threads, silver and metal embellishments go into making these one of a kind creations that come in clutches, totes and hold-alls. For those of you who dont know your baguette from your saddle these offer a great freedom from trends, seasons and horrible big logos.

JANTZEN

WOMEN'S BOUTIQUE

1-35-16 Ebisu-Nishi, Shibuya-ku, Tokyo
03-5728-5631
www.jantzen.com
🕐 11:00–20:00
📅 Not fixed
🗺 MAP 2-35　　¥|¥-¥|¥|¥

American retro casual inspired by the 60s and a love for water, thanks to Jantzen's origins as a swimwear maker. The present collection here, which is unique to Japan, is inspired by this history. Silk marine striped tops, bright T-shirts in block stripes, silk frocks with pleats and stripes, leg warmers, lace dresses, and cute little woolen suits—and a lot of ornithological motifs—characterize this freewheeling brand.

J. CREW

MEN'S/WOMEN'S BOUTIQUE

Aqua City, 1-7-1 Daiba, Minato-ku, Tokyo (Others)
03-3599-4700
www.jcrew.com
11:00–21:00
Not fixed
MAP 22-1
¥¥¥¥¥

Ruffled striped shirts, skinny gilt button cardigans, and nipped-waist polka-dot dresses are what you will find here, so if you are looking for short shorts or sky high hemlines you would be better off down the street. Fashion forward but never too racy, they also make winning knits and superb totes, perfect for the weekend. Collegiate, classic, and preppy, J. Crew looks best on tall athletic, sunkissed people.

JEAN PAUL GAULTIER

MEN'S/WOMEN'S DESIGNER

2-1-1 Marunouchi, Chiyoda-ku, Tokyo (Others)
03-5224-5032
www.jpgaultier.fr
11:00–20:00
Not fixed
MAP 7-15
¥¥¥¥-¥¥¥¥¥

This brand is now thirty years old, yet still continues to challenge the couture establishment (don't forget, he dressed men in skirts back in 1985, put Madonna in a conical bra, and is the brilliant creative director for Hermès). His couture lines are one of the few that still remain true to the sensibilities of haute couture. The women's collection remains the best thing here, with perfect trouser suits but in men's fabrics with lots of volume. His trademark trenchcoat dresses, double-breasted peak lapel redingote coats, capes, sailor striped hoodies and Ts, and lots of other no-nonsense fashion stuff is for women who like to take matters in their own hands.

J. F. REY

KIDS'/MEN'S/WOMEN'S EYEWEAR

12-18 Daikanyama-cho, Shibuya-ku, Tokyo
03-5458-0019
www.jf-rey.jp/
11:00–20:00
Wednesdays
MAP 2-36
¥¥¥

French designer J. F. Rey's eyewear is inspired by contemporary graphic design and modern architecture. Each of the pieces are sculptural, in shapes that are never ordinary, such as the award winning "boz" with circular temples, and the "ding dong acetate," inspired by African and Asian cultures and even incorporating leaves and dried flowers. The JF 2180 integrates the stainless steel structure fitting the lenses only halfway at the front, so the glasses—with acetate temples and lattice work—seem extremely light. Most of the frames have vibrant and contrasting inside-outside coloring and a superb lightness and flexibility of face, endpiece, and temple. Their excellent children's stainless steel models are made of clipped together metal parts, without screws or welding, and can be entirely taken apart to avoid any breaking. Cutting-edge technology peaks with style.

JILL STUART

WOMEN'S DESIGNER

6-19-20 Jingumae, Shibuya-ku, Tokyo (Others)
03-3409-0484
www.sanei.net/
11:00–20:00
Not fixed
MAP 6-49 ¥¥-¥¥¥

Japanese love Jill Stuart. In fact, the collection you see here is like her collection in any other country—but the sweet, pretty aesthetic is of course more prevalent here than anywhere else. Peasant-style skirts made of strips of variously hued lace, equestrian jackets, and velvet jackets cinched with a wide belt—basically the collection is really about how you wear it. There is something here for every woman of style.

JIL SANDER

MEN'S/WOMEN'S DESIGNER

6-3-16 Minami-Aoyama, Minato-ku, Tokyo (Others)
03-5778-0601
www.jilsander.com/
11:00–20:00
Not fixed
MAP 1-56 ¥¥¥¥¥

This brand has been revived by Belgian designer Raf Simons, who stays true to Jil Sander's esoteric yet understated aesthetic with comfortable and very feminine iconic pleated sheaths, sharp jackets, simple fly-front coats, and lots of smart tailoring. The men's collection has great sporty shirts in vivid colors and wonderfully light flat front trousers. A staple among high-end creative types, Sander's clothes are an investment that is worth its minimalist style.

JIMMY CHOO

WOMEN'S SHOES

Omotesando Hills Mailn Bldgg. 1F, 4-12-10 Jingumae, Shibuya-ku, Tokyo
03-5410-0841
www.jimmychoo.com
11:00–21:00
Not fixed
MAP 5-35 ¥¥¥¥-¥¥¥¥¥

The king of three-inch heels finally sets his bejeweled foot down in Tokyo, at his first independent boutique in Omotesando. Classic, but perfect, patent leather slip-ons are always the safest bet; otherwise, the latest collection in dark, brooding burgundy, brown, and black in patent leather with metallic studs serves best for the confident woman. The bestselling shoe is the Macy—a great, perfectly balanced 10.5cm-high platform sandal that safely defends its comfort criteria. Despite the small collection of shoes, the shop oozes luxury with its 40s style velvet boudoir interiors. You can also find a few other bags, small accessories, and the most recent collection of flat shoes and boots for a casual look.

J.LINDEBERG

MEN'S/WOMEN'S DESIGNER

5-5-25 Minami-Aoyama, Minato-ku, Tokyo (Others)
03-5464-3631
www.jlindeberg.com/
🕐 11:00–20:00
🗓 Not fixed
🚉 MAP 1-57   ¥|¥|¥-¥|¥|¥|¥

If you thought that the skinny pants look was only for women, think again, and visit the J. Lindberg shop where you'll find the deadliest darkest skinny pants, Russell Crowe style, for men. A truly international lifestyle brand, based on the private likes and dislikes of its ex-Diesel guru Johan Lindeberg, the brand cites various influences, starting with Marlon Brando, Robert Redford, and old golfing heroes in bow ties and plus fours, and moving on through rock stars and pop legends. While they make the usual basics, it is the mood and styling here that sets them apart: one year it could be rock n' roll, and the next year the rock n' roll party might be off to the Hamptons. Their sports collection is located in the Tokyo Midtown complex.

J.M. WESTON

MEN'S SHOES

5-11-5 Minami-Aoyama, Minato-ku, Tokyo
03-5485-0306
www.jmweston.com
🕐 11:00–20:00
🗓 No holidays
🚉 MAP 1-58   ¥|¥|¥|¥-¥|¥|¥|¥|¥

This master shoemaker from France has been storming the world with his classics that are still being made in century-old factories. Their oxfords, derbies, loafers, and ankle-length boots have sharp silhouettes, comfortable shapes, a polished finish, and cutting edge classic details. This shop does not do bespoke but J.M. Weston *speciales*—a collection of pattern order shoes where you chose any shape from those on display and the shop re-makes it for you in your size and choice of leather. Choose from a variety of colors in calf, including bordeaux, pink, green and blue, and from leathers like shark, ostrich, and croc. RTW offerings go up to size 9 and include a wide range of sporty styles, matching belts, and an array of small accessories like wallets and key holders.

JOHANNA HO

WOMEN'S DESIGNER

Roppongi Hills West Walk 2F, 6-10-3 Roppongi, Minato-ku, Tokyo (Others)
03-5785-2339
www.johannaho.jp
🕐 11:00–20:00
🗓 No holidays
🚉 MAP 12-21   ¥|¥-¥|¥|¥

This Hong Kong designer has a mind of her own, dressing girls of the moment in clothes that are never outlandish but with details interesting enough to get you noticed. Knit lines come with layers of ruffles in the front, so do form-fitting cotton shirts, but other detailing is fun too, like tank tops in khaki and navy with red and pink piping, knit secretary dresses with 60s glamor, and animated T-shirts that are a bit quirky. And since no muse goes without the prettiest of shoes, Johanna does them in ballet flats, heels, and sandals in rainbow colors.

JOHN LOBB
MEN'S SHOES

3-2-3 Marunouchi, Chiyoda-ku, Tokyo
03-6267-6011
www.johnlobb.com/
⊙ 11:00–19:00 (Sun/Holidays until18:00)
▦ No holidays
⌶ MAP 7-16 ¥¥¥¥-¥¥¥¥¥

Haberdashery and fine tailoring for gentlemen has been undergoing great changes in the recent past, with most major houses trying to ride down Savile Row and ride up the high street. John Lobb, purveyor of shoes to James Bond, has not been spared, and after undergoing some great changes, has thankfully returned to what it does best—shoes: Oxford, Derby, monk, loafer, and dandy ankle boots. They also offer six kinds of made-to-measure models that take more than a year to make, and include wood lasts of your feet. For the equestrian, John Lobb makes a superb pair of riding boots. And, for ladies looking for a great gift for their men, there is no better choice than the handmade calfskin accessories here, like the all-leather key rings, a superbly macho money clip, a coin purse, and the inevitable business card case.

JOHN SMEDLEY
MEN'S/WOMEN'S KNITWEAR

5-2-7 Jingumae, Shibuya-ku, Tokyo (Others)
03-5766-6442
www.johnsmedley.jp/
⊙ 11:00–20:00
▦ Not fixed
⌶ MAP 6-50 ¥¥-¥¥¥

Straight from Derbyshire, England with a knitting history of more than 250 years, John Smedley undoubtedly makes the finest knitwear in the world, and at the best prices. In knitwear jargon this means thirty guage, a fineness that few knitwear makers can hope to achieve. Houndstooth sweaters with matching mufflers, twin sets in almost thirty colors, sweaters with mesh down the sleeves, and fine patterns make up their collection in this shop. Each sweater, on an average, has 1.5 km of yarn and 1.2 million stitches, and the necks and collars have always been hand cut and hand sewn. The intarsia patterns in this shop have been specially woven for the Japan market and, as everyone loves a great collaboration, John Smedley has also worked with the famous Japanese knitwear brand Intoca to make beautiful cardigans and pullovers in grey and cream with raglan sleeves, bell sleeves, and elbow detailing. Everything here is famously made from New Zealand Merino wool and can be machine washed. In summers, witness a flourish of similar basics in cotton and silk.

JOSEPH
MEN'S/WOMEN'S BOUTIQUE

9-7-4 Akasaka, Minato-ku,
  Tokyo (Others)
03-5413-7889
www.joseph.co.jp/
🕐 12:00–20:00
📅 Not fixed
🔍 MAP 12-22   ¥|¥|¥-¥|¥|¥

Set up by former hairdresser Joseph Ettegui, whose pants are the holy grail of all pants. Every season sees new fabrics and colors. But it isn't just the pants that are great here. Come winter and his jackets are tailored with the same fineness and neatness, especially in shearling and fur. While most worry about prices, his fur pieces are definitely worth the trip to the bank and come much cheaper than those of other labels. His shirts and knitwear follow the same lines of high-end luxe, and are traffic stopping no matter what your size.

JOURNAL STANDARD LUXE
WOMEN'S BOUTIQUE

1-5-7 Jinnan, Shibuya-ku, Tokyo (Others)
03-5457-0844
journal-standard.baycrews.co.jp/
🕐 11:00–20:00
📅 No holidays
🔍 MAP 8-22   ¥|¥|¥

Farm fashion, rustic chic, and quiet boho minimalism pervade this store that reminds shoppers to slow down with an extensive collection of free spirited designers such as Universal Utility, Karen Mansfield, and Isabel Marant. Lots of linen, crochet and lace, organic quilted jackets, comfortable denims, long shorts, and beautiful wraparound knits in offwhite, beige, and indigo. Airy, chic, and lightweight ideas for weekends and country homes. Now all you need is a Double RL Ranch, Ralph Lauren as a husband, and a cookbook on the way.

JUANA DE ARCO
LINGERIE

hpgrp, 6-9-16 GInza, Chuo-ku,
  Tokyo (Others)
03-5537-2740
www.ante-buenosaires-hpfrance.com/
  shop.html
🕐 12:00–20:00
📅 3rd Tues.
🔍 MAP 4-17   ¥|¥|¥

Argentinian label Juana de Arco unleashes her full palette of colors in this shop, immediately transporting you to her Buenos Aires atelier. Handmade candy-colored bras, panties in neon colors, thongs with pretty ribbons, camisoles with patchwork and golden piping, boxer shorts, pajamas, Arabian pants, baby-dolls, yoga clothes, and tulle skirts all in a riot of color. No two items are the same; in fact, no two pajama legs are the same, since she uses only dead stock from her favored textile factories. Her reds are a treat and her llama knits made by the Budi Budi twins in a village in Argentina offer color and comfort in the winter. Though men will have to be satisfied with just one design of boxer shorts in stripes, your floor could not look better covered in her Turkish cushions, also in deadstock fabric. Let your imagination fly and—as one size fits all—cross your fingers and snuggle.

JUDGEMEK
MEN'S/WOMEN'S BOUTIQUE

Akita Bldg.2F, 6-12-22 Jingumae,
Shibuya-ku, Tokyo
03-5774-6921
www.palgroup.co.jp/judgemek/
🕐 11:00–20:00
📅 No holidays
📍 MAP 6-51 ¥¥-¥¥¥

Everything at Judgemek has possibilities. T-shirts with interchangeable necks, shirts with three sleeves, coats with attached ties, and cloth tags that also double up as necklaces; plus a lot of accessories of the made-from-tarp type, and shoes with a leaning towards patent leather. A long favorite has been the tutaee, a superb Japanese-inspired jacket whose lining can be removed to make it wearable all-season. With lots of monotones and eccentric ideas, Judgemek takes creativity seriously, with clothes that definitely break the ice.

JUICY COUTURE
MEN'S/WOMEN'S BOUTIQUE

5-5-5 Minami-Aoyama, Minato-ku,
Tokyo (Others)
03-5766-2237
www.sannfreres.co.jp/brands/JUICY/
index.html
🕐 11:00–20:00
📅 No holidays
📍 MAP 1-59 ¥¥¥-¥¥¥¥

Sexy comfort for women in a fabric that you never would have touched until Juicy Couture came along. Designers Pam Skaist-Levy and Gela Nash have gone all-out luxury and in their first flagship store outside the States, replete with men's floor, you can find all their usual celeb casual staples, including sunglasses, shoes, watches, fragrance, babywear and even dogwear. Decorated in pop colors, the first floor carries bags, accessories, soft toys, and other sundries, including teapots. The upper floor carries their high-end clothes line, Couture Couture, which consists of American classic couture-inspired clothes. And for the men for whom pajamas are after-five uniform, you can grab some of the finest in town from the men's floor.

JUNKO SHIMADA
WOMEN'S DESIGNER

Matsuya Ginza Main Dept 3F, 3-6-1
Ginza, Chuo-ku, Tokyo (Others)
03-5250-4160
www.junkoshimada.co.jp/
🕐 10:00–20:00
📅 Not fixed
📍 MAP 3-11 ¥¥¥¥-¥¥¥¥¥

Junko Shimada's creations are the least cerebral and most feminine of all her fashion contemporaries in Japan. For starters, she keeps her hems really high, so it is advisable to have killer calves if you want to look great in her miniskirts and dresses. In winter she is always into knit dresses in big checkerboard patterns, shiny vinyl numbers, cheongsam-style dresses and tartan flared mini dresses. In summer the look is simple and offers city chic with soft white cotton dresses, small tartan-check flared dresses, and simple figure-hugging numbers. She has a following among women who love her totally chic modern aesthetic.

JUNYA WATANABE
MEN'S/WOMEN'S DESIGNER

5-2-1 Minami-Aoyama, Minato-ku, Tokyo (Others)
03-3406-3951
none
🕐 11:00–20:00
📅 Not fixed
📍 MAP 1-60   ¥|¥|¥|¥

A product of the mentor-disciple tradition of Japanese culture, Junya Watanabe has gained as much fame as his mentor Rei Kawakubo of Comme des Garçons, where he started as a pattern cutter. Today he works both at Comme des Garçons with the Tricot line, and at his own label. His staple is the biker's jacket in calf leather, which sometimes comes with a washed or purposely stressed look. Adept at using wool gabardine, he manages to use it in dresses and gets away with surprising softness. Drapes are also used, often to soften the glambot appearance of tight black, shiny leather jackets. And he often plays around with trompe l'oeil—like using different fabrics in one garment. A dress that is made of part knit on one side and jaquard satin on the other is an example of looks that are avant garde yet really wearable.

JURLIQUE
COSMETICS

2-8-5 Jiyugaoka, Meguro-ku, Tokyo (Others)
03-3718-8006
www.jurlique-japan.com/
🕐 12:00–20:00 (Sun/Holiday 11:00–19:00)
📅 No holidays
📍 MAP 11-8   ¥|¥|¥|¥

While the world is moving towards stem cell creams, micro derma abrasions, and fridges full of injectable stuff, many like Stella McCartney and Nicole Kidman are going back to mother earth as the real secret to beauty. Jurlique is considered the purest in the market, with such obsessive control over their ingredients that they have their own fields to cultivate all that goes into their magic potions. Imagine fields of organic geraniums, roses, mint, calendula, and lavender that go into their excellent bath and massage oils, silk dust masks, natural lipsticks, and a whole array of just pure goodness for the skin. Head upstairs to their rejuvenating spa to quickly recharge your skin with these heavenly products.

JUVENILE DELINQUENT

MEN'S BOUTIQUE

2-26-14 Dogenzaka, Shibuya-ku, Tokyo
03-3770-6220
www.jd-zoot.com/
🕐 12:00–21:00
📅 Not fixed
∫ MAP 8-23   ¥|¥-¥|¥|¥

This is where Al Capone would have shopped had he visited Japan. He would have especially loved the tailored pinstripe baggy suit with matching vest, and extra long coats ideally paired with a really bright shirt in red or orange. Known as the Zoot Suit, it also comes in a Hollywood baggy style with a shorter blazer. The Sunningdale suit has box pleats at the shoulder blade, and the zip-up leather suit is entirely in leather. Derby hats and Spanish hats are the best advised accessories, along with wingtip shoes and gold tipped walking sticks. A person who dresses like this at night would surely wear jeans with kimono patches, gold medallions, and the essential P. Diddy snow-white fur coat during the day.

KALISTE-UN DIMANCHE A VENISE

WOMEN'S SHOES

5-9-8 Minami Aoyama, Minato-ku,
  Tokyo (Others)
03-5778-3628
www.akakura.jp/kalliste/
🕐 11:00–20:00
📅 No holidays
∫ MAP 1-61   ¥|¥|¥-¥|¥|¥

A sudden wave of sexy Italianess on feet has been brought about by the merger of these two brands, now sold under one roof. Their strappy sandals, decorated with turquoise and other stones, can tread up the high streets and burn the dance floor at the same time. In winter, the sexy leather boots, mules with pointy toes, and superb pumps carry many feet to work. Some might be disappointed, as the shop does not sell sizes over 24.5cm.

KAMI

WOMEN'S BOUTIQUE

Daikanyama 8953 Bldg.1F, 1-35-17
  Ebisu-nishi, Shibuya-ku, Tokyo
03-5459-6600
www.kami-daikanyama.jp/
🕐 11:00–10:00 (Sat/Sun/Holidays
  starts from 10:00)
📅 Not fixed
∫ MAP 2-37   ¥|¥-¥|¥|¥

Saucy LA style dresses with loud flashy prints, bling accessories with eyewear to match, and the only shop in town that dares to sell perfect copies of the latest Marc Jacobs and Fendi spy bags with unashamed pizzazz in a posh fashion district.

KAPITAL

MEN'S/WOMEN'S DENIM

Gaia Ebisu Bldg 1F, 2-20-2 Ebisu-minami,
Shibuya-ku, Tokyo (Others)
03-5725-3923
www.kapital.jp/
🕐 12:00–20:00
📅 Not fixed
♪ MAP 10-4   ¥|¥|¥

The most traditional brand of jeans in the country from the world's center of denim, the Okayama area of western Japan. Since the early eighties they have been producing jeans through a laborious, hand-crafted process where the dyeing, designing, cutting, and stitching takes place between designer and craftsmen to create long-lasting denim pieces that don't necessarily follow any trend. With more than twenty different patterns of jeans, the label also stocks dungarees, bags, and other denim accessories. A brilliant example of weaving tradition with cool.

KARTELL

INTERIOR

6-1-3 Minami-Aoyama, Minato-ku, Tokyo
(Others)
03-5468-2328
www.kartell.it/
🕐 11:00–19:30
📅 Wednesdays
♪ MAP 16-62   ¥|¥|¥|¥

Plastic, once the outcast of the design world, still makes certain lips curl up in disdain. But Achille Castiglioni, Philippe Starck, Ron Arad, and Antonio Citterio—who surely couldn't all be wrong—decided to collaborate with this manufacturer to put plastic where peoples' hearts are. As a result, people are still lining up to buy the 4970/84 container units (no bolts and a simple, neat appearance) originally designed by their inhouse designer in 1967. The shop now stocks them in silver, cream and in many sizes. Philippe Starck's Louis Ghost and Dr No chairs that look like thrones in plastic, Charles Ghost in various colors, and la Boheme stools in the shape of ancient Roman urns are a quick way to add humor to any room. Ron Arad's curving Bookworm bookshelf, and Feruc-cio Laviani's Take table lamp, a plastic version of a baroque-styled crystal lamp, easily become focal points for any interior space. The T-table, with its curiously intricate tabletop, can take any amount of roughhousing, and their enviable collection of children's stackable furniture available in Dr. No and La Marie forms, offer the same fun factor for kids' rooms.

KATE SPADE

MEN'S/WOMEN'S ACCESSORIES

Amon B Tower, 5-2-11 Minami-Aoyama,
Minato-ku, Tokyo (Others)
03-5468-8161
www.katespade.com/
🕐 12:00–20:00
📅 Not fixed
♪ MAP 1-63   ¥|¥|¥-¥|¥|¥|¥

Kate Spade has a cult following in Japan for her sweet and air-ily charming accessories. She makes fairytale handbags, totes, and clutches in leather, fabric, canvas, nylon and straw combinations that are good for both day and night. While the materials seem ordinary, the exquisite detailing and sunny colors are something girls can't say no to. There is also a neat collection of matching canvas platforms, sandals, and beautiful heels. There's a small collection of Jack Spade items for men that is perfect for the beach. The shop also stocks some Kate Spade stationery and a pretty baby buggy.

K-DIARY
MEN'S/WOMEN'S
SPORTSWEAR/SHOES

3-18-23 Jingumae, Shibuya-ku, Tokyo
03-5775-7908
www.k-swiss.jp/
🕚 11:00–20:00
📅 No Holidays
ℐ MAP 5-36 ¥|¥

From frumpy tennis court gear to high fashion, this company, originally created by two tennis-loving brothers in 1966, has smartly undergone a chameleon change that has put the five stripes and ubiquitous double D rings on the same level as the swoosh. More classic than its contemporaries, K-Swiss still sells its very first model—the all leather tennis shoe first released in 1966. But, while famous for their tennis, running and training shoes, they have finally launched into leisure apparel famously peddled by tennis's dream girl Anna Kournikova.

KEITA MARUYAMA TOKYO PARIS
MEN'S/WOMEN'S DESIGNER

Roppongi Hills Hill Side B1F, 6-10-2
    Roppongi, Minato-ku, Tokyo (Others)
03-5775-7773
www.keitamaruyama.com
🕚 11:00–20:00
📅 No holidays
ℐ MAP 12-23 ¥|¥|¥-¥|¥|¥|¥

Keita Maruyama's obsession with all colorful things Chinese has lead to collections that may change in silhouette and form but are always heavily embroidered and come in a riot of colors and embroidery. Quite like a bird with beautiful plumes, he does long evening dresses in silk with colorful silk embroidery of flowers, birds, and trees on the corners. His skirts and shirts are also in heavy satin with delicate imagery. In winter, the sweaters come in heavy cable knit embroidered in wool, and his down jackets come in printed silk. The look is 1930s Shanghai girl meets Tokyo boy. For the boys, there is a small corner that stocks ties, socks, wallets in silk, and embroidered shirts and sweaters.

KENZO
MEN'S/WOMEN'S DESIGNER

3-6-1 Ginza Chuo-ku, Matsuya 4F, Tokyo
    (Others)
03-3564-5777
www.kenzo.com
🕚 10:00–20:00
📅 Not fixed
ℐ MAP 1-12 ¥|¥|¥|¥-¥|¥|¥|¥|¥

Kenzo remains a triumph of collective memory, exquisite detailing and nouveau boho. This is the original home of this Franco-

Japanese brand. To shoppers making an entrance, it is a peagantry of color and bohemia, but they are instantly taken hostage by the effervescent prints, cardigans, skirts, and shoes—all in one swift stroke of Kenzo's Asian-inspired creative genius. Now that he no longer works here, his legacy is kept alive by Sardinian Antonio Marras, with lots of floral prints, embroidery, fantastic tartan, velvet, and crochet everywhere possible. Many may have removed Kenzo from their must-have list, but those in the know swear that the way to wear this post-bohemian is to mix and match with clean lines and simple basics.

KIRA KIRA PROJECT

INTERIOR/ACCESSORIES

Laforet Harajuku 1F, 1-11-6 Jingumae,
  Shibuya-ku, Tokyo
03-5414-3628
www.kirakirajapan.com/
🕐 11:00–20:00
📅 No holidays
Ⱶ MAP 5-37   ¥¥¥

In its post-punk phase, Tokyo is now all about adult sweetness and a nostalgia for childhood comics. The very decorated hot pink toy-and-clothes stores Kira Kira is a collaboration between cool Tokyoites such as Dresscamp designer Toshikazu Iwaya, *Memoirs of a Geisha* actress Kaori Momoi and stylist Tetsuro Nagase. Stock up on stuffed toys that have evolved beyond the kid's bedroom: Tamashii-kun, Shigeru-kun, Muupiru Seaser, Kumapiru, and Oui Oui are all made of cloth and are soft, expressionless, and strangely inspiring. If it's clothes you're after, try the ShinYa sleeveless "hair print" T-shirts or the cute Spiderman knit shirt that will instantly make you feel like the world's most wanted.

KITON

MEN'S/WOMEN'S DESIGNER

Roppongi Hills Keyaki Street 1F, 6-12-
  2 Roppongi, Minato-ku, Tokyo (Others)
03-5786-7760
www.kiton.it
🕐 11:00–20:00
📅 No holidays
Ⱶ MAP 12-24   ¥¥¥¥¥

As every smart man knows, single-breasted suits make the sharpest outfits. And smart men also know that the best cuts in the business come from Italy, with Kiton in the lead when it comes to fine cashmere pinstripes, wool worsted, or more casual fabrics like jute and linen. All the suits here are still handmade and half finished, and there are shirts, ties, and shoes to make this a one-stop gentleman's shop. The same sharpness is used in tailoring for the women's collection that comes with accessories such as superb mink stoles that nestle remarkably well on the shoulders.

KIWA SYLPHY
WOMEN'S BOUTIQUE

Omotesando Hills Main Bldg B4F, 4–12–10 Jingumae, Shibuya–ku, Tokyo
03–5785–1177
www.kiwasylphy.jp/
🕐 11:00–21:00
🗓 Not fixed
📍 MAP 5-38
¥¥¥¥

While Swarovski takes center stage here (the owner is Japan's largest importer of Swarovski crystals), Kiwa Sylphy also has a clothes line that is about getting the looks for less but with a lot of style. Chic elegance comes in tops with feminine detailing using silk and lace; wide pants, frills, and chiffon lace tops bring classic styles back with a modern twist; and while the styling uses volume as the trend dictates, it is timeless in its appeal.

KNOLL
INTERIOR

6-5-55 Minami-Aoyama, Minato-ku, Tokyo
03-5774-6007
www.knoll.com/knoll_home.jsp
🕐 11:00–19:00
🗓 Wednesdays
📍 MAP 1-64
¥¥¥-¥¥¥¥

Bauhaus fans know there is only one place they can shop: Knoll, the only design house that continues to bring Bauhaus to homes and offices. The manufacturer won its design laurels thanks to owner Hans Knoll's wife, Florence, who worked with Eero Saarinen, Walter Gropius, and Marcel Breuer as a student, then later on went on to produce Eero Saarinen's Tulip chair, a petal-shaped, one legged chair where the seat, back, and armrests in plastic-coated aluminum and fiberglass form a unified whole. Their chaise lounge in tubular steel and leather padding, the Diamond armchair with rectangular legs and scooped seat, and their Pollock executive swivel chair still remain totemic design icons of this century.

KOTUCA
WOMEN'S SHOES

6-6-2 Jingumae, Shibuya-ku, Tokyo
03-3406-8863
www.kotuca.com/
🕐 12:00–20:00
🗓 No holidays
📍 MAP 6-52
¥¥-¥¥¥¥

For all you tall, beautiful, amazon goddesses who never find their shoe size in Japan, this is the answer to your traumatized feet. Kotuca stocks large sized pumps, flats, ballerinas, sandals, espadrilles, sneakers, and just about everything else needed to complete your wardrobe. Miu Miu, Jimmy Choo, Kenneth Cole, Anne Klein, Hermès, Chanel, and loads of Nine West models are usually easily available—and Kotuca's private order system means that you are just an email away from your favorite pair of shoes. (Once a month, Kotuca's extremely friendly English-speaking staff goes abroad on a shopping spree to get what you want.)

KRIZIA

WOMEN'S BOUTIQUE

Imperial Hotel Plaza, 1-1-1 Uchisaiwai-
cho, Chiyoda-ku, Tokyo (Others)
03-3595-2731
www.sanki-brand.com/
🕐 11:00–20:00
📅 No holidays
👣 MAP 4-18   ¥|¥|¥|¥-¥|¥|¥|¥

One would think that Krizia would be given a run for its money in this country that produces the best knits in the world. But despite the mind-boggling variety of knits available in town, none can beat Krizia for its sex appeal. Figure-hugging dresses and the most flattering sweaters have been the trademark for the last fifty years, and the injection of fresh blood (in the form of designer Hamish Morrow) has seen fantastically colored collections in ultra high-tech Italian fabrics that—because of their clean cut tailoring—look great on any body type. Look for brightly colored mini cocktail dresses, perfectly tailored pant suits and coats with blown up Peter Pan collars.

KUMA B

BRIDAL

Asteon 301, 2-2-20 Fukasawa, Setagaya-
ku, Tokyo
03-3704-7791
bears_field@hotmail.com
🕐 11:00–20:00
📅 No holidays
👣 MAP 11-9   ¥|¥|¥|¥

The best-dressed brides in town all get their wedding outfits from one source. The highly secretive designer Kuma B undertakes dresses on order exclusively by appointment. Prices are surprisingly reasonable and come with superb service to your doorstep with just a phone call. He knocks on the door and, in perfect English, will show you a plethora of sketches of the latest and best in wedding dresses. Kuma B is the man, if you are looking for that perfect ultra-luxurious, pale silk bare top bustle or long lean mermaid silhouette, embroidered skirts, or just a simple bias cut silk chiffon dress. His Ikebana experience also makes him adept at bouquets for you and boutonnieres for the bridegroom. Rumor has it that his wedding gowns have been flown to ladies as far away as France. Whether you are looking for the long romantic dress, the short, easy-to-dance-in dress, or the cocktail style dress, his outfits are one of a kind. You'll be the most talked about bride in town.

KYOSHO

TOYS

Omotesando Hills B3F, 4-12-10 Jingumae,
Shibuya-ku, Tokyo
03-5785-0280
www.kyosho.com
🕐 11:00–21:00
📅 No holidays
👣 MAP 5-39   ¥|¥-¥|¥|¥

The man with a passion for toy cars and aircraft models was once just a geek—and perhaps a bit weird. Kyosho, the toyshop, has changed all that. Class, quality, and chutzpah with bespoke models are waiting to decorate the home of the übersexual. Kyosho makes the humble toy go hybrid with RC circuit models of Lamborghinis, catamarans, yachts, and gliders. And while men at Kyosho give women a run for their money in the shopping game, the ladies could sip a cocktail or a beer at the well appointed bar counter area featuring a toy racing course, of course.

LACOSTE

MEN'S/WOMEN'S SPORTSWEAR

Shibuya Seibu Department Store, 20-2 Udagawa-cho, Shibuya-ku, Tokyo (Others)
03-3462-0111
www.lacoste.co.jp
10:00–20:00
Not fixed
MAP 8-24
¥¥

Under Christophe Lemaire's sporty energy, Lacoste retails its original French functionality, effortlessly blending the luxurious with the practical. His signature designs are all that you see here in the way of printed shirts, zipped jackets, and pants. His blazers for women with sporty piping and large logos are well on the way to becoming daytime icons. The shop also spotlights Ts, T-shirt dresses in myriad colors, and sporty shoes that should never be called "sneakers."

LA FORET

MEN'S/WOMEN'S DEPARTMENT STORE

1-11-6 Jingumae, Shibuya-ku, Tokyo
03-3475-0411
www.laforet.ne.jp/
11:00–20:00
No holidays
MAP 5-40
¥¥¥-¥¥¥¥

La Foret is Tokyo's definitive fashion haunt. Brave young fashionable things loaded with cash come here to visit more than seventy in-store shops: global label Top Shop Top Man, cool Britannia at Side by Side, the hottest in street fashions from WJK and Silas and Maria, a mini golf course, St. Gregory's Spa, nail salon, etc. If the demographic here leaves you feeling a bit vintage, head down to the café where you can enjoy a hot chocolate al fresco while taking style notes from passing girls-of-the-moment and moody stylists who raid the place for the newest looks. Don't forget to stroll on Takeshita Dori only a minute away. This is the road dotted with shops selling everything street outrageous socks, hip hop gear, costume play, and goth outfits. On the weekends you can stock up on vintage kimonos on sale at the intersection just outside this store.

LA GRANDE AQUAGIRL
WOMEN'S BOUTIQUE

3-15-7 Minami-Aoyama, Minato-ku, Tokyo
03-5414-1260
aquagirl.ne.jp/
🕐 12:00–20:00
📅 Not fixed
🚇 MAP 1-65

The buyers of La Grande Aquagirl have a thing for shoes that really tweak your conscience and then your wallet. Enter the shop and get tipsy toes at a shoe bar that stocks a great cocktail of it-shoes from Celine, witty Japanese label Pippi, Pierre Hardy, Dove Nuotane Gli Squalli, and the French master Louboutin. The rest of the shop is dedicated to collections that would suit these shoes and is arranged so you can mix and match with the high and low styling of top French maisons as well as their own pretty collections of knits and other basics.

LAMP HARAJUKU
WOMEN'S BOUTIQUE

4-28-15 Jingumae, Shibuya-ku, Tokyo
03-5411-1230
www.hpfrance.com/Shop/Brand/Lamp_harajuku.html
🕐 12:00–20:00
📅 No holidays
🚇 MAP 5-41

Inspired by the 1966 New Wave Czech film, *Daisies*, in which the two main characters are sweet but cruel girls, robbing men, wearing lace shawls and flower headdresses, and generally leading destructive, decadent lifestyles. The shop translates this image into really sweet, dangerous creations, largely from Japanese designers. The first floor is dedicated to lacy creations such as those of Aski Katski, who uses vintage and natural fabrics in her own dyeing technique to create light, airy, rust colored dresses with details like detachable bottom halves that can be worn as shirts. Yoshiko, a basket maker, features items all hand-woven by her, with ribbons, polka dots, and flowers. Le Briqueabraque takes hankies and stitches them together into cute little dresses. The second floor stocks lines similar to the ground floor, but in slightly darker moods. Nozomi Ishiguro's ghost-like creations might be in vintage lace and stressed, but plunging necklines and short dresses add a really sexy edge. For a sweet touch the shop is decorated all over with butterfly brooches in leather from Japanese designer Torquata. And it features Swati's candles in cake, chocolate, and bread.

LANVIN
MEN'S/WOMEN'S BOUTIQUE

7-9-17 Ginza, Chuo-ku, Tokyo
03-3289-2788
www.lanvin.com/
🕐 11:30–20:00 (Sat/Sundays untill19:00)
📅 No holidays
🚇 MAP 4-19

This most French of brands (now under Chinese ownership, and with Moroccan-born Israeli Alber Elbaz as creative director) has made a stellar impact in the world of couture with bold, feminine designs. The slip still remains a forte, while his scissors turns whatever they touch into high fashion. Though his trench coats look dark, flat and heavy on a hanger, they transform into something really arty when worn. The cocktail dresses have also become legendary, and even if you decide not to make a big purchase here, you are sure to leave with one of the loveliest pair of ballerina flats in one of ever so many colors.

LA PERLA
WOMEN'S LINGERIE

6-4-9 Ginza, Chuo-ku, Tokyo (Others)
03-3289-2077
www.laperla.com/
🕐 11:00–21:00
📅 No holidays
🎵 MAP 4-20　　　¥|¥|¥-¥|¥|¥|¥

La Perla's saucy intimates make the best gifts any woman could give herself. And the price is justifiably forgotten when these lace bras, combined with silk shorts, suspender tights, and ultra sexy camisoles, have their desired effect on the senses. But La Perla is not just about lacy nothings. Their collection of tops and skirts is pretty and sensual and understandably loyal to its lingerie inspirations, with the occasional flashes of bare skin, and comes padded for comfort. The most sensational thing, however, is their resort line of bathing suits that are jewels in the pool. With a silky finish and superstar colors: they come in black satin, fuschia pink, gold, and turquoise, with beads, heavy embroidery and brocade lace. For the men's collection of briefs, head to Barneys New York.

L'ARTISAN PARFUMEUR
PERFUMERY

Bellcommons 3F, 2-14-6 Kita-Aoyama,
　Minato-ku, Tokyo (Others)
03-3475-8070
www.artisanparfumeur.jp
🕐 11:00–20:00
📅 Not fixed
🎵 MAP 16-6　　　¥|¥-¥|¥|¥

L'Artisan Parfumeur casts a spell on you with perfumes handcrafted from secret formulas. The best is the Odeur series, a collection of perfumes created by traveling parfumers which includes the Bois Farine, a mysterious fragrance with the smell of flower created by perfumer Jean Claude Ellena after his visit to the Reunion Islands, Timbuktu, with patchouli and vetiver base notes inspired by Mali, while Sicilian oranges have been peeled in a perfume called Mandarine. This shop is dedicated only to their perfumes, but their corner in the Takashimaya Department Store has the new Jatamansi collection of skin care products (and you can also enjoy a free hand massage while trying the products). Perfumes for the house are available in a wide variety of sprays, while Amber balls are scented decoration that you can put anywhere in the house. Cars and men have not been left out, with Four Flour Clover and Amber fragrances for a scent-filled ride to work, and Fou d'Absinthe a big hit with any style of man.

LAX

MEN'S/WOMEN'S DENIM

Lumine est B2F, 3-38-1 Shinjuku,
    Shinjuku-ku, Tokyo (Others)
03-3341-3927
www.lax-hpfrance.com/
🕐 10:30–21:00
🗓 Not fixed
📍 MAP 9-17   ¥-¥¥

LAX is a small haven of imported jeans from LA. The shop has been the hit of the season, upping the cool quotient of ubiquitous denim wear. It essentially stocks ladies' and men's collections from Paper Denim&cloth, Serfontaine, Hudson, and Ernest Sewn in skinny, boot cut, and straight for women, and loose or wide for men. The range of belts in stressed and colored leather come at reasonable prices, while retaining their edge—and all women look good in a pair of Serfontaine denim skirts and cute T-shirts from Cobson Images. But it is the Bravestar jeans that the shop's stylist swears by. These are the ultimate original, woven from machines circa 1905 and dyed in a grey blue resulting in a structured look and stiff fall. The emphasis is on clean denim and, at this price, shopping here means you understand its true value, not just its surface appeal.

LAZY SUSAN

INTERIOR/ACCESSORIES

3-3-11 Kita-Aoyama, Minato-ku,
    Tokyo (Others)
03-3403-9546
www.lazysusan.co.jp
🕐 11:00–20:00
🗓 Not fixed
📍 MAP 5-42   ¥¥-¥¥¥

The overall feel of this mega store might be a little too yuppie for some, but look carefully and you will discover at least a couple of items that you absolutely love. For most, the choice is found in their extensive collection of glassware and china. For others it could be the home accessories, with center tables and floor cushions in approximation of the Hamptons lifestyle. But if you're armed with a bit of cash, head upstairs for the real treasures—a great collection of Ikepod and handcrafted Gata watches for men and real vintage costume jewelry for women from Chanel and Dior. Lazy Susan is really what you make of it—from preppy gear to things for the slick and smart lady.

LE CHARME DE FIFI ET FAFA

KIDS'

5-4-3 Minami-Aoyama, Minato-ku, Tokyo
03-5774-0853
none
🕐 12:00–20:00
🗓 No holidays
📍 MAP 1-66   ¥¥-¥¥¥

This shop is a big draw for those urbane dads and super mamas who beautifully balance their work and private life. They come here to dress their kids in whimsical creations of frocks, T-shirts, and trousers that use vintage liberty prints and fabrics sourced from vintage markets in London. With bits of lace, eyelets, and really soft fabric, these are one-of-a-kind pieces that are sugar and spice and all that's nice.

L'ECLAIREUR

MEN'S/WOMEN'S BOUTIQUE

4-21-26 Minami Aoyama, Minato-ku, Tokyo
03-6406-0252
www.leclaireur.jp/
🕐 11:00–20:00
📅 Not fixed
🎫 MAP 1-67   ¥|¥|¥-¥|¥|¥

As the Tokyo branch of the Paris cult shop, L'Eclaireur's dark brooding leather scented interior played host to the renaissance of Belgian designers a couple of years ago. Today, the shop might have lost its appeal while Tokyo looks for sunny cheer, but it is still home to the brilliant collections of Ann Demeulemeester, Dries Van Noten, Carpe Diem, Martin Margiela, and others from Antwerp. Cutting-edge leather accessories include fitted alligator jackets in brown and black, alligator and python shoes and bags of great quality from lesser-known designers. A bit spectacular, a bit dangerous, this shop is a rock chic must.

LE COQ SPORTIF

MEN'S/WOMEN'S SPORTSWEAR

4-25-9 Jingumae, Shibuya-ku, Tokyo (Others)
03-5413-4620
www.descente.co.jp/lecoqsportif-jp/
🕐 11:00–20:00
📅 Not fixed
🎫 MAP 5-43   ¥-¥|¥

Hot on the heels of the sports brands, with their loud designer collaborations and trumpeted marches up the high street, comes Le coq sportif. They are making the same transition, but in a subtle, discreet French way. Set up in the late 1940s, le coq sportif has essentially been sportswear for soccer, running, tennis and recently, yoga. But the sporty cock now also adorns patent white-and-silver sports bags that are a great alternative as smart cabin luggage; slim soled sneakers in muted colors for men, women, kids, and babies; gloves, hats, and mufflers for a run in the park; and an extensive range of yoga gear for Sunday morning inner reflection. Reasonably priced with low key styles.

L.E.D. BITES

MEN'S ACCESSORIES

Roppongi Hills West Walk 2F, 6-10-3 Roppongi, Minato-ku, Tokyo (Others)
03-5785-1600
www.ledbites.com
🕐 11:00–20:00
📅 No holidays
🎫 MAP 12-25   ¥|¥-¥|¥

This homegrown label gives a lot of bite to men's accessories. Think python totes in moon white, patent red messenger bags, shagreen briefcases, stressed Bostons in beige, and a range of ideas in croc. Looking for a nifty little gift? Grab their exotic leather iPod nano covers that come in lizard, python, and shagreen—and in a lot of colors too. How to pull all this off is the hard part. Our suggestion is to stick to the basics—unless, of course, you are a P. Diddy wannabe.

LE DEPOT MILLES FILLES

WOMEN'S ACCESSORIES

Shibuya Center Bldg. 3F, 16-8 Udagawa-cho, Shibuya-ku, Tokyo
03-3477-1230
millefilles.web.fc2.com/
12:00–19:00
No holidays
MAP 8-25
¥¥-¥¥¥

Rumor has it that 60 percent of Japanese girls own at least one Vuitton bag, so expect to get bumped by at least one of the whopping 75 *million* LVs as you make your way around town. Some of them make it in remarkable condition to this mecca of previously loved brand bags and their great collection of Vuittons at really cheap prices. Also a great place for vintage Chanel bags, Chanel jewelry, and lovingly restored Dior, Prada, and Fendi bags. A must shop for those with a pathological addiction to logos.

LEELA

WOMEN'S BOUTIQUE

4-28-5 Jingumae, Shibuya-ku, Tokyo
03-5770-3905
www.leela.co.jp/
11:30–20:00
No holidays
MAP 5-44
¥-¥¥

Leela brings bright punchy prints, spicy combinations, and sizzling colors from India into its range of reasonably priced clothes and bags. Each item is specially styled in the subcontinent, so the tops hug the body, the sweaters are warm enough for any winter, and the bags come in a wonderful variety of shapes, colors, and finishes guaranteed to put a bit of color wherever you are—even on the most cloudy day.

LE GARAGE

DRIVING ACCESSORIES

AXIS Bldg 1F, 5-17-1 Roppongi, Minato-ku, Tokyo
03-3587-2785
www.legarage.jp
11:00–19:00
Not fixed
MAP 12-26
¥-¥¥¥¥

High octane shop for driving fanatics, Le Garage sells everything that any serious driver would love. They stock such essentials as cubic bags made from convertible car canvas, Freitag bags, made-in-England Dent's driving gloves, including cashmere lined ones, Japanese label Dover Club jackets that are perfectly cut in flashy red, and aviator goggles, helmets and race wear—plus books and bags to keep you right on track

LE LIGNE ROSET
INTERIOR

3-5-17 Kita-Aoyama, Minato-ku, Tokyo
03-5771-5800
www.ligne-roset.com/
🕐 11:00–19:00
🗓 Tuesdays
♪ MAP 5-45　　¥|¥|¥|¥-¥|¥|¥|¥

Sumptuous sofa luxury with understandably chic Gallic origins that are different from the leather, steel, and plastic favored by the Danish companies. Upholstered furniture in luscious colors, and barely there legs give interiors panache without the tiresome cult fetishist image some chairs seem to demand in the slow changing world of product design. The pretty little Tazia settee with a wooden backrest created by Pascal Morgue is inspired by Morocco and CB Lefebrve's saddle-high chairs are not for those who suffer from vertigo. Be it their Pop chair armless, with joint curving backrest and four simple steel legs, or the Togo sofa in wine red that looks like a giant comfy cushion, or the more recent Facett sofa and arm chair by brothers Ronan and Erwan Bouroullec, the entire Ligne Roset collection brings instant haute couture inspirations to the house.

LEONARD
WOMEN'S BOUTIQUE

Roppongi Hills Keyaki St. 1F, 6-10-2
　Roppongi, Minato-ku, Tokyo (Others)
03-5786-9781
www.sankyofs.co.jp
🕐 11:00–21:00
🗓 No holidays
♪ MAP 12-27　　¥|¥|¥|¥

Since 1961 Leonard has been spinning their vivid floral silk jersey dresses year after year. A dress from Leonard will ensure an unforgettable entrance to any party. Elegantly draped from the shoulder, they do a great job of defining the waist, and the bold print graciously helps for a slimmer silhouette. Designer Vèronique Leroy keeps the label looking young with ideas such as pretty floral silk jersey leggings that look oh-so-*now* when worn belted with her dresses (that, by the way, have started coming with cool silver leather shoulder straps). Once the preserve of the Parisienne *bourgeoise,* Leonard's new look is definitely for the young at heart while keeping the label's signature prints alive and blooming.

LE SPORT SAC
MEN'S/WOMEN'S ACCESSORIES

6-29-1 Jingumae, Shibuya-ku,
　Tokyo (Others)
03-3407-4343
www.lesportsac.co.jp
🕐 11:00–20:00
🗓 No holidays
♪ MAP 6-53　　¥-¥|¥

Le Sport Sac might never have been destined for greatness until *The OC*, the hit American TV series, came along with a range of cute and sporty canvas bags designed for actress Mischa Barton. Immediately, its diaper bag image was transformed to totes for the party babe. The latest funky *tokidoki* series is tremendous, too, with wild prints of crabs, fish, forests, and monkeys, or in solid colors like neon orange and chic smoke gray. All the other self-confessed Le Sport Sac fans can find the regular collection of totes and pouches in grosgrain webbing and tough rip stop nylon with the classic Le Sport Sac logo. If you are still not satisfied, go all the way and have a bag made to measure in one of many funky prints and logo tape colors.

LES TOILES DU SOLEIL
INTERIOR

2-8-2 Jiyugaoka, Meguro-ku, Tokyo
03-3777-7035
www.grams.co.jp/
⊘ 10:00–20:00
▦ Not fixed
⌐ MAP 11-10

¥|¥|¥|-|¥|¥|¥|¥

If you are looking for colorful sturdy curtains in a thick material like canvas that last forever—and you are ready to pay a premium price for it—look no further. Les Toiles du Soleil, a traditional French dying and weaving method in flatweave, has all the answers for you. Bolts of fabrics in a riot of colors line the back of the shop and make for curtains that kill in every color under the sun. If you came for the curtains and was shocked by the prices, but fell in love with the fabric, don't depart the shop without one of their equally lovely aprons, travels bags, wallets, and totes—all in the same trademark stripes.

LE TANNEUR
MEN'S/WOMEN'S ACCESSORIES

Shinjuku Mitsukoshi Alcott 4F, 3-29-1
Shinjuku, Shinjuku-ku, Tokyo
03-3354-1111
www.letanneur.com
⊘ 11:00–21:00
▦ Not fixed
⌐ MAP 9-18

¥|¥|¥

This French fave finally swims the pond and makes it to the shores of Tokyo. Practical city chic is in this brand's DNA so no "It-bag arm candy" here. Women get softly structured bags while the men's look is sharp and official. A brand like this is always in tune with trends, so there is enough saddle inspiration, rounded shapes and smart trimmings in contrasting colors to keep every bag addict happy. Their small accessories, like clutches and wallets, that come in many color variations with occasional metallic accents feel like important finds as they are free from logos. Goat leather, jacquard, calf, lamb, mock croc, and nubuck go into totes, shoulder handbags, and simply pretty evening bags. The men's briefcases are cleverly structured, offering room and a sharp silhouette, and there are plenty of top quality gift ideas for him: small leather accessories, belts, bracelets, scarves, hats, and key chains.

LHP

MEN'S BOUTIQUE

4-32-12 Jingumae, Shibuya-ku,
Tokyo (Others)
03-5474-0808
www.lhp-japan.com/
⊘ 11:30–20:30
No holidays
MAP 5-46 ¥¥¥-¥¥¥¥

Lazy Hazy planet makes appealingly blokey clothes for the kind of guy who watches Prime Sports, loves to get a beer or two in the evening, and has a bit of cash to spend on his casual luxury wardrobe. Collections from Soe, Givenchy, Levi's Red, Diamond Dogs, and G.Guaglianone, combined with items like polka dot teddy bear jerseys, Wendy&Jim illustration T-shirts, and a nice collection of Japanese heartthrob Hiromu Takahara's Roen line with dark Mickey Mouse jerseys. Serious fashion stuff with the occasional whimsical touch.

LIFT ECRU

MEN'S/WOMEN'S BOUTIQUE

17-5 Daikanyamacho, Shibuya-ku,
Tokyo (Others)
03-3780-0163
www.lift-net.co.jp/
⊘ 11:00–20:00
No holidays
MAP 2-38 ¥¥¥¥

Despite the way the shop and its arty staff look, the collections are quite spectacular, infinitely wearable and come with a timeless quality. More arty than its sister shop nearby, you'll find a great collection of Rick Owens along with collections from new designers such as Israeli Sarah Lanzi, who makes great sculptural sheaths in wool. All the clothes are dark, anti-modernist, and extremely minimal bordering on the experimental. With patient and extremely informative service in English, one stop here will get you back on the fashion radar.

LIFT ETAGE

MEN'S/WOMEN'S BOUTIQUE

16-5 Daikanyamacho, Shibuya-ku,
Tokyo (Others)
03-3780-0163
www.lift-net.co.jp/
⊘ 11:00–20:00
No holidays
MAP 2-39 ¥¥¥¥

Another place where the customers, the salespeople, and the collections look arty and identical. It stocks one of the cleverest collections for men, where the styles could be appropriately mixed for smart casual daywear or office hybrid. Ace Japanese designer Kiminori Morishita's extremely masculine separates and jackets are lined up at the entrance. With sharp military jackets from Veronique Branquihno and Dries von Noten, and shirts and jackets from Stephan Schneider, this is definitely one of the few shops in Tokyo that houses lots of testosterone.

LILITH

WOMEN'S DESIGNER

5-2-11 Minami-Aoyama, Minato-ku, Tokyo
03-3423-6333
www.lilith-japan.com
🕐 11:00–20:00
▦ Not fixed
🔍 MAP 1-68   ¥|¥|¥-¥|¥|¥

Lilyth, the fierce, mythological first wife of Adam, inspired French designer Lily Bareth to create this brand. If your fashion spirit agrees with Comme des Garçons, but your office dress code doesn't, this is the store for you. On the right side of avant-garde, Lily picks up skirts, blouses, and trouser suits and adds unabashed strokes of originality. Big bows adorn most clothes, layered blouses can be teamed with heavy fabric skirts that are at once voluminous and beautifully draped, and the humble trouser suit becomes jackets with mid-length bell sleeves to be paired with humungous pants. Fairy tale-like pinstripes on billowy skirts in tulle offer a refreshing change from stuffy pencil skirts. Keeps the spotlight on you without raising eyebrows.

LIMI FEU

WOMEN'S DESIGNER

6-6-11 Jingumae, Shibuya-ku, Tokyo (Others)
03-5464-1752
www.limifeu.com/
🕐 11:00–21:00
▦ No holidays
🔍 MAP 6-54   ¥|¥|¥

Limi is the daughter of Yohji Yamamoto and has taken the design world by storm with her neat girly collections. Check out the shirts with ruffles, great shorts, and the beautifully tailored white blouses stitched around the body to fit like a glove. Limi also does some excellent tunics in a heavy gabardine fabric that can be worn as such or over jeans. In winter, there is usually a great collection of leg warmers, and woolen versions of her creations—always stoic and sophisticated. A great charismatic collection, very independent from papa's school of cool.

LISTE ROUGE

MEN'S BESPOKE

7F, 1-6-13 Azabudai, Minato-ku, Tokyo
03-3582-7462
www.listerouge-japan.com/
🕐 11:00–20:00
▦ weekends
🔍 MAP 14-1   ¥|¥|¥-¥|¥|¥

Liste Rouge is only about bespoke shirts, proud French tailoring, and ease of ordering through a really detailed catalogue (with over 200 swatches) that is sent to your house. While ordering a shirt might be by appointment only, be heartened by the fact that your entire order can be placed in English. With more than 50 kinds of collars, sleeves, and buttons from which to choose, you can custom design your own shirts, including details like the collar style. With the best range of textiles to choose from neatly presented in both autumn/winter and spring/summer collections, your passport to a perfectly tailored shirt is just a phone call away.

LIVING MOTIF

INTERIOR

5-17-1 Roppongi, Minato-ku, Tokyo
03-3587-2784
www.livingmotif.com
🕐 11:00–19:00
📅 No holidays
👣 MAP 12-28   ¥|¥-¥|¥|¥

Three floors of the most haute houseware and lifestyle solutions offered by Japan's oldest purveyor of modern design. For bibliophiles, the best starts on the ground floor, which stocks a fine collection of English mags and lazy coffee table books, including some special collectors items such as the Assouline edition of *Rajasthan,* the 1940s photo book encased in heavy brocade silk. The second floor has a great collection of goods designed to travel from Globetrotter and others, and extremely desirable haute stationery from Lamy, Faber Castell, and Mont Blanc. Also some great solutions for those who take their office home, such as an adjustable computer table with an attached leg rest so you can lie back comfortably and type at the same time. If you buy a gift, don't forget to get it wrapped in the super graphic Chihone and Lorenz wrapping paper.

LLADRO

INTERIOR

7-8-5 Ginza, Chuo-ku, Tokyo (Others)
03-3569-3377
www.lladro.com
🕐 11:00–20:00
📅 No holidays
👣 MAP 4-21   ¥|¥|¥|¥-¥|¥|¥|¥

Previously just an expensive and exquisite obsession among porcelain doll enthusiasts, under designer Jaime Hayon, Lladro is moving up in homemaker's hearts. Their range of expensive but functional extravagances: salt and pepper holders, porcelain soap dishes, incense burners, jewelry boxes, pencil holders, mugs, keychains, and, specially for Tokyo, a figure of an adorable infant on a trunk with "Tokyo" engraved on it, is indulgence that can be understood by very few. Hayon's lyrical Re-Deco collection of figurines in traditional porcelain with platinum colored details gives a new definition to decoration.

LOEWE
MEN'S/WOMEN'S BOUTIQUE

ONE Omotesando, 3-5-29 Kita-Aoyama,
Minato-ku, Tokyo (Others)
03-5771-4811
www.loewe.com/
🕐 11:00–20:00
📅 No holidays
📍 MAP 5-47　　　　¥|¥|¥|¥|¥

Loewe's claim to fame started with leather and some very wealthy citizens of Spain. While the catwalks are always charged with designer José Enrique Oña Selfa's rubberized glamazon hot looks, the shop has a more old-money feel to it. The ultimate must-buy item here still remains leather, though in simple designs but aggressive style. Think turquoise suede leather suits perfectly color matched with a silk satin top, or a collarless silk tafetta coat dress with a balloon silhouette cinched with a thick black patent leather belt, and black gloves in shiny nappa.

LOFT
INTERIOR

21–1 Udagawa–cho, Shibuya–ku, Tokyo
03–3462–3807
www.loft.co.jp/
🕐 10:00–21:00
📅 Not fixed
📍 MAP 8-26　　　　¥|¥|-¥|¥|¥

Six floors of lifestyle items that can be one man's necessity, another man's clutter. Poke through mini scissor-shaped paper shredders that do not take up any space, window curtains that induce deeper sleep, pure vitamin C drops from Obagi, good design award-recipient salad leaf drying bowls and, for the couch potato, a slimming band to strap around your waist while you watch TV. Give the newly created munchies corner a miss for the healthier option of mineral waters from around the world. Also a great collection of every accessory you could ever need for a day on the beach, and an extensive range of men's cosmetics for men with personality.

LOIS CRAYON
WOMEN'S BOUTIQUE

b6 1F, 6-28-103 Jingumae, Shibuya-ku,
Tokyo (Others)
03-5766-1811
www.lois.co.jp/
🕐 11:00–21:00
📅 Not fixed
📍 MAP 6-55　　　　¥|¥|¥|-¥|¥|¥|¥

The polite Belgravian version of Anglomania chic with dresses in tweed, shirts with high collars and ruffles, girly cashmere cardigans, and lots of very beautiful skirts: short skirts, high waisted skirts, boho skirts, tight skirts with bustles, and skirts with bell shapes. Clothes for nice polite girls, far from risky and very business-friendly.

LONGCHAMP

WOMEN'S ACCESSORIES

2-4-2 Ginza, Chuo-ku, Tokyo (Others)
03-5524-3888
www.longchamp.com/
🕐 11:00–20:00
📅 No holidays
📍 MAP 3-13   ¥/¥/¥/¥

Ask any experienced travelista and she will insist that the unspoken accessory code for traveling is either a Longchamp or rival Lancel bag. While Longchamp's foldable nylon and leather duffels, called Le Pliage, come in eight different sizes and all the colors under the sun, unless you are in the market for wallflower style, the advice is to spend your money on the fun stuff. At Longchamp they have succumbed to an injection of youth, with designs in patent leather and boxy pockets, vintage suede slouchy looks, and colorful antique prints.

LORO PIANA

MEN'S/WOMEN'S KNITWEAR

6-12-2 Roppongi, Minato-ku,
    Tokyo (Others)
03-5770-5700
www.loropiana.com
🕐 11:00–20:00
📅 No holidays
📍 MAP 12-29   ¥/¥/¥/¥/¥

The Hermès of cashmere, long a purveyor of the finest fabrics for suits available only at the finest tailors around the globe, has finally descended into the retail world. This means excitement and a flurry of shopping for those who are addicted to premium knitwear, pants, shirts, and the finest of jackets for both men and women in nothing else but the very best cashmere in the world, the sheerest of silks and super-fine, 100-percent wool.

LOUIS VUITTON

MEN'S/WOMEN'S ACCESSORIES

5-7-5 Jingumae, Shibuya-ku,
    Tokyo (Others)
03-3478-2100
www.louisvuitton.com/
🕐 11:00–20:00
📅 No holidays
📍 MAP 6-56   ¥/¥/¥/¥/¥

Yet another outstanding architectural landmark that stocks a stellar collection of luggage, luxury wallets, clutches, totes, suitcases, pens, diaries, and many status bags. Under Marc Jacobs' creative hand, Vuitton's clothes' line has made its way back into people's wardrobes. If you need just one thing, let it be a red leopard print wrap-around dress.

LOVELESS
MEN'S/WOMEN'S BOUTIQUE

3-17-11 Minami-Aoyama, Minato-ku, Tokyo
03-3401-2301
None
🕐 12:00–22:00 Sun/Holidays until20:00
🗓 Not fixed
⌘ MAP 1-69 ¥¥¥¥-¥¥¥¥¥

Eschew trends and embrace the Japanese labels known as the *new romantic*: edgy Mastermind, flawless Green for women, Green Man for men, and ephemeral Mosslight. This cult shop Loveless has the biggest and best collection of hot new Japanese talent, plus RT by Ramdane Touhami, Nili Lotan shirts for women, and budding Parisian designer Guillame Lourmiel's waiter coats and tuxedo shirts. There is also a great music collection and a formidable selection of Akira comics in English. John Galliano and Karl Lagerfield are said to make a point of stopping in here every time they are in Tokyo.

LUCIEN PELLAT-FINET
MEN'S/WOMEN'S DESIGNER

5-2-5 Jingumae, Shibuya-ku, Tokyo
03-5774-6333
www.lucienpellat-finet.com/
🕐 11:00–20:00
🗓 No holidays
⌘ MAP 6-57 ¥¥¥¥-¥¥¥¥¥

Lucien Pellat-Finet makes sweaters look like the big new fashion idea, in painstakingly soft (and expensive cashmere) with big Swarovski skulls, flowers, or guns. These are stocked in summer too, along with shorts, pants, and blousons. Equally coveted as his cashmere are the scented candles with secret ingredients and a big dose of undiluted perfume.

LULU GUINNESS
WOMEN'S ACCESSORIES

Roppongi Hills Hillside B1F, 6-10-2 Roppongi, Minato-ku, Tokyo
03-5412-7588
www.luluguinness.com/
🕐 Mon–Fri/12:00–21:00 Sat, Sun/11:00–21:00
🗓 No holidays
⌘ MAP 12-30 ¥¥-¥¥¥

Lulu's bags with candy stripes, vintage glam totes, and screen siren creations offer a very ladylike style. These are the perfect ingredients for any girl looking to make a quick new lease on life. Lulu therefore has a lot of fans and, with her characteristic wit, has even recently launched into luxury. Take "Lucille", a beautifully embroidered mini-doctor's purse, or the egg-shaped "Penelope" in python skin which thankfully remains free of the current trend for slouchy. If you are a recent Lulu convertee and want to stick to her basics, then Guinness's classic puppy print umbrellas and boudoir makeup bags are also on sale here.

LUSH

AROMATHERAPY

Kunimatsu Building, 2-23-13 Dogenzaka,
Shibuya-ku, Tokyo (Others)
03-5459-3630
www.lushjapan.com
🕐 11:00–21:00
📅 No holidays
📍 MAP 8-27   ¥-¥¥

Inspirational soaps that are good enough to eat (all articles are vegan just in case you can't resist a bite). Lush not only makes soaps but body scrubs, creams, shampoos, and fragrances. Long time favorites include "honey I washed the kids" soap—a slice of which comes with a honeycomb on the top—creamed almond and coconut smoothie shower gel, and the delicious cupcake face mask. Five and forty-five kilogram soaps also available, along with an extensive men's "happy daddy" series.

M0851

MEN'S/WOMEN'S LEATHER/
ACCESSORIES

3-3-11 Ginza, Chuo-ku, Tokyo (Others)
03-5524-3153
www.sannfreres.co.jp/brands/m0851/
index.html
🕐 11:00–20:00
📅 No holidays
📍 MAP 3-14   ¥¥¥-¥¥¥¥

Tokyo is best known for minimal simplicity, cerebral styling, and androgynous clothing in the most pastel of colors, and this shop does it all—albeit only in calf leather. Bags from messengers to duffels, biker jackets, pants and skirts in beige, peach, brown and red, all with equally easy prices, in soft leather of basic quality but with subtle styling.

MAC

COSMETICS

Omotesando Hills West Bldg. 1F, 4-12-10
Jingumae, Shibuya-ku, Tokyo (Others)
03-5410-1122
www.maccosmetics.co.jp
🕐 11:00–21:00
📅 No holidays
📍 MAP 5-48   ¥¥-¥¥¥

Fashion's favorite face maker mixes shades of fuschia, gold, green, and canary yellow and a dash of their own effervescent spirit for a the most up-to-date styles in makeup. With MAC you have the ultimate carte blanche to channel your inner Nicole Kidman, Naomi Campbell, or Gwen Stefani. The fun part is that some of their products have multiple uses, like the cream color base that could be used as a highlighter, eye shadow, or just above the cheekbone for a sculpted look. The foundation spreads like butter over the face for a smooth even texture and the great thing about MAC is that it suits you whichever part of the world you are from.

MAKER'S SHIRT
MEN'S/WOMEN'S BESPOKE

Marunouchi Bldg. B1F, 2-4-1 Marunouchi,
Chiyoda-ku, Tokyo (Others)
03-5220-3718
www.shirt.co.jp/
🕐 11:00–21:00 (sun/Holidays
until20:00)
▦ Not fixed
🍴 MAP 7-17 ¥|¥-¥|¥¥

Bespoke shirtmaker for both men and women, with unbelievably cheap prices. Easy fit, tight fit, many collar solutions, side pleats, box pleats, shoulder pleats, shoulder yoke and shirttail solutions, and cuff options. More than this, they offer in-depth professional advice on how to wear shirts with different textures and choose a matching tie of the right color, style and length.

MANGO
WOMEN'S BOUTIQUE

6-10-9 Jingumae, Shibuya-ku,
Tokyo (Others)
03-5467-0343
www.mango.com
🕐 11:00–20:30
▦ Not fixed
🍴 MAP 6-58 ¥-¥|¥

Yet another high street genius taking the world by storm with vividly colored minis and A-line dresses combined with knit tops. They are obsessively up-to-date with their weaves, so look for their skinny Ts or trousers in the summer and reasonable woollen coats in the winter. For those who have just graduated from college and are taking the first steps down the career lane, Mango's business suits offer a good option until the bonuses start kicking in.

MARC JACOBS
MEN'S/WOMEN'S DESIGNER

6-4-14 Minami-Aoyama, Minato-ku,
Tokyo (Others)
03-5464-3001
www.marcjacobs.com/
🕐 11:00–20:00
▦ 3rd Wednesday
🍴 MAP 1-70 ¥|¥|¥|¥-¥|¥|¥|¥

This recently built shop stocks both Marc by Marc Jacobs and Marc Jacobs. For the insatiable Marc Jacob groupies who must have the latest Jacobs bag or shoe just as it hits the shelves, most collections of his mysteriously floating skirts (with and without bows), trapeze coats, sunglasses, and boxy chunky bags are on the top floor. The ground floor houses the simpler baggy jeans, bubble skirts, denim, corduroy, and a reasonable amount of simpler shoes. The collection here might be much smaller than his Paris shop but is still good enough to make you feel like fashion's front girl.

MARIAGE FRERES

TEA SALON/INTERIOR

5-6-6 Ginza, Chuo-ku, Tokyo (Others)
03-3572-1854
www.mariagefreres.co.jp/
🕐 11:00 – 20:00
📅 No holidays
📍 MAP 4-22   ¥|¥-¥|¥

For teapots, teas, and divine fragrances look no further. Mariage Freres, the last purveyors of fine tea in the world, is not just a place for tea lovers; it is the best shop in town for teapots that are not just functional but great decorative pieces. They come in every shape, size, color, and material imaginable under the sun. But choose with caution: Mariage Freres advises that with mild, delicate and fragrant teas like Formosa oolong and Darjeeling, one should use their china, porcelain, glass, or enamel cast iron. They have four varieties of the Japanese *tetsubin* cast-iron teapots, which can be used not just for green teas but just about any tea in the world. Their vintage-inspired shapes of glass teapots are best for teas rich in tannin, like Ceylon and Assam. After the tea tour, let your spirits soar with their exquisite collection of aromas for the house from candles and incense. There are Himalayan rose and Darjeeling fragrances and the exquisite Ambre, that fragrance derived from whales!

MARIANELLI

LINGERIE

Ginza Komatsu 3F, 6-9-5 Ginza, Chuo-ku, Tokyo
03-3572-5798
www.eishin-kk.co.jp/marianelli/
🕐 11:00–20:00
📅 No holidays
📍 MAP 4-23   ¥|¥|¥-¥|¥|¥|¥

Lingerie-starved people should know this tiny boutique in Ginza; though it might not have the largest collection of intimates in town, it keeps enough stuff of quality for even the most well-endowed among us. The owner is understandably biased towards Aubade, with their trademark oversized flowers on tulle in contrasting colors with half-cups, strapless, and plunge bras, paired with Brazilians, tangas, strings, and mini boxers. For lacy corsets and fine slips, there is Italian Naory, and the shop also sells smart sexy peignoirs and baby-dolls. There is a small collection of pretty stockings in sizes 3 and 4 and even though the shop is tiny, there is enough intimate armor here to make you feel really bold and beautiful.

MARIMEKKO

INTERIOR/ACCESSORIES

Espoir Omotesando Annex 1, 4-25-18 Jingumae, Shibuya-ku, Tokyo (Others)
03-5785-2571
www.marimekko.com/eng
🕐 11:30–20:00
📅 Not fixed
📍 MAP 5-49   ¥|¥-¥|¥|¥

This Finnish textile company, set up in 1950, had a breakthrough when Jackie Kennedy wore their dresses in bold colors and non-figurative designs during JFK's election campaign in 1960s. Since then, they have been selling clothes, interior deco, and bags all around the world. Some three thousand fabric patterns have been printed at Marimekko and the hottest item here—sold to over 15 million people, is the striped "Tasaraita" cotton-jersey line, first made in 1968. Another thing to buy is one of the oldest but most fun basic items, the Jokapoika unisex shirts in printed cotton that have been hot favorites since 1956. In this, their Japanese flagship store, they also sell a lot of specially made accessories for the home, such as aprons, tea cups, and place mats in the brand's signature bold and beautiful prints.

MARINA RINALDI
WOMEN'S BOUTIQUE

3-5-30 Kita-Aoyama, Minato-ku, Tokyo (Others)
03-5474-4896
none
🕐 11:00–20:00
📅 No holidays
📍 MAP 5-50   ¥|¥|¥|¥|-¥|¥|¥|¥|¥

Marina Rinaldi offers plus-size styles with a lot of pizzaz. Blousons, simple jackets, trousers, cotton shirts, business-appropriate clothes, and weekend casual elegance all come with a slight nod to current trends. And as no Italian label is complete without high quality shoes, this shop stocks everything from beautiful slingbacks to croc embossed boots. With the right amount of frills and a range of styles, Rinaldi fashions fill your wardrobe with clothes that fit right and have staying power too.

MARITHÈ AND FRANCOIS GIRBAUD
MEN'S/WOMEN'S DENIM

5-4-29 Minami-Aoyama, Minato-ku, Tokyo (Others)
03-3406-3171
www.girbaud.co.jp/
🕐 11:00–20:00
📅 No holidays
📍 MAP 1-71   ¥|¥|-¥|¥|¥

Decades after starting their alchemy, Marithè and Francois Girbaud still remain the jeans creators du jour. Of course, the jeans are the best things here, and the silhouettes are fantastic: they make legs look long due to a three-dimensional cut that shames the flat appearance of most other labels. The denim comes in different weights so you can choose the fabric most comfortable on your skin, and their revolutionary enzyme processes means that each new pair feels like your most comfy battered well-worn pair. While they also do shirts, stressed knits, and sneakers, the style balance understandably weighs heavily towards the denim. As these are the most wanted jeans in Japan, the shop stocks a huge range with really superb rock style, and the service comes without superfluous attitude.

MARKS AND WEB
AROMATHERAPY

Omotesando Hills Main Bldg B2F, 4-12-10
Jingumae, Shibuya-ku, Tokyo (Others)
03-5410-0821
www.marksandweb.com/
🕐 11:00–21:00
Not fixed
MAP 5-51   ¥|¥

Create your own spa at home with the handmade organic soap, herbal creams and bath essence, and the extremely popular facial sprays with essential oils ylang ylang, bergamot, olive, mandarin, germanium, etc. Marks and Web also has a wonderful series of bath towels and gowns made with organic cotton specially grown in Peru, and the lightest maple wood hairbrushes, soft body brushes and bathroom furniture. A bathroom like this is guaranteed to make you feel good even on your worst day, and with such great prices, you'll soon be scrubbing away with a smile.

MARNI
MEN'S/WOMEN'S DESIGNER

2-1-1 Marunouchi, Chiyoda-ku,
Tokyo (Others)
03-3215-0390
www.marni.com
🕐 11:00–20:00
No holidays
MAP 7-18   ¥|¥|¥|¥-¥|¥|¥|¥|¥

When Marni started out, no one thought they could get away with their seeming artlessness, curvy seams, layering, and those awful, dusty colors. But today, Marni is in every metropolitan girl's wardrobe, and has singularly and cleverly rewritten fashion rules to suit themselves. Designer Consuelo Castiglione's trademark buttonless coats adorn many famous shoulders over the leggings on many famous legs. Her sack dresses and balloon skirts, often with color block printing and big bow detailing sculptural belts, are what people save up for, and the innocent, curved leather block color necklaces and matching totes are recognizable from a mile away. Absolutely no logos and still so recognizable . . . nobody does fashion today like Marni.

MARTINIQUE
WOMEN'S BOUTIQUE

Daikanyama Address 2F, 17-4
Daikanyama-cho, Shibuya-ku,
Tokyo (Others)
03-5428-1018
www.melrose.co.jp/martinique/index2.
html
🕐 10:00–20:00
Not fixed
MAP 2-40   ¥|¥-¥|¥|¥

Tokyo's continuous thirst for foreign designs means there sometimes seems to be one such boutique around every corner. And each time a new one opens, it draws crowds mooching about for the hottest stuff off the catwalk. Martinique's woody interior hosts Maurizio Pecoraro, Menichetti, Mon Cler, Thakoon, Louboutin, and great accessories from Nathalie Costes. And whatever the season, this is the place to head for luxe camisoles designed by their own team in beautiful colors finished with lace.

MARTIN MARGIELA
MEN'S/WOMEN'S DESIGNER

Minami Aoyama SO Bldg Room 301,
  5-3-10 Minami-Aoyama, Minato-ku,
  Tokyo (Others)
03-5778-0891
www.maisonmartinmargiela.com
🕐 10:00–20:00
📅 No holidays
🎚 MAP 1-72   ¥|¥|¥|¥-¥|¥|¥|¥|¥

One might see stuff like this elsewhere, but somehow Martin Margiela always makes it look new. Making skirts and suits may seem staid, but that's where his creativity literally rips tradition apart. Yes, there are a lot of slashes and wide slits on everything from trousers to skirts. This also is where you should go if you need jackets with the humungous shoulder padding that was seen on every model at his shows in 2007. This is also where you can get his famous calf leather ankle-high boots. His men's collection is definitely more wearable, with wide pants and chunky knit lines with the trademark four hand stitches at the back, and loose but structured dinner jackets with velvet lapels. Arty students also love his complicated stuff.

MATSUYA
DEPARTMENT STORE

3-6-1 Ginza, Chuo-ku, Tokyo
03(3567)1211
www.matsuya.com
🕐 10:00–20:00 (Mon/Tue, until19:30)
📅 Not fixed
🎚 MAP 3-15   ¥|¥|¥|¥-¥|¥|¥|¥|¥

In its latest incarnation, Matsuya is home to absolutely everything hot. Japanese brands here include Kolor, Scye, and Halb, and there is also a super collection of Moncler and John Smedley. The import shoes corner has everything desirable among major European brands. There is an excellent array of chocolates, desserts, and Japanese sweets downstairs. The seventh floor hosts the shop-in-shop Design Collection, a design store that makes this place worth a visit by itself.

MATSUZAKAYA
DEPARTMENT STORE

6-10-1 Ginza, Chuo-ku, Tokyo
03-3572-1111
www.matsuzakaya.co.jp/
🕐 10:30–19:30 (Thur, Fri, Sat until
  20:00)
📅 Not fixed
🎚 MAP 3-24   ¥|¥|¥|¥-¥|¥|¥|¥|¥

In today's Tokyo of trash and Hollywood glam, Matsuzakaya may have lost its appeal, but it still remains the ultimate reference in kimono shopping. Pretty young twenty-somethings come shopping here for their coming-of-age-ceremony kimonos, brides to be come here to be kitted out in white kimono finery, and moms come here for heavily embellished black silk kimonos.

MAX & CO
WOMEN'S DESIGNER

5-2-5 Jingumae, Shibuya-ku, Tokyo
03-3498-7201
none
🕐 11:00–20:00
No holidays
MAP 6-59   ¥|¥|¥-¥|¥|¥|¥

Made in Italy diffusion line from sophisticated MaxMara. While keeping the quality but cutting down on prices Max & co has a following among fashion icons like Liya Kebede and Naomi Campbell, who love it for its edgy image. Neatly displayed on two floors are formals and casuals, jackets, jewelry, and shoes, and many combinations of looks from sexy go-go millennium, to granny chic, to boardroom elegance.

MAXMARA
WOMEN'S DESIGNER

5-9-19 Minami-Aoyama, Minato-ku, Tokyo (Others)
03-5467-5604
none
🕐 11:00–20:00
3rd Tuesday
MAP 1-73   ¥|¥|¥|¥-¥|¥|¥|¥|¥

Cashmere, often in coats, is what MaxMara fans buy and keep on coming back for. The suits are beautifully cut too with a tailored softness that spills around you when you wear it. Beautiful materials, sometimes unusual (such as a suit in cream leather) can make their way into your wardrobe before you know it. Of late men's tailoring for women has been seen at MaxMara in the form of jackets paired with pretty cocktail dresses. With great tailoring, superb materials and pastel colors MaxMara might be predictable to some and revered as consistent to others, but in any case it is always about being beautifully dressed up without trying too hard.

MERCIBEAUCOUP
MEN'S/WOMEN'S DESIGNER

3-10-11 Minami-Aoyama, Minato-ku, Tokyo (Others)
03-6805-1790
www.a-net.com
🕐 11:00–20:00
Not fixed
MAP 1-74   ¥|¥|¥-¥|¥|¥|¥

Mercibeaucoup's designer Eri Utsugi loves theatrics. While their runway show once had models dressed in animal heads pretending to sweep a street while bumping into each other, and once featured attacking fruit monsters, their shop in Aoyama has a roulette wheel for amusement. These theatrics stretch to the collection itself: their clothes are pop, with a kind of uncerebral naïvité. Fruit monsters, safari animals, sheep, and bears come out in ruffled dresses, coats with balloon sleeves, and really sexy, short A-line dresses and bra tops. For men it can't get any cuter—with Dennis the Menace, candy stripes, and even polka dots fighting for attention on baggy pants, tees, and vests. You can look for the deeper meaning if you like or you can just team all this with a cool pair of jeans and up the fun quotient.

MICAN HP FRANCE EXCLUSIVE
WOMEN'S BOUTIQUE

La Foret Harajuku 1F, Jingumae, Shibuya-ku, Tokyo
03-3404-3288
www.hpfrance.com/Shop/Brand/exclusive.html
⊘ 11:00–20:00
▦ Not fixed
♪ MAP 5-52   ¥¥-¥¥¥¥

Fine quirky accessories define this excellent collection of exclusive brands handpicked by the shop's star buyers. For a whiff of excitement zero in on Argentinian fashion guru Tramand. Björk's own designer, and a darling of the Tokyo fashion crowd, is a hero back home. Originally a textile designer, his skirts, dresses, and sweaters are first stitched and then printed using a special printing technique he developed which results in cool hues, ice cream colors, and clothes that flow serenely. With all this creativity, he still finds space for innovative ideas, such as flattened beads stuck on the sleeves on both sides without sewing. The silhouette is structured and the comfort level very high. Combine this with Japanese designer Hisui's knit casuals and trousers with polka dots, and South Korean Lim Hyun's layered and crocheted tops and gypsy skirts, and you are choosing from the most coveted new designers in town. If you like your accessories dainty and funny there is enough in store: Q-pot rings with choco carres will give you and those around you a tickle anytime of the day; American Leo Works' oxidized and beaten link bracelets are dark and brooding; and cult e.m. Design's layers of rings and bracelets bring on the fun.

MICHAEL KORS
WOMEN'S DESIGNER

Shibuya Seibu A 7F, 21-1 Udagawa-cho, Shibuya-ku, Tokyo (Others)
03-3462-0111
www.michaelkors.com/
⊘ Mon/Tue/Wed/Sun (10:00–20:00)
  thu/Fri/Sat (10:00–21:00)
▦ Not fixed
♪ MAP 8-28   ¥¥¥¥-¥¥¥¥¥

Michael Kors designs always feel in tune with the age no matter what year or season. His is a constant American dream far from boho, far from this season's cocoon coats, and frilly details. Chic sporty looks, in tailored opulence in silks, suedes. and cashmeres in colors as flashy as an airstrip. Jokes aside, his style is luxury at its simplest, without taking the minimalist lane.

MIDWEST
MEN'S/WOMEN'S BOUTIQUE

1-6-1 Jinnan, Shibuya-ku, Tokyo
03-5428-3171
None
⊘ 11:00–20:00
▦ Not fixed
♪ MAP 8-29   ¥¥¥¥

This shop is haunted by young fashion wannabes who scour the collections to find the finer threads and handpick the best shoes.

The list of collections reads like a who's who of stellar style giants. To name a few foreign ones: Bless, Buttero, Guidi, Jil Sander, Kris van Assche, and Balenciaga, Pierre Hardy, and Premiata for shoes. But the spirit of the shop is kept alive by the Japanese designers: Anrealage, Ato, Cosmic Wonder light source, Diet Butcher Slim Skin Julius, Mihara Yasuhiro and his Puma collaborations, Volga Volga, and Yeah Right.

MIHARA YASUHIRO (SOSU)
MEN'S/WOMEN'S DESIGNER

B1F, 5-2-6- Jingumae, Shibuya-ku, Tokyo
03-5778-0675
www.sosu.co.jp/
🕐 12:00—20:00 Sat/Sun/Holidays until11:00
📅 Not fixed
📍 MAP 6-60   ¥|¥|¥-¥|¥|¥|¥

While their women's theme is described in their own words as "twinkle conflict," in reality, it is a great mixture of nostalgia and futuristic weaves. Feminine and far-from-girly—think short leather skirts with tight shirts, at once edgy and classic. For men, his most famous creations are half-sleeved jerseys with Smileys, but on a more serious note he does cyber chic, such as tie shirts and seersucker half-sleeved shirts with frills. His best, though, are the shoes: half sneakers that look like your average sneaker in the front and a regular lace-up at the back, or the special Puma edition where the white rubber sole covers the top section in an ink splatter design.

MIKIHOUSE
KIDS'

Ginza Matsuya 6F, 3-6-1 Ginza, Chuo-ku, Tokyo (Others)
03-3535-3557
www.mikihouse.co.jp
🕐 Mon/10:00—19:30.Fri/10:00—20:00/ Wed, Thu, Sat, Sun/10:00—20:00
📅 No holidays
📍 MAP 3-16   ¥|¥-¥|¥|¥

You'll love the selection at Mikihouse, the Mecca of children's wear for boys and girls under seven. Here, parents and kids see eye-to-eye on cheerful, age-appropriate clothing that is famously fade resistant. For back-to-school or birthday gifts, Mikihouse's bags, hats, toys, picture books, denim and formals are everything kids—and grownups—will love.

MIKIMOTO
ACCESSORIES

2-4-12 Ginza, Chuo-ku, Tokyo (Others)
03-3562-3130
www.mikimoto.co.jp/
🕐 11:00—19:30
📅 Not fixed
📍 MAP 3-17   ¥|¥-¥|¥|¥|¥|¥

It is the diamond that is a women's best friend; the humbler pearl finishes second. But when it is packaged and sold in a superb building created by none other than Toyo Ito, and comes in a neat little box stamped "Mikimoto," it suddenly becomes as appealing as a diamond. The world headquarters of Japan's favorite pearls is housed in a nine-floor extravaganza of taste where the jewelry is limited only to the ground floor. Here are simple white, yellow, and black pearl studs, small pearl necklaces, and even pearl mobile phone straps. Their younger range, titled "mizesse," are rings made of diamond and gold set on leather bands. The second floor has numerous gift ideas that include metal and pearl bookmarks, wallets, bags, jewelry boxes, eyewear, and ties. On the floors above you will find a dedicated service of cosmetics and one entire floor of bridal advice. If all this makes you hungry, grab a quick bite at any of the three gourmet restaurants upstairs.

MILK
WOMEN'S DESIGNER

6-29-3 Jingumae, Shibuya-ku, Tokyo
03-5467-6555
www.milk-web.net
⊘ Mon–Fri/12:00–20:00. Sat,
   Sun/11:00–20:00
▦ Not fixed
𝄃 MAP 6-61   ¥ ¥

This shop is almost exclusively targeted at cosplay Lolitas in search of a bit of milkmaid charm. There's not much else in clothes here than lacy tops with bows, tulle skirts with polka dots, and net petticoats with matching shoes. But just as you curl your lips in distaste reading this, you should know that the accessories here are something else—chains with poodle pendants, poodle earrings, heartclips, ice cream rings, poodle keyrings, black and white knee length stockings, red patent leather heart-shaped bags, and pink wallets with matching pink diamante tiaras. Just about everything that could only be called "Gothic chic."

MILKFED
WOMEN'S BOUTIQUE

18-4, Sarugakucho, Shibuya-ku, Tokyo
03-3780-6627
www.milkfed.jp
⊘ 12:00–20:00 Sat/Sun/Holidays
   until11:00
▦ Not fixed
𝄃 MAP 2-41   ¥ ¥ ¥

Sophia Coppola's affair with Japan started way before the iconic film *Lost in Translation*. One of her most tangible creations is the brand Milkfed, a hot favorite among Tokyo teens and twenty-somethings. Quite in her own style, Milkfed is a brand about sexy success and sky high skirts, insouciant T-shirts, Mary Janes in so many colors, quirky loafers, beautiful undies in silk and embroidery, Birkin inspirations for bags, and a collection of soundtracks from her movies, including *Lost in Translation*, of course.

MINA PERHÖNEN

WOMEN'S DESIGNER

3F, 5-18-17 Shiroganedai, Minato-ku, Tokyo
03-5420-3766
www.mina-perhonen.jp/
🕐 12:00–20:00
📅 Mondays
🚩 MAP 23-1   ¥|¥|¥

Slightly eccentric, very romantic, and outlasting the vagaries of fashion trends, Mina Perhönen always uses smoky colors and lots of nuance, with patterns such as flowing rivers and green fields on all her boho clothes. Silk and cotton blouses with cap sleeves, skinny aloha shirts, silk nylon skirts ruched at the top and gathered at the bottom, and many other sweet nothings. Most items remain quite girly, and with their very own in-house textile team they have been weaving their way through hot spots around the world including Le Bon Marche, Colette, and Barneys.

MISSONI

MEN'S/WOMEN'S KNITWEAR

5-7-4 Jingumae, Shibuya-ku, Tokyo (Others)
03-5468-5678
www.missoni.com/
🕐 11:00–20:00
📅 No holidays
🚩 MAP 6-62   ¥|¥|¥|¥-¥|¥|¥|¥

Another mom and pop story that has gone global. Pop was competing at the 1948 Olympics in London in a neat little tracksuit made by his own company, mom was watching, and the rest is history. The much loved knitted zig zags were born, thanks to the "flame-dye" technique. Now in the hands of spirited daughter Angela, Missoni makes forever modern, knee-length skirts, kimono dresses, wraparound sweaters, wide legged trousers, tiny skirts, sexy bikinis, and scene-stealing ties or short sleeved cotton shirts for men.

MISS SIXTY

WOMEN'S CASUAL

Jingumae Media Square Bldg. 1F, 6-25-14 Jingumae, Shibuya-ku, Tokyo (Others)
03-5464-1426
www.misssixty.com/
🕐 11:00–20:00
📅 No holidays
🚩 MAP 6-63   ¥-¥|¥

Under Libyan-born designer Vicky Hassan, Miss Sixty has finally gone all denim, with body suits cropped at the ankle, short puffy sleeves, denim pants with a leather front and embroidered dungarees. Lately they have been inspired by a love of all things Napoleon, meaning military jackets over crisp white shirts. The high-waisted denim pencil skirts are particularly refreshing. You can find everything in a range of dark colors, as well as white, black, and light blue. The rest of the collection combines varying elements of beach party and 60s hippie style. For rock royalty there is plenty of black, leather and rhinestone.

MITSUKOSHI

DEPARMENT STORE

1-4-1 Muromachi, Chuo-ku,
  Tokyo (Others)
03-3241-3311
www.mitsukoshi.co.jp
🕐 10:00–19:30
▦ Not fixed
📍 MAP 21-1   ¥¥-¥¥¥¥¥

While Aristide Boucicaut in Paris had the brilliant idea of offering all daily necessities under one roof at a fixed cost in 1838, a concept that was the precursor to the modern day department store, Japan was already a hundred years ahead of the game with Mitsukoshi, a department store that opened its doors in 1673, and was one of the first stores in the country to allow customers to wear outdoor shoes inside. More than three centuries later, Mitsukoshi still remains the revered shopping destination and at its main Nihonbashi store you have an extensive range of men's and women's clothing and beauty ideas. Besides providing a superb collection of brands, Mitsukoshi provides golf services, travel services, school uniforms, and an excellent gallery space on the sixth floor that often has important ikebana events.

MIU MIU

MEN'S/WOMEN'S DESIGNER

5-5-8 Minami-Aoyama, Minato-ku,
  Tokyo (Others)
03-5778-0511
www.miumiu.com/
🕐 11:00–20:00
▦ Not fixed
📍 MAP 1-75   ¥¥¥¥-¥¥¥¥¥

Miu Miu is Miuccia Prada's line for younger women where she gives vent to her unconventional and idiosyncratic tendencies. Big sharp bags for both men and women, shoes that glitter and wink, platform sandals and blocks of color on patent wedges. Her printed flared skirts are a cult item among knowledgable women, as are the men's three button jackets with pants free of tucks among men. A must visit for girls and boys with intellect and heavy Miu Miu wallets.

MOLAB

YOGA

b6 1F, 6-28-6 Jingumae, Shibuya-ku,
  Tokyo
03-3486-5102
www.gests.jp/molab/
🕐 11:00–21:00
▦ Not fixed
📍 MAP 6-64   ¥¥-¥¥¥

A collection of yoga basics all under one roof provides the answer for every yogini's style woes. The collection starts with camisoles and full-sleeved tops that are not only superstretch but have pretty lace trimmings and layering. Good trousers are the hardest thing to find and this shop offers a whole range of wide legged ones in lycra, modal, and cotton fabrics. The shop also stocks yoga mats, relaxing music, and essential oils. Strike a pose not only in great style but also great comfort.

MONITOR MIND

WOMEN'S BOUTIQUE

Coredo Nihonbashi 1-4-1 Nihonbashi,
    Chuo-ku, Tokyo (Others)
03-3278-5637
www.crossplus.co.jp/shop/c_group09.
    html
🕐 11:00–21:00 (Sun/Hol. 11:00–20:00)
📅 Jan. 1
🚇 MAP 21-2   ¥|¥|-¥|¥|¥

Monitor Mind essentially stocks designer Atsuro Tayama and a few other like-minded creators. A former protege of Yohji Yamamoto, the designer is well known in Tokyo circles for his radical (for a designer) anti-American views. His brand for women, A.T., sold at this shop, takes its name from the film E.T. , but thankfully his clothes are free of any radicalism or sci-fi leanings. What Tayama gives you is a collection full of basics, with a bit of thrill, in colors like black, beige, and grey, playful but serious. A long grey sweater, closed on the side with a long strip of ruffle ideally worn over skinny jeans, formal threads with down jackets cut close to the body, empire waist dresses, and surf shorts. All his stuff can be teamed with the two other brands sold here: Italian label February, with classic but funky tailored pieces like bandeau fan skirts or shirts with a fun cut, and Colcci from Brazil that offers sexy casuals with a great fit.

MONT BLANC

MEN'S/WOMEN'S ACCESSORIES

7-9-11 Ginza, Chuo-ku, Tokyo (Others)
03-5568-8881
www.montblanc.com/
🕐 11:00–20:00
📅 No holidays
🚇 MAP 4-25   ¥|¥|¥|¥|¥

The pen is mightier than the sword, and this German power pen is the mightiest of all. Celebrating more than a century in power, here you'll find the entire range of the regular Mesiterstück and Starwalker, plus the centenary diamond-studded versions and all the gold, platinum, metal, and diamond combos. Enough pens already? You could match your treasured Mont Blanc with other Mont Blanc items, like watches, pen cases, perfumes, sunglasses and even jewelry.

MORABITO

MEN'S/WOMEN'S ACCESSORIES

Tokyo Midtown 9-7-1 Akasaka,
    Minato-ku, Tokyo (Others)
03-5413-0628
www.yanase.co.jp/other_sales/
    morabito/
🕐 11:00–21:00
📅 No holidays
🚇 MAP 12-31   ¥|¥|¥|¥|¥

One man's craft is another woman's life, and Morabito's collections have, over the last few centuries, been bringing grace and history to leather. The shapes for women's bags and men's briefcases remain elegant and classic, and serve as a wonderful canvas for their treatment of exotic leathers—croc, galucha, lizard, and ostrich—that come in small wallet, diaries, and key holders.

MORIMAE
BONSAI

7-9-10 Ginza, Chuo-ku, Tokyo
03-3571-4114
www.morimae.jp/
🕐 10:00–19:00
🗓 No holidays
🗺 MAP 4-26　　　¥|¥|¥-¥|¥|¥|¥

A delectable little shop with a dour service that does nothing to smother the glory of all the bonsai artistry that is on display. Both the formal *koten* and informal *bunjin* styles are available here, along with all the tools that you need to let your green thumb have a go at this exquisite Zen pastime.

MORGAN DE TOI
WOMEN'S DESIGNER

4-11-4 Jingumae, Shibuya-ku,
　Tokyo (Others)
03-5410-1492
www.morgan.fr/
🕐 11:00–20:00
🗓 Not fixed
🗺 MAP 5-53　　　¥|-¥|¥

Morgan de Toi has feminine clothes with a saucy style that never look vulgar on an intelligent woman. Their clothes are divided into casual workwear with tight skirts and many jacket possibilities, weekend styles with tight sexy shirts, chiffon blouses, and jeans, and for special nights out, figure-hugging tube tops with frills, and killer dresses with flashes of red. As the clothes are never expensive, it is always uplifting to step inside, grab a dress, and pay pennies for it.

MOROKO BAR
WOMEN'S BOUTIQUE

Shibuya Parco Part3 2F, 15-1 Udagawa-
　cho, Shibuya-ku, Tokyo
03-3477-8730
None
🕐 10:00–21:00
🗓 Not fixed
🗺 MAP 8-30　　　¥|¥|¥

Summer has us rushing to Moroko Bar for their great collections of caftan dresses, sleeveless tops, and shorts. The waists are cinched for an hourglass appeal, and decoration and other flounces are minimal. Colorful withot being cheesy, Moroko Bar's owner Rumiko Imamura, who was once a bored "office lady," brings a lot of sunny cheer, and a convertible-cars-and-wide-open-fields feel to collections that never fail to reflect Tokyo's swiftly shifting fashion trends.

MOSCHINO

WOMEN'S DESIGNER

Shinjuku Isetan 4F, 3-14-1 Shinjuku,
    Shinjuku-ku, Tokyo (Others)
03-3357-8740
www.moschino.it/
🕐 10:00–20:00
📅 Not fixed
✆ MAP 9-19   ¥|¥|¥|¥-¥|¥|¥|¥

The woman who wears Moschino is beyond fashion. Not only does she know a lot about it, she knows how to play around with it. Under Rosella Jardini's watchful eye, Moschino's clothes continue to be woven with irony, wit, and humor. For women like burlesque star and big fan Dita von Teese, come tailored pants, mannish shirts, chunky mixed tweed jackets with velvet trimmings or buttons which are coquettish but still elegant. Then there are, of course, the unusual color combination prints that come in refined patterns, and lots of fiery red on skirts, pants, and even in jersey Ts. This is a label not for the faint-hearted, but for the fun-loving, high-spirited trailblazers.

MUJI

INTERIOR/MEN'S/WOMEN'S
CASUAL

2,3F, 3-8-3 Marunouchi, Chiyoda-ku,
    Tokyo (Others)
03-5208-8241
www.muji.net/
🕐 10:00–21:00
📅 No holidays
✆ MAP 3-18   ¥-¥|¥|¥

When Muji, Japan's biggest design export, started 25 years ago, they only sold nine household products and a bit of food. Today, under the philosophy of "love with no frills," Muji sells 4000 different items, all in neat colors with clean lines and generic packaging. Business suits, Indian cotton T-shirts, unit sofas, DVD players, flashlights, mouse pads, espresso coffee makers, shampoo, bicycles, international foods, brown rice and banana cake—in short, a zillion good ideas. Looking to stock up on a modern design classic? Take home the neat wall hanging CD player designed by Naoto Fukasawa. This is Muji's mega-store and it stocks all of their products, including flowers and eyewear. Come once and you'll keep coming back.

MULBERRY

WOMEN'S ACCESSORIES

Roppongi Hills Hill Side Terrace B1F, 6-10-
    2 Roppongi, Minato-ku, Tokyo (Others)
03-3746-0806
www.sanki-brand.com
🕐 11:00–20:00
📅 No holidays
✆ MAP 12-32   ¥|¥|¥

The launch of their Bayswater and Roxanne range has clearly put Mulberry firmly back on the fashion radar. This shop supplies you with the latest of these cool swinging accessories from Britain's luxury label. If you are not into their editor's series, the saddle inspired range is small and sharp, with a lot of gaucho spirit.

MYSTIC

WOMEN'S BOUTIQUE

Akita Bldg. 2F, 6-12-22 Jingumae,
    Shibuya-ku, Tokyo (Others)
03-5774-8116
www.palgroup.co.jp/mystic/
⊘ 11:00–20:00
🗐 No holidays
🍴 MAP 6-65   ¥-¥¥

Mystic makes funny stuff, such as down jackets with frills, matching down bags, and lots of other clothes with a difference. They might not be great for the quality of fabrics but score high on creativity. The shop also often carries a great collection of really original bags, sometimes with maps on them, that even come with matching socks. There might be seasons when there are no down jackets with matching bags; and for these seasons the really reasonable items and lots of ideas for layering make this shop worth a casual visit. Don't miss Judgemek, the shop next door with eccentric clothing.

NAIVEWATER

WOMEN'S BOUTIQUE

1-34-28 Ebisu-nishi, Shibuya-ku, Tokyo
03-5784-2401
None
⊘ 11:00–20:00
🗐 Not fixed
🍴 MAP 2-42   ¥-¥¥

Purveyor of ideas for a slow life, Naivewater provides fashion solutions in a world where time is luxury. These ideas, essentially for women, come in the form of tops, trousers, and skirts in natural fabrics in grey, white, and beige—often embellished with handwoven lace or eyelets. In winter, they keep a fuzzy series of mufflers and gloves, leather trainers, as well as boots from Puma. In summer, shoes take on the different colors and hues of the espadrilles.

NANETTE LEPORE

WOMEN'S DESIGNER

3-18-15 Minami-Aoyama, Minato-ku,
    Tokyo
03-5410-0191
www.nanettelepore.com/
⊘ 11:00–20:00 (Sun/Holidays untill
    19:00)
🗐 Not fixed
🍴 MAP 1-76   ¥¥¥-¥¥¥¥

If you are looking for serious clothes, don't step in here. American designer Nanette Lepore is pretty much only about fun—bright cocktail frocks, incredibly feminine and deadly sexy in a gamine kind of way. When combined with a pair of shoes from her extensive designer collection and one of Nanette's much-coveted bags, it's really a va-va-voom spectacle just perfect for Tokyo.

NANO-UNIVERSE

MEN'S/WOMEN'S BOUTIQUE

1-19-14 Jinnan, Shibuya-ku,
Tokyo (Others)
03-5456-8172
www.nano-universe.jp
🕐 11:00–20:00
🗓 Not fixed
📍 MAP 8-31   ¥|¥

One of the most revered boutiques, thanks to their winning combinations of both men's and women's accessories and clothes, plus their collection of luxury ready-to-wear on the second floor. Shopping here is relaxing in a dark, warm, cozy kind of way, with wooden floors and hushed lighting. The best things are the large Balenciaga bags, top quality basics like silk cotton camisoles and T-shirts, and selected items from Alexander McQueen. Apart from these, they stock Rogan, Loomstate, Bark Tannage, Nu For Men and Selvedge, Miu Miu for women and many other brands. If you head upstairs, there is a quiet room at the back that stocks John Malkovich, Veronique Branquinho, and Marco Tagriaferri.

NAOKI TAKIZAWA

MEN'S/WOMEN'S DESIGNER

3-18-11 Minami-Aoyama, Minato-ku,
Tokyo (Others)
03-3423-1408
www.isseymiyake.co.jp/
🕐 11:00–20:00
🗓 No holidays
📍 MAP 1-77   ¥|¥|¥|¥-¥|¥|¥|¥

Creative heir to Issey Miyake, now at the helm of APOC, Takizawa stays true to his mentor's tradition of creating fluid garments that fit and flow comfortably with the body. Like Miyake, Takizawa uses incomparable tech fabrics and materials. His recent collections continue to feature nostalgic sporty colors but it is his earthy, ethnic offerings that constantly show up in all his collections. Be it green, white, gold, orange, or dusty brown, his comfortable vests and lose trousers are very popular and are perfect for loitering at country clubs or urban haunts. For women, the pant suits are particularly ingenuous, and are cut wide for an easy fit.

NAPAPIJRI

MEN'S/WOMEN'S SPORTSWEAR

Omotesando Hills Main Bldg. 2F, 4-12-10,
Jingumae, Shibuya-ku, Tokyo (Others)
03-5410-0260
www.howdy99.com/
🕐 11:00–21:00
🗓 Not fixed
📍 MAP 5-54   ¥|¥-¥|¥|¥

If the countryside beckons, head here to this Italian brand with a Finnish name (the name means Arctic Circle and is pronounced Napapiri). It pays homage to the Arctic expeditions of the early twentieth century and is named after the Norwegian island of Napapijri which was the last place to buy rations before heading to the North Pole. Well known for their pricey urban casuals with big logos, at their only flagship store in Asia you can find an extensive collection of down jackets, plaid shirts, pants, belts, scarves, embroidered Norwegian sweaters, and woolly hats for the entire family plus lots of backpacks to carry everything in. Napapijri collections always come in many colors, have big logos and use expeditions as inspiration. Unsurprisingly, they also have a ski collection with matching parkas, trousers and sweaters, but most of their stuff is for the casual urban adventurer: think shopping, frisbees, and the occasional countryside walk.

NARA CAMICIE
MEN'S/WOMEN'S BOUTIQUE

3-17-15 Minami-Aoyama, Minato-ku, Tokyo (Others)
03-3479-8954/5
www.naracamicie.co.jp
🕑 11:00–20:00
🗓 No holidays
📍 MAP 1-78 ¥¥-¥¥¥

A haven for those looking to indulge in a quick shirt fix. While the looks might be hit and miss, choose carefully and you'll come across winners for both men and women. Resort style frilly tops in blue and white, formal office looks in sharp white, blue, and pink, and classy evening looks in silk and organza, all laid out neatly on shelves and brought to you by eager-to-please sales staff. While the collections favor women, there is also a small men's collection in the corner.

NARCISO RODRIGUEZ
WOMEN'S DESIGNER

Catherine, Imperial Hotel Plaza, 1-1-1 Uchisaiwai-cho, Chiyoda-ku, Tokyo
03-3501-0555
www.narcisorodriguez.com/
🕑 11:00–20:00
🗓 No holidays
📍 MAP 4-27 ¥¥¥¥-¥¥¥¥¥

You can always count on Narciso to quench your thirst for minimalism no matter what the trend of the season. Structure and fall flow from his scissors in black, white, grey, cream and, occasionally, in dark jewel tones. His drainpipe trousers for women are cut slightly above the ankles and paired with simple V-necked tops. Geometry and complex seams that give volume are a constant thread in his creations—clothes that please his fans for their practicality in a daily urban environment. This shop stocks a small collection of his dresses, tops, skirts, and trousers for women in plus sizes.

NAUTICA
MEN'S/WOMEN'S BOUTIQUE

6-17-10 Jingumae, Shibuya-ku, Tokyo (Others)
03-5485-1316
jp.nautica.com/
🕑 11:00–20:00
🗓 Not fixed
📍 MAP 6-66 ¥-¥¥

Nautica is understandably proud of its best-selling Ts from the Competition line that also features really comfortable tracksuits and knit shirts that fit like a glove *and* keep you dry. Their extensive casual and outdoor wear has all that you would ever need to brave the winds and the high seas: shirts, sweaters, pants, down jackets, and windbreakers—often in high performance fabrics.

NEIL BARRET
MEN'S/WOMEN'S DESIGNER

6-2-7 Minami-Aoyama, Minato-ku, Tokyo
03-5774-6097
www.sannfreres.co.jp/brands/NEIL/
⊘ 11:00–20:00
▦ No holidays
♪ MAP 1-79   ¥|¥|¥|¥

The Italian soccer team lifted the World Cup trophy in outfits designed by this Brit. With a cult following not only in Italy but also NYC and LA, this former head of men's wear at Prada is best known for his suave, tailored look—especially for men. Greatly inspired by archeology, his claim to fame is for the fine line he strikes between formality and informality. His trousers are streamlined and cut smart and low around the waist, for a perfect silhouette. This he pairs with everything from fine knits to T-shirts and tuxedos and then equips you with classic white Puma sneakers. His signature casual designs in luxe fabrics are repeated in his women's collections too.

NEW YORKER
MEN'S/WOMEN'S BOUTIQUE

4-3-5 Ginza, Chuo-ku, Tokyo (Others)
03-5809-3577
www.newyorker.co.jp/
⊘ 11:00–20:00
▦ Not fixed
♪ MAP 3-19   ¥|¥|¥

This is not the shop to look for prized possessions, but fans of New Yorker—who are mostly business women and men—come here for finer cuts, like the super 130 wool and cashmere 30 suits for men and women, and a range of natural suits in the summer.

NEXT
MEN'S/WOMEN'S/KID'S
BOUTIQUE

2-9-7 Jiyugaoka, Meguro-ku,
   Tokyo (Others)
03-3731-2227
www.next.co.uk
⊘ 11:00–20:00
▦ No holidays
♪ MAP 11-11   ¥-¥|¥

Next might not solve all your sartorial conundrums, but it is a quick answer for basic neighborhood shopping if you live around Jiyugaoka. Neatly laid out on three floors—women's wear, children's wear, and men's wear—are clothes for all occasions and total coordinate solutions of matching accessories that are comfortable, with clean lines. All at amazingly cheap prices.

NICOLAI BERGMANN SUMU

INTERIOR

Tokyo Midtown, 9-7-4 Akasaka,
Minato-ku, Tokyo
03-5647-8331
www.nicolaibergmann.com/
⊘ 11:00–21:00
▦ Not fixed
⌐ MAP 12-33 ¥|¥-¥|¥|¥

The real world couldn't feel farther away than when you're in this store. Beautiful Danish design feels like a fashion spread until you come to flower designer Nicolai Bergmann's creations. These are mostly vivid flowers tucked into one spot in their vases, with beautiful colors and foliage all together, including cucumbers, orchids, and lily of the valley—which he uses down to the roots—to create great ideas for your house or party.

NICOLE MILLER

WOMEN'S DESIGNER

24-4 Sarugaku-cho, Shibuya-ku,
Tokyo (Others)
03-5784-3671
www.nicolemiller.com/
⊘ 11:00–20:00
▦ No holidays
⌐ MAP 2-43 ¥|¥|¥-¥|¥|¥

While the display in the front part of the shop might be a bit too preppy for any critical acclaim, head to the back section for a dazzling selection of beautiful long dresses, perfect for an evening out on the town. They come in vibrant turquoise, green, gold, and magenta, and are off-shouldered, halter-necked or with spaghetti straps. The shop offers to alter them to your size for the perfect, fun-to-wear party frock.

NIKE

MEN'S/WOMEN'S SPORTS-
WEAR/SHOES

Marui Jam, 1-22-6 Jinnan, Shibuya-ku,
Tokyo (Others)
03-3464-0101
www.nike.jp
⊘ 11:00–20:30
▦ Not fixed
⌐ MAP 8-32 ¥|¥

For a few more swooshes in your wardrobe or shoe collection, head here to the city's largest Nike store. Apart from their extensive offering of active wear, accessories, and shoes for every activity, check out the more recent additions to Nike sport clothing. There are articles with pouches perfect for the iPod Nano, and a sport kit with iPod that quickly solves motivation problems at the gym. You can even track your progress and goals through a sensor in the pocket of the special Air Zoom Moires shoes. Nike's sneaker history is often described as pre-Air Max and post Air-Max, and the power running shoe built on air comes in the latest 360 models, on sale here in many colors. For the ultimate in bespoke trainers hit the Nike iD web page where you can have a say in the design of every part of your kicks (even Giorgio Armani confesses to be a fan). And finally even class is on sale at Nike; their White Label Elite series uses black patent leather and fake pony skin, in sneakers, vests and jackets for hot looks at the club.

NINE WEST
WOMEN'S SHOES

6-3-9 Jingumae, Shibuya-ku,
Tokyo (Others)
03-6418-8870
www.ninewest.com
⊘ 10:00–21:00
▦ Not fixed
↑ MAP 6-67 　¥¥-¥¥¥¥

If you thought that Nine West was just a place for high school kids to stock up on shoes, spin around in your heels and take another look, because in their cheeky reincarnation they sell superbly sexy shoes that are inspired by classics: Gucci's loafers, Christian Louboutin's lacy toes, Ferragamo's flats, and whole shelves of accessories, such as bags with trimmings of the moment in gold cord, leather and silk. Delightfully low prices, superb service and exquisite colors (like poppy red and turquoise blue), will make you want to return often. If Nine West is still not for you, don't miss out on the dapper collections of Enzo Angiolini on the top floor. In metal and embossed leather, the look is luxe while prices remain Nine West.

NO CONCEPT BUT GOOD SENSE
MEN'S/WOMEN'S CASUAL

6-30-3, Jingumae, Shibuya-ku, Tokyo
03-3498-1951
www.no-con.net/
⊘ 11:00–20:00
▦ No holidays
↑ MAP 6-68 　¥¥-¥¥¥

Does the shop's name make sense? Who cares; shopping here is easy—men's takes center stage on the ground floor level, women's wear takes up the top floor. Clothes are laid out by articles, such as coats, trousers, shirts, and sweaters in dark colors with bundles of street style. The local DJ community comes looking, mostly for coats that are always in tune with the current trends and colors that are unusual to find in men's clothes—even the season essential biker's jackets are not limited to black. The women's collections have the same edgy street vibe as the men's.

NONNATIVE

MEN'S CASUAL

Grace Daikanyama, 26-13, Sarugaku-cho,
Shibuya-ku, Tokyo (Others)
03-3463-9151
www.nonnative.com/
🕐 13:00–19:00
📅 Wednesdays
📍 MAP 2-44

¥|¥-¥|¥|¥

This streetwear emporium has no patience with famous labels or limited editions or any other marketing moniker employed by clothes makers. What they want you to do is to mix and match, styling your own look from the melting pot of street style labels on offer. To make this possible, the shop stocks homegrown and imported labels of T-shirts, sneakers, shorts, pants, and jackets and also CDs and little accents for the interior, such as cushions. In a place not shy of difficult shades or styles, shopping suddenly feels like, yes, freedom.

OBJ EAST

MEN'S/WOMEN'S EYEWEAR

2-8-9 Ginza, Chuo-ku, Tokyo (Others)
03-3538-3456
www.obj.co.jp/
🕐 11:00–20:00
📅 No holidays
📍 MAP 3-20

¥|¥|¥-¥|¥|¥|¥

Even a flashy pair of glasses will get attention, but the right kind of attention comes with a pair that is discreet and cutting edge. Head to Obj East for the latter type of frame. The range of vintage round shapes, classic ovals, teardrops , moddish Wellingtons, butterflies, and the latest iconic squares ensures a perfect fit for every face. Some frames come with special features like aluminum hoods or wood temples. And if it is labels you are looking for, Obj stocks them all—from the most wanted Alain Mikli to sporty Oakley.

OBJET STANDARD

WOMEN'S DESIGNER

Tokyo Midtown, 9-7-1 Akasaka, Minato-
ku, Tokyo (Others)
03-5464-2305
www.objetstandard.com
🕐 11:00–20:00
📅 No holidays
📍 MAP 12-34

¥|¥|¥-¥|¥|¥|¥

Objet Standard makes stuff that not only looks good, but feels great. In spring they do skinny pants and pretty white cotton blouses in clean, straight lines, A-line skirts in luxe fabrics, and jackets worn with bikinis. In winter they are best at suits, with little out-of-the-ordinary touches such as silk piping, leather, white satin fabrics, slashed side pockets on coats, all in a skinny, tight fit.

OILILY

WOMEN'S ACCESSORIES

Ikebukuro Seibu 7F, 1-28-1 Ikebukuro,
  Toshima-ku, Tokyo (Others)
03-3987-1802
www.oilily.nl
🕐 10:00–21:00 (Sun/Holidays until
  20:00)
📋 Not fixed
📍 MAP 17-2   ¥|¥|¥|¥

Back in Holland, these lively colorful bags are style icons. With a handmade romantic feel to each, they are definitely the most stylish bags mommies could hope for. A patchwork of different materials finished off with dark detailing means you can easily coordinate it with any outfit. Everything comes in matching colors and sizes and it is only in Japan that you can also buy the cute makeup bags. The best selling items are the multifunctional mommy bags with many pouches, kitted with cute diaper covers. Oilily also makes heavenly clothes for kids in loads of color combinations, so the bag fashion/ tot combo offers a great respite for trend-loving mothers.

OJEWEL

JEWELRY

6-9-16 Ginza, Chuo-ku, Tokyo
03-5537-2740
www.hpfrance.com/shop/brand/o-jewel.
  html
🕐 12:00–20:00
📋 3rd Tues.
📍 MAP 4-28   ¥|¥|¥-¥|¥|¥|¥

It's rare that precious jewelry gets so avant-garde; but this shop is dedicated to those designers from around the world whose works have a museum-like quality. Take, for example, Annelie Planteydt, who is a sculptor first and then a master jeweler. Her necklaces in gold (and many other materials like tautalum) are strips of metal linked to create various geometric shapes and cascade around the neck. Gesine Hackenberg uses textile, urushi lacquer, silver, and steel to make brooches that look delicious in brightly colored candy and chocolate flower shapes. Jiro Kamata's jewelry becomes a topic for conversation as he incorporates everyday objects into his ear- rings. This little jewelry empire also includes irrepressibly upbeat creations from designers like Dorothea Dahnick , Felix Lindner, Peah, Iris Nieuwenburg, Joke Brakman, Yutaka Minegishi, and Mirei Takeuchi. The materials are so precious and the designs so unique that this undoubtedly becomes one of the best shops in the this part of the world for wedding rings.

ONITSUKA TIGER

MEN'S/WOMEN'S SHOES

Roppongi Hills West Walk 4F, 6-10-
  1 Roppongi, Minato-ku, Tokyo (Others)
03-5772-2660
www.onitsukatiger.com/
🕐 11:00–21:00
📋 No Fixed
📍 MAP 12-35   ¥-¥|¥

Onitsuka Tiger's retro cool sneakers have the same camp connec- tion to cool people of both sexes today as in the 50s and 60s, when they became really popular. With their low tops and fine soles, they seem just barely there, but the gorgeous color combinations are rare among the other breeds of retro sneakers doing the rounds of the city. The Tiger sneakers come in chocolate, beige, white, black, and yellow with colorful red, yellow, and white stripes on the side. Pair this with their great range of trainer tops for the original made-in-Japan retro vibe.

OPAQUE
DEPARTMENT STORE

2-1-1 Marunouchi, Chiyoda-ku, Tokyo (Others)
03-5220-6655
www.opaque.ne.jp
🕐 11:00–20:00 (Sun/Holidays untill 20:00)
🗓 Not fixed
🎯 MAP 7-19   ¥|¥-¥|¥|¥|¥

Opaque enhances your lifestyle with small but fun ideas. Skip the clothes and head straight for the first floor, which offers the best collection of OPI nailcare products, including the razor-sharp diamond peel nail file and foot scrub. Buy expert aromatherapy from Rose de Marrakech, hundred percent bio beauty products from German company Tautropfen, Lavere and Weleda. Some of these products are used at the spa upstairs. For the perfect smile, there is even a teethcare salon and all this, topped with the cute florist at the entrance, makes you feel good just to be there.

OPTICIEN LOYD
MEN'S/WOMEN'S/KIDS' EYEWEAR

4-26-35 Jingumae, Shibuya-ku, Tokyo
03-3423-0505
www.loyd.co.jp
🕐 10:30–20:00
🗓 Not fixed
🎯 MAP 5-55   ¥|¥-¥|¥|¥

If you're looking for really good quality glasses for you or your child, head to Opticien Loyd, who stock more than 1300 kinds of frames on the optical floor, around five hundred sunglasses on the top floor, and an extensive range of kids eyewear in the basement. As Japan makes the best quality lightweight titanium frames in the world, it makes sense to get a pair while you are here. The open display of material, color, and size makes it really easy to choose. Be warned that the staff politely refrain from giving advice on what best suits you, so it is better to go equipped with a friend.

ORLA KEILY
WOMEN'S ACCESSORIES

Shibuya Mark City East Mall B1, 1-1-12-3 Dogenzaka, Shibuya-ku, Tokyo (Others)
03-3447-9770
www.orlakely.com/
🕐 11:00–21:00
🗓 No holidays
🎯 MAP 8-33   ¥-¥|¥

Irish-born designer Orla Keily brings you her world of brash bold color with geometric prints on totes, bags, wallets and printed T-shirts. With a cult following, Keily creates everything herself in a '60s and '70s graphic style with a Scandinavian accent and hyper functional design. She always sets off super strong colors on a very neutral beige or faded tone, quickly adding spice to any background.

ORREFORS KOSTA BODA

INTERIOR

Roppongi Hills Keyakizaka Terrace, 6-15-1 Roppongi, Minato-ku, Tokyo
03-3404-8729
www.kostaboda.se
🕐 11:00–20:00
📅 No holidays
↕ MAP 12-36

¥¥¥¥

This century-old Swedish glassware manufacturer is best known for the delicate engravings and figurative motifs in Neo-classical style that they started creating in the early 1920s. Since then, they have been striving to create spectacular glass pieces that grace homes and offices at fairly reasonable prices. Of late, contemporary design has been injected into the collections through designers Martti Rytkonen, Lena Bergstorm, and Ingegerd Raman who make series of heavy bowls, vases, candleholders, and tumblers in unique shapes. If the vivid colors prove to be too adventurous, stick to the basics in clear glass, and you will treasure your purchases like pieces of art.

OSH KOSH B'GOSH

KIDS'

1-25-17 Jiyugaoka, Meguro-ku, Tokyo (Others)
03-3718-8390
www.oshkoshbgosh.com/
🕐 11:00–21:00
📅 Not fixed
↕ MAP 11-12

¥-¥¥

Kids take center stage in this store that has become a stateside legend. Tiny overalls for newborns, plaid shirts for the older ones, corduroy pants for teens and tons of T-shirts, sportswear, shoes, and accessories for all ages. Their durable fabrics and casual designs endure reckless play or the arduous bike race home from school.

PAOLA FRANI

WOMEN'S DESIGNER

Aoyama Bell Commons 1F, 2-14-6 Kita-Aoyama, Minato-ku, Tokyo
03-3475-8001
www.paolafrani.com
🕐 11:00–20:00
📅 Not fixed
↕ MAP 16-7

¥¥¥-¥¥¥¥

Who wouldn't look pretty in Italian Paola Frani's sexy outfits? Just about everything has lace, barely stays on and is extremely tiny. But if you do manage to get into any of her tops, tight skirts, or skinny pants, winter or summer, she'll make you look refined, sophisticated, sexy, and in the know.

PATAGONIA

MEN'S/WOMEN'S KIDS'
SPORTSWEAR/ACCESSORIES

6-16-8 Jingumae, Shibuya-ku,
Tokyo (Others)
03-5469-2100
www.patagonia.com
🕐 11:00–20:00
📅 Not fixed
🚹 MAP 6-69   ¥¥-¥¥¥

Patagonia's honest approach to the environment has won it many fans among well-to-do sea-and-sun lovers for their extensive range of sportswear made from recycled materials. Like the board shorts made out of 100% recycled polyester spun from trash, or the organic cotton Ts, camis, dresses, shorts, rashguards and hoodies—even to the surfboards made with natural epoxy resins. While the ground floor shop is dedicated to casuals for men, women, and kids, trek up three wooden stairs to Patagonia Ocean that stocks a range of wetsuits manufactured in Japan from recycled polyester, and knee pads lined with organic merino wool.

PATRIZIA PEPE

WOMEN'S DESIGNER

Shibuya Parco Part1, 15-1 Udagawa-cho,
Shibuya-ku, Tokyo (Others)
03-3464-5111
www.orizzonti.co.jp/pepe/index.html
🕐 10:00–21:00
📅 No holidays
🚹 MAP 8-34   ¥¥¥-¥¥¥¥

Patrizia Pepe's clothes are great for people built like cheese straws. This one-stop, fuss free shop can dress you in fantastic semi formals and casuals for the whole day. Clothes are cut sharp and close to the body, meaning that winter overcoats fit like a dress with skinny long sleeves. Even the casuals are ultra feminine, with detailing such as Swarovski-studded V-neck sweatshirts with plunging necklines or elegantly draped knits. The dresses are the best—if you can manage to squeeze into them, that is—with perfect necklines and hems with cinched waists.

PAUL & JOE ACCESSORIES

WOMEN'S ACCESSORIES

B6 1F, 6-28-6 Jingumae, Shibuya-ku,
Tokyo (Others)
03-5778-2045
www.kuipo.co.jp/pauljoe/index.html
🕐 11:00–21:00
📅 No holidays
🚹 MAP 6-70   ¥¥-¥¥¥

Irreverent accessories from French designer Sophie Albou's collection, Paul and Joe, can be found at this gem of a boutique. For style, she maintains the same tone as her free-spirited line of clothes, and creates original whimsical items based on her own personal collection of much-loved bags. She offers oversized versions of evening bags made from the softest crinkled or aged leather, as well as glossy bags with flower prints or acid bright colors. The heavy detailing with gold writing and gold plated metal is inspired by her jewelry range. In combinations of crochet and leather, colorful piping, and pretty vintage shapes, these accessories go well through the week and into the weekend whether you are in Tokyo or Bali.

PAUL & JOE
MEN'S/WOMEN'S DESIGNER

Seibu Dept. Store, 2–5–1 Yurakucho, Chiyoda–ku, Tokyo (Others)
03–5218–5107
www.paulandjoe.com/
🕐 🗓 Wed, Thu, Fri/11:30–21:00; Sat, Sun, holidays/11:00–20:30; Mon, Tue/11:30–20:30
⌐ MAP 3-21   ¥|¥|¥|-¥|¥|¥|¥

Sophie Albou started off as a designer in her father's luxury shirts brand La Garage. In 1995 she then set up Paul and Joe, originally only a men's brand named after her two sons, before venturing into women's clothes. So her forte understandably remains shirts, in all colors, varieties and hues—cute shirts, pretty shirts and shirts with individuality well known for the dynamic prints. If you want to convey a more radical original style, it's best to pair these shirts with something a bit more avantgarde. The shop also stocks the men's collection and the recently started Paul and Joe beauty line.

PAULE KA
WOMEN'S DESIGNER

5-5-18 Ginza, Chuo-ku, Tokyo (Others)
03-6274-3100
www.euromoda.co.jp/
🕐 11:00–20:00
🗓 No holidays
⌐ MAP 4-29   ¥|¥|¥|¥|-¥|¥|¥|¥|¥

French-born designer Serge Cajfinger's label comprises a great bouillabaisse, mixing the best of Porto Alegre's Brazilian warmth (it's where he grew up), with elegant French sensibilities. Here you can find his entire collection, with accessories, pretty skirt and jacket combinations in luxurious fabrics—and the cruise collection in summer with its tight stretch cotton poplin dresses, cotton twill peddle pushers, and beautiful linen crepe dresses. Whether it's net, neoprene, a puffed ball dress or large silk trousers, Paule Ka's women remain elegant, in tune with the trends of the moment and impeccably turned out in a Jackie O kind of way.

PAUL SMITH
MEN'S/WOMEN'S DESIGNER

6-3-10 Minami-Aoyama, Minato-ku, Tokyo (Others)
03-3486-2649
www.paulsmith.co.jp
🕐 11:00–20:00
🗓 Not fixed
⌐ MAP 1-80   ¥|¥|¥|¥

For the uninitiated, Sir Paul Smith's quintessential take on English fashion is all a bit strange. Step into the shop, and, before you know it, you are hypnotized by the stripes and prints that are anglomaniac with brushes of the eccentric. Take for example the series of skirts, matching shirts, and pullovers in French tapestry prints that has ignited a whole trend of antiquity in fashion. Men should not leave without at least a pair of classic boxer shorts and, of course, some multicolor cuff links. That is, if the fuschia cargo shorts, pink shirts, fluoro belts, embroidered waistcoats and red seersucker jackets prove to be too much for your senses.

PAUL STUART
MEN'S/WOMEN'S DESIGNER

5–7–20 Jingumae, Shibuya–ku, Tokyo (Others)
03–3406–8121
www.paulstuart.com
🕚 11:00–20:00
🗓 Not fixed
📍 MAP 6-71   ¥|¥|¥|¥-¥|¥|¥|¥

Paul Stuart offers all possible combinations for dressing up for the boardroom. The shop stocks suits, shirts, and knits combined with matching high-quality, semi-hand-made shoes, striped silk ties, and silk cuff links in all possible colors with matching handkerchiefs and car coats, and impossibly preppy clothes for women. Even then, the label manages to be modern, slick, and unfussy and with a bit of creativity, he can also be perfect for After Six.

PEACH JOHN
LINGERIE

109 Bldg., 2-29-1 Dogenzaka, Shibuya-ku, Tokyo (Others)
0120-066-107
www.peachjohn.co.jp
🕚 10:00–21:00
🗓 No holidays
📍 MAP 8-35   ¥-¥|¥

This homegrown brand is all for pretty pink and peach ideas for intimates that stress comfort and put you in a warm, fuzzy mood whatever the time of the day. Their stuff comes in a huge variety of colors and prints and is very reasonably priced. Bra and panty sets, camisoles, boxers and sleep wear almost always come with frills and they also make accessories like lacy boxes and satin pouches to protect these frilly incumbents while traveling.

PIERRE MANTOUX
WOMEN'S LEGWEAR

5-11-8 Minami-Aoyama, Minato-ku, Tokyo (Others)
03-5467-1110
www.pierremantoux.jp
🕚 11:00–20:00
🗓 No holidays
📍 MAP 1-81   ¥|¥

Purveyor of stockings to royalty, Pierre Mantoux has been hugging beautiful legs since 1930. Mantoux is skilled at delicate embellishments, fine fishnets, just a hint of sparkle all over, a slight lace design, or a single thread running over the calf of a sheer tight— and despite all this everything is surprisingly reasonable. You'll also find knee length socks, lacy numbers to wear at home, and pure cashmere, cotton, and woolen tights that feel really light to wear and soft to touch.

PINKO

WOMEN'S BOUTIQUE

Glass Square B1F, 4-20-7 Ebisu, Shibuya-
ku, Tokyo
03-3446-1517
www.pinko.it/
🕐 11:00–20:0
📅 Not fixed
🚇 MAP 10-5

¥-¥¥

Featuring saucy celeb casuals well worn by the fashion pantheon, the shop recently opened its doors in Japan. Pinko's slinky drapes for the evening, sequined denim wear, snow white waiter's jackets, and knee high boots are favored mostly by celebs like brand ambassador Mariah Carey.

PLEATS PLEASE

WOMEN'S DESIGNER

La Place de Minamiaoyama, 3-13-21
Minami-Aoyama, Minato-ku,
Tokyo (Others)
03-5772-7750
www.pleatsplease.com/
🕐 11:00–20:00
📅 No holidays
🚇 MAP 1-82

¥¥¥¥

This gravity-defying fabric suits every body perfectly, including expecting mothers, power women and all those in between. With a sharp clean look in an unending range of colors, each garment has a very delicate pleated surface. This is created by heat-setting the fabric in a finely pleated paper mold. Miyake holds the patent for this technique. Loads of prints and shapes are available every season in an impossible variety of colors. Travel-perfect, iron-free and very shapely, some local women are known to wear only this label. This shop not only stocks their largest and latest collection, but is the cheapest in the world, with a duty-free service.

PORSCHE DESIGN

ACCESSORIES

5-3-9 Ginza, Chuo-ku, Tokyo (Others)
03-5568-7232
www.porsche-design.com
🕐 11:00–20:00
📅 No holidays
🚇 MAP 4-30

¥¥¥¥

For those who don't have the car yet, be heartened to hear that the clothes use the same leather lining as the seat covers and the 3110 range of precision pens uses the same material as the tubing around the engine of those legendary cars. Porsche design also stocks the 1972 first generation of style goods created by Ferdinand Porsche—cutting-edge, stainless-steel Faber Castell pens, forty-year-old briar wood pipes and the namesake Roadster luggage with the exact same wheel design in miniature. Simply the best industrial design at your finger-tips, period.

PORTER
MEN'S/WOMEN'S ACCESSORIES

Marunouchi Bldg. 3F, 2-4-1 Marunouchi,
    Chiyoda-ku, Tokyo (Others)
03-5220-2555
www.yoshidakaban.com/
🕐 11:00–21:00 (Sun/Sat untill 20:00)
🗓 Not fixed
♪ MAP 7-20   ¥|¥|¥

Designer Kurachika Yoshida's luggage and accessories have
become much-coveted items among edgy, fashion-driven young
businessmen in town. He makes shoulder bags, tote bags, day-
packs, Bostons, briefcases, wallets, and card cases in dark leather,
vinyl, and nylon, and is a favorite for his simple, fashion-friendly
styles that efficiently protect your things from the effects of the
daily grind.

PRADA
MEN'S/WOMEN'S DESIGNER

5-2-6 Minami-Aoyama, Minato-ku,
    Tokyo (Others)
03-6418-0400
www.prada.com/
🕐 11:00–20:00
🗓 Not fixed
♪ MAP 1-83   ¥|¥|¥|¥

Twenty years ago, after decades of making only leather, Mario
Prada's daughter Miuccia launched a sturdy, reasonably priced
parachute nylon bag series that made Prada instantly recognizable
worldwide. Apart from the bags, most of her skirts have also become
collectors' items, with graphic prints, and elegantly waisted shapes.
There are also, of course, the It shoes for both him and her, and
minimal dressing for men available on the upper floors. If you have
too much Prada gear already, a visit to the shop's premises would
not disappoint. Designed by Swiss duo Herzog and de Meuron, it is
an architectural gem by itself. Tokyo being Prada's "epicenter," as
the building is known, ensures that this store is privy to most collections prior to their hitting the shelves elsewhere in the world.

PRINTEMPS GINZA
DEPARTMENT STORE

3-2-1 Ginza, Chuo-ku, Tokyo
03-3567-0077
www.printemps-ginza.co.jp/
🕐 Tue–Sat 11:00–20:00, Sun/Mondays
    untill 19:00
🗓 Not fixed
♪ MAP 3-22   ¥|¥-¥|¥|¥

The Tokyo branch of the ritzy Parisian departmental store, Printemps Ginza enacts its Frenchness to the hilt. There are announce-
ments in French and French sounding (homegrown) labels like Le
Souk, Viva You, Gaminerie, Ined, Vigny, etc.. While its Parisian
counterpart has pulled up its socks and stocks the most cutting
edge brands, this one hardly goes beyond the twenty-something,
Ginza-gamine style of shorts, stockings, taffeta dresses, and chiffon wraps. They even offer culture classes—flower arrangement,
table setting, golf, and tennis lessons—only for women. So you
might want to save your time and stick to the ground floor, with

the Tsumori Chisato Carry series for accessories and bags, and a nice floor full of cosmetics that include L'Occitane, Paul&Joe, Shu Uemura, and a Cosme clinic that stocks all kinds of wonder oils and ointments.

PSLING
INFANTS

17-6 Daikanyama-cho, Shibuya-ku, Tokyo (Others)
03-3780-0222
www.psling.co.jp/
🕚 11:00–20:00
📅 No holidays
🕴 MAP 2-45   ¥ ¥ ¥ - ¥ ¥ ¥ ¥

While the likes of fashionmag cheerleaders have made babies a pre-requisite fashion accessory, Psling makes slings for babies a prerequisite fashion accessory. Find the best collection of slings in town in this shop that stocks hundreds of strikingly beautiful varieties in jute and cotton in myriad colors and gradations. There are enough varieties to kit your every outfit, and stoic ones that look extremely stylish on daddies, too. Don't miss the killer collection of mommy bags in patent and jungle prints.

PUMA STORE HARAJUKU
MEN'S/WOMEN'S/KIDS' SPORTSWEAR

Harajuku Quest Bldg., 1-13-14 Jingumae, Shibuya-ku, Tokyo (Others)
03-3401-6100
www.puma.jp
🕚 11:00–20:00
📅 No holidays
🕴 MAP 5-56   ¥ - ¥ ¥

These are the guys who married sport to fashion, and they remain fiercely committed to the cause. This store is their second concept store in the world after California. Stocked with carefully chosen Puma products from their collections worldwide, the store has an extensive fitness collection with running, swimming, and yoga gear. Their golf collection of Ts, pants, bags, and shoes is especially lightweight for ease of travelling, and if their extensive range of shoes from past and present collections doesn't please you, design your own at the Mongolian shoe BBQ corner. With laces, tongue trimmings, toe overlays, and heel caps in many different colors, your bespoke sneaker is bound to raise temperatures at the gym.

Q-POT
WOMEN'S ACCESSORIES

6-11-4 Jingumae, Shibuya-ku, Tokyo (Others)
03-5467-5470
www.gramme.jp
🕚 12:00–20:00
📅 No holidays
🕴 MAP 6-72   ¥ - ¥ ¥

Qpot makes hilarious jewelry at their tiny little flagship tucked away in the back lanes of Omotesando. Trinkets couldn't get more entertaining than this: cheese rings made of gold and acrylic, and portions of cheese in a pendant or ring motif. The wisdom tooth key holder in brass and polyester and the tooth cuff buttons too are compellingly funny. But a real dose of aching humor awaits you with rum raisin ice cream rings, strawberry marble ice rings, pink whipped cream rings, biscuit rings, strawberry rings, coffee biscuit necklaces, and cake hair ornaments. If that isn't enough, they have entire boxes of chocolate rings available to endulge your accessory tooth.

QUIKSILVER
MEN'S/WOMEN'S SURFWEAR

Omotesando Hills Main, 4-12-10
 Jingumae, Shibuya-ku, Tokyo (Others)
03-5410-0270
www.quiksilver.com/
🕐 11:00–21:00
▦ Not fixed
𝍏 MAP 5-57   ¥-¥¥

Quiksilver immediately transports you to the world of *Point Break* and *The Endless Summer.* As the waves are not that far from town, you should get seriously interested in their bathing suits, surfing shorts and logo-emblazoned T-shirts and hoodies. Of course they have all the other necessary things, too: five- and six- metre surf-boards, wet suits, and waterproof watches. Quiksilver's winter sport range equips you with heavy weather suits, goggles, and headwear for skiing or snowboarding. Even for those who don't indulge in extreme sport pastimes, the accessories here are superb gift ideas for the budding skier or surfer among friends or family.

QUIKSILVER BOARDRIDERS CLUB
MEN'S/WOMEN'S/KIDS' SURF SHOP

Shibuya Parco UP/S4, 2-1 Udagawa-cho,
 Shibuya-ku, Tokyo (Others)
03-3477-5991
www.quiksilver.jp
🕐 11:00–21:00
▦ No holidays
𝍏 MAP 8-36   ¥-¥¥

Surf wear and surf gear, mostly in Hawaian-style prints for both men and women. As you may have guessed, the styles are not much more than beach shorts, bikinis, and footwear. The shop also stocks Ts, bags, rash guards, and wet suits (in kids's sizes too). The image is Backdoor Pipeline, Oahu, Hawaii, while you might be actually hanging around your building's rooftop pool.

RAFFINE LIVING
INTERIOR

2F, 1-35-5 Ebisu-nishi, Shibuya-ku,
 Tokyo (Others)
03-3770-6992
www.raffine-living.jp/
🕐 11:00–20:00
▦ Wednesdays
𝍏 MAP 2-46   ¥-¥-¥

Never mind that the collections are not as refined as the name sounds; this store stocks a bit of everything that can ease your life with design solutions. Sure they have the necessary sofas, glassware, and design objets, but they also have a neat collection of home electronics from Amadana, and gadgets like the humidifier chimney for the dry season. This is also a great address to know because they can build your dream sofa from scratch: just give them the design and they do the rest. They also upholster sofas at reasonable prices. You can choose the fabric from their selection or you can give them any fabric of your choice. After an expert visit, they'll pick up your sofa, redo it and drop it back in pristine condition. Perfect solution for busy bodies in search of a perfect sofa to unwind upon.

RAGTAG

MEN'S/WOMEN'S SECOND
HAND

1-17-7 Jinnan, Shibuya-ku, Tokyo (Others)
03-3476-6848
www.ragtag.jp/
⊘ 12:00–21:00
No holidays
MAP 8-37

¥-¥ ¥ ¥ ¥

The greatest consignment shop in town for those with a yen for designer clothes on a budget. Always buzzing with activity, the four floors offer Dolce Gabbana, Miu Miu, Prada, Missoni, Issey Miyake, Comme des Garçons, Yohji Yamamoto, Gucci, Versace, Christian Louboutin, and almost every designer under the sun. Stocks everything from Hermès accessories, Louboutin shoes, Paul Smith jackets and Comme des Garçons purses all neatly arranged on three floors—so there's always something to please every brand as fashionista, especially the cash-strapped ones.

RALPH LAUREN

MEN'S/WOMEN'S DESIGNER

4 25 15 Jingumae, Shibuya ku,
Tokyo (Others)
03-5412-8700
www.polo.com
⊘ 11:00–20:00
No holidays
MAP 5-58

¥ ¥ ¥ ¥ ¥

Japan's largest ever retail venture, by the four-inch tie maker and lifestyle hero. This season will see the ultimate in bespoke craftsmanship with suits, sweaters and shirts in a luxe palette of dull greys and vivid pastels dandified with soft pink and lilac for the gentleman and the baby face. Uptown chic for the park-avenue princess comes in light blue, pink and brown while Ralph takes the rest of us Mata Hari adventurer überbabes to Cote d'Ivoire, on the set of the film "White Mischief." It's a natural palette that says safari and ranch with suede skirts and jackets, embroidery, fringe and western detailing. So much fun; so many options. And don't forget the accessories, especially Stella, the red pump, and Donna, the gold woven espadrille, and the hottest accessory on the block—the Ricky bags in alligator.

REALMAD HECTIC

MEN'S CASUAL

Protect Bldg. B1F, 4-26-21 Jingumae, Shibuya-ku, Tokyo
03-3405-6933
None
🕐 12:00–20:00
📅 Not fixed
🚇 MAP 5-59   ¥-¥¥

The Star Wars-themed entrance is a male shrine to all things wildly popular. The owner brings back his skate boarding youth experience in the States, so for a long time the shop was best known for its statement skate board wear from Polo Ralph Lauren and Helly Hansen. But in its zeal to produce the coolest activity-appropriate clothing the three brands designed by the shop—PKG, Teenage Wolf and Seesaws basics—are sold here so that you can go supermarket shopping and on a date in the same clothes. Skate boarders love his layered looks with Tshirts, tanks and cotton shirts with relaxed trousers and the designer is proud of the minimum five year shelf life of the entire collection.

REBIRTH (LUMP)

MEN'S CASUAL

J-Hill Side 2F, 3-15-4 Jingumae, Shibuya-ku, Tokyo
03-5785-2644
None
🕐 12:00–20:00
📅 NoT fixed
🚇 MAP 5-60   ¥-¥¥

A cult shop for street wear, especially for the rock and roll elite, Rebirth offers clothes with handcrafted flair and detailing—such as hats embroidered with an eye, jackets and denim with flashy red piping, and key chains with a hand motif. Designer Shimano is particularly fascinated by things like the coverage of war on television, and has even visited the Auschwitz camp for inspiration. His fashion is dark and brooding; hence the rock and roll appeal. Quieter in colors than other streetwear vendors, this is a real layering mecca, as the colors never stray beyond the blues, blacks, and whites of denims. Coordination is superbly simple, even for the color blind among us.

RENATO NUCCI

WOMEN'S DESIGNER

4-21-24 Minami-Aoyama, Minato-ku, Tokyo
03-3479-5785
www.renato-nucci.com
🕐 11:00–20:00
📅 No holidays
🚇 MAP 1-84   ¥¥¥¥-¥¥¥¥¥

The way Nucci's collection is dyed in beautiful colors and made of luxe fabrics knitted in a fine gauge means that they fall well on you no matter what your size. As Nucci designs especially for the more well-endowed woman, the tall, curvy type loves to shop here for beautiful ideas, like pant suits, skirts, and flimsy tops.

RENE CAOVILLA

WOMEN'S SHOES

6-6-9 Ginza, Chuo-ku, Tokyo
03-3571-5501
www.renecaovilla.com/
🕐 12:00–20:00 (Sat/Sun/Holidays
　　11:00–19:00)
🗓 No holidays
📍 MAP 4-31　　　　　　　¥¥¥¥¥

Some of us just can't get enough of these jewels for the feet. Extravagantly displayed in this tiny boudoir with the most attentive service, Rene Caovilla performs magic, with dazzling stones gripping ankles and snaking around calves on four-inch rhinestone heels. He pinches silk fabrics with great dexterity, creating the most difficult knots and drapes on sandals, and then adorns the platform with crystals. Snakes are a recurring theme and so is lace. His lasts are legendary, ensuring that his pumps fit like a glove. If you want to live a true Cinderella story, make sure that these are the shoes you leave behind.

REPUBLIC OF FRITZ HANSEN

INTERIOR

6-8-18 Minami-Aoyama, Minato-ku,
　Tokyo
03-5778-3100
www.fritzhansen.com/
🕐 11:00–20:00
🗓 No holidays
📍 MAP 1-85　　¥¥¥¥-¥¥¥¥¥

In 1958, Fritz Hansen stormed the world with Arne Jacobsen's Egg armchair and Swan armchair. Since then the Republic of Fritz Hansen (as it has become known) has been spinning out irresistible furniture, all of which is reasonable and starkly functional—making it one of the most recognized furniture labels in the world. The best here is undoubtedly the seven designs of arm chairs from Arne Jacobsen that, apart from the Egg, Swan, Seven, Eight and Grand prix include the Ant chair series with curving seats and back rests in a riot of colors, supported on a tubular, three-legged steel frame. Proof again that Fritz Hansen is just full of ideas that really work.

RESTERÖDS

MEN'S/WOMEN'S UNDERWEAR

20-23 Daikanyamacho, Shibuya-ku,
　Tokyo
03-3770-8182
www.resterods.com
🕐 12:00–19:00
🗓 Not fixed
📍 MAP 2-47　　　　　　　¥¥

Really hip underwear from Sweden that is undergoing a great revival. Originally set up in 1935, everything is still made in the tiny village of Resterods in Sweden, and true to the brand's Scandinavian origins, the colors remain vibrant and simple, and the design is refreshingly free of lace and unnecessary embellishment. Winter items usually work better than summer stuff with long shirts, striped knitted long johns, mile-long high school charm knitted scarves, long V-neck sweaters with knitted legwarmers, roll-up Ts, tank tops, and mittens. The comfortable boxers and hipsters for men and women are classic pieces in bright colors, and the classic logo on the elastic waistband has a lot of style even when it peeps over low waist jeans.

RESTIR
MEN'S/WOMEN'S BOUTIQUE

4-2-2 Ginza, Chuo-ku, Tokyo (Others)
03-5159-0595
www.restir.com/
🕐 11:30–20:30 (Sundays/Holidays
11:00–20:00)
📅 Not fixed
🚇 MAP 3-23   ¥|¥|¥|¥-¥|¥|¥|¥

Cutting edge luxury is the shop's credo and it sells a great selection of all that you ever wanted. Puma's collaboration with McQueen, Galliano Homme, the hot, hot Rick Owens, and Alexander McQueen are only some of what's here for men. Women are also offered a great selection of must-haves, from Miu Miu, Christian Louboutin, Zac Posen and Alessandro Dell'Acqua. Precious feet would find their desires with the many offerings from Rene Caovilla, Jimmy Choo and Manolo Blahnik. The shop also has one of the most user-friendly websites around. Though all sizes are not available, the shop is a must visit for all fashion lovers.

RE-STYLE KIDS
KIDS'

Shinjuku Isetan 6F, 3-14-1 Shinjuku,
Shinjuku-ku, Tokyo
03-3352-1111
https://www.isetan.co.jp/icm2/jsp/store/
shinjuku/index.jsp
🕐 10:00–20:00
📅 Not fixed
🚇 MAP 9-20   ¥|¥-¥|¥|¥

For parents tired of too basic or too simple, this corner of Isetan makes children's clothes that will be topics for dinner conversation. Little denim wonders from True religion jeans or Paper denim and cloth, to be styled with belts with antique buckles that cost as much as the jeans, Marni dresses, Undercover rock chic, Mina Perhönen's colorful styles, Baby Dior, and Bonpoint for parents who love couture styles for their 0-4 year-old kids. All the clothes for kids under two are tested for formalyn piece by piece and thoroughly cleaned—an impressive combination of service and style. The collections are as good as the rag trade gets for kids.

REVISITATION
WOMEN'S BOUTIQUE

5-9-15 Minami-Aoyama, Minato-ku,
Tokyo (Others)
03-5467-6866
www.abahouse.co.jp/
🕐 11:00–20:00 (Sun/Holidays untill
20:00)
📅 No holidays
🚇 MAP 1-86   ¥|¥|¥

Revisitation revisits the old British classics of tweed wool knits, prints, long cardigans, and lacy tops. The collections might be a bit too saccharine, but there's a long list of dreamy mix-and-match feminine pieces that you could stock up on. There is also a huge collection of silk and taffeta outfits to wear for weddings, evenings, and other dressy occasions.

REVOLVER

MEN'S DESIGNER

2-7-15 Jingumae, Shibuya-ku, Tokyo
03-3478-7008
www.revolholic.com
🕐 11:30–19:30
🗓 Not fixed
⌐ MAP 5-61   ¥·¥

Revolver is where value systems rarely stray beyond casual and super cool. Designers Kiri and Arata's brand was long a hot favorite among Tokyo models. The designers themselves have been inspired by their own experiences as models in Paris; not so much by the shows, but what went on backstage, including the clothes everyone wore. This resulted in their first collection many years ago, among which the multicolored hooded jerseys in colors like rust, scarlet, and sea green remain their hottest selling items. Collections are always built around shirts, pants, and casual gear but are infused with a lot of spirit and ideas like artistic illustrations, pop imagery, and brilliant colors.

RICHARD JAMES
MEN'S BESPOKE

Tokyo Midtown 9-7-1 Akasaka,
  Minato-ku, Tokyo (Others)
03-5413-0054
www.richardjames.co.uk/
🕐 11:00–21:00
🗓 No holidays
⌐ MAP 12-37   ¥·¥·¥·¥

Richard James' stitches are the most contemporary of Savile Row tailors. While the other labels are all into affordable luxury, this one remains true to its finest of cuts. Bespoke tailoring with a vengeance sees the finest of cashmere and herringbone in sharply cut one, two, and three-button coat suits, with strong shoulders and sleeves cut high. In the winter you'll find equally superb overcoats.

RMK
COSMETICS

3-10-8 Kita-Aoyama, Minato-ku,
  Tokyo (Others)
03-5468-6815
www.rmkrmk.com
🕐 11:00–20:00
🗓 No holidays
⌐ MAP 6-73   ¥·¥·¥

Make-up artist Rumiko's cosmetics label RMK is perfect for a milky white complexion. Their transparent RMK makeup base is a light foundation that delivers glow and evens skin tone too. The super basic powder is light and silky and adds a beautiful sheen. Their color theory is very different from other makeup artists in that it uses only a basic seven-color pastel shade chart, from light blues, pinks, beiges to greys—hues which work great when you try to get the smoldering eye effect or strong cheeks. They also do an exhaustive range of blushes and lipcolors. If you decide to buy some of their products, you can call and reserve a make-up lesson. And the staff will also help you apply a replenishing face mask and the latest nail polish.

ROBERTA DI CAMERINO
WOMEN'S ACCESSORIES

7-6-19 Ginza, Chuo-ku, Tokyo (Others)
03-3571-5970
www.robertadicamerino.com/
🕐 11:00–20:00 (Sun/Holidays untill 19:00)
🗓 No holidays
🚇 MAP 4-32 ¥|¥|¥|¥-¥|¥|¥|¥

In Roberta Di Camerino's shop, red soprarizzo velvet leads the way, and trompe l'oeil takes center stage in an ironic pop kind of way (but with Venetian good taste). Widely hailed as the first creator of an It bag in the 40s, their bags have been quietly sported by every-one from Coco Chanel to Madonna. Her Bagonghi handbag, made famous by Grace Kelly, can be found in this shop. The bag, which comes in two sizes in black and red velvet, has a small handle and opens up like a doctor's bag. The bag has also inspired a famous red and blue silk scarf where the Baghonghi appears in little motifs. They're adept at trompe l'oeil on satin, nappa leather, and suede, so if you are looking for something contemporary, do not hesitate to grab the classic scarlet and navy blue clutches or the really beau-tiful velvet wallets and clutches in the more contemporary beige. This tiny little shop also stocks some of her pretty pret-a-porter col-lections in trompe l'oeil that are as close to art as fashion gets.

ROEN
MEN'S/WOMEN'S DESIGNER

B1F, 3-6-19 Kita-Aoyama, Minato-ku, Tokyo (Others)
03-5468-6871
www.roen.jp/
🕐 11:00–20:00
🗓 No holidays
🚇 MAP 6-74 ¥|¥|¥|¥-¥|¥|¥|¥

Hiromu Tahara's world of skull and bones greets you as you step down the black and red stairs to his label's flagship store. Dark brooding collections in black whisper from the shelves as fanati-cal fans of this darling of the Tokyo Collection stock up on his long sleeved T-shirts with skull and crossbones, nylon blousons, deerskin coats, and Mickey sweats in black n' white. The shop also stocks Roen jeans, and reigning bad boys love his shoe line that has such stuff as python retro sneakers.

ROSE BUD
WOMEN'S BOUTIQUE

1-23-18 Shibuya, Shibuya-ku,
Tokyo (Others)
03-3797-3290
www.rosebud-web.com
🕐 11:00–20:00
📅 No holidays
ℾ MAP 8-38

¥¥¥

No one does trends better than Rose Bud! Must-have items for winter include leg warmers with chunky buttons, knit caps with fur, patchwork casquettes, cuddly sweaters, skinny denims, and lots of fur hobos. In summer this translates to silk bomber jackets, lightweight gilets, skimpy tops, and loads of really trendy sneakers, plus Adidas's hottest selling items. Among other things you can also find the cult classic skinny stretch jeans from JBrand, favorite of Kate Moss, Angelina Jolie, and Sienna Miller.

ROYAL CHIE LAVISH
FUR

Imperial Hotel B1F, 1-1-1 Uchisaiwai-cho,
Chiyoda-ku, Tokyo (Others)
03-3503-6344
www.chieexcellence.com/
🕐 10:00–19:00
📅 No holidays
ℾ MAP 4-33

¥¥¥¥¥

Furrier to the Japanese emperor and his family, Royal Chie's fur collection is designed by owner Chie Imai and produced in Finland. As expected of fur, her coats are lavish, but the difference she makes is in the use of color, lightness, and sometimes reversibility, features that are normally impossible to achieve. Her Mosaique series, for example, is made of pink, yellow, and blue mink pieces that are hand stitched together to create a coat that can be teamed with a dress without dwarfing it. She's revered for this technique, and each one of her coats is unique. Sometimes she combines different colors such as shades of gray, black, and navy blue to create a checkered effect never seen elsewhere. She also does tiny sleeveless fur jackets with matching mink scarves that look great with any outfit, casual or formal.

ROYAL FLASH
MEN'S/WOMEN'S/KIDS'
BOUTIQUE

6-18-8 Jingumae, Shibuya-ku,
Tokyo (Others)
03-3498-2973
www.royalflash-jp.com/
🕐 11:30–20:30
📅 Not fixed
ℾ MAP 6-75

¥¥¥¥-¥¥¥¥¥

A serious school of cool, this shop is not for the faint hearted. Designer casuals in LA gorgeous hippie and outlaw style led by Dolce & Gabbana for men, and Matthew Williamson and Rick Owens for women. Thomas Wylde's skull scarves and skull-studded handbags have also scored serious points with the ladies. However, those in the know come here in search of underground Japanese labels such as Le Grand Bleu's layered, reworked casuals T-shirts, denim shorts, jackets, or arty remakes from If Six Were Nine. The men's section is a lot more fun, though, with stressed pierced jeans also from If Six Were Nine, Junker trousers for real rock stars, and original American South Paradiso leather biker jackets perfectly structured to fit around rippling muscles. Dig Design for kids of rock royalty makes unbelievable outlaw rocker style mini-versions of T-shirts, trousers and skirts for kids.

RYKIEL WOMAN

WOMEN'S DESIGNER

28-7 Sarugakucho, Shibuya-ku, Tokyo (Others)
03-5428-8754
www.onward.co.jp
11:00–20:00
Wednesdays
MAP 2-48 ¥¥¥¥

Gifts, naughty and small, brought to you by the Rykiels. There are pillows in the shape of a women's breasts, pillows embroidered with the words "sex" and "happy," lacy underwear, lipstick and "come hither" T-shirts. They also do a great range of clothes for the gym, comfortable but daring in black and pink with crystal decoration, that you can accessorize with their yoga bag or black crystal studded dumbbells. The same black crystal is used in the hot designer pet carrier bag. With the lacy nothings and the toi and moi candles, you can get back in bed without leaving much to the imagination, and while the fashion-friendly sex toys have been taken off the shelf recently, there is still enough sexy items to keep the flame burning.

RYUGI

MEN'S/WOMEN'S/
PET'S BOUTIQUE

b6 3F, 6-28-103 Jingumae, Shibuya-ku, Tokyo (Others)
03-5778-0312
www.c-smen.com/
11:00–20:00
No holidays
MAP 6-76 ¥¥¥

A shop that sells the intimidating Japanese *yanki* style clothes. *Yankis* are Japanese patriotic youth who are attracted to right-wing ideas and love to use Chinese and Japanese characters to decorate their clothes and bikes. With shaved eyebrows and hairlines, the strong colors of their clothes, and a penchant for yakuza style, they are style blazers in their own right. This shop cuts down on the ideology and focuses on the clothes: silk bomber jackets with embroidered dragons, Chinese characters, and the word "Japan" embroidered in bright silk thread that can be accessorised with baseball hats and trainers that are in the same style too. They even do *yanki* vests and cardigans for pets.

SALOTTO

WOMEN'S BOUTIQUE

6-11-1 Minami-Aoyama, Minato-ku, Tokyo
03-5469-2015
www.salotto-inc.com/
🕐 11:00–20:00
📅 No holidays
📍 MAP 1-87   ¥|¥-¥|¥|¥|¥

Behind the huge wooden doors of Salotto lies a beautiful world of sartorial obsession with daytime luxury. The treasures here start with Japanese designer Mikako Nakamura, whose A-line cashmere jackets are the softest and most coveted in town. Nakamura's stuff is reasonable and comes with a life time guarantee. A great range of boots, pumps, and sandals from Proenza Schouler, Celine, and Manolo, along with a superb collection of Stella McCartney separates and Roberta di Camerino accessories in trompe l'oeil are other reasons to browse around here. Japanese designers include Mihoko Saito with Edwardian trend fabrics, tweed, and lace, denim from Lux Luft and Takei Ippei. They have an extensive wedding line too.

SAMANTHA KINGZ

MEN'S ACCESSORIES

4-29-4 Jingumae, Shibuya-ku, Tokyo (Others)
03-5775-4570
www.samantha.co.jp/
🕐 11:00–21:00
📅 Not fixed
📍 MAP 5-62   ¥|¥-¥|¥|¥

The Samantha Thavasa empire strikes again, this time for men. The recently opened shop is not something one would want to desperately hunt down, but behind its massive wooden doors lies a whole world of fun. Totes, briefcases, and hold-alls are the staple here, in wacky combinations and textures such as embossed croc and obvious inspiration from Bottega Veneta intericciato. Most totes announce their masculinity with dagger and skull motifs, while good taste gets snubbed with their leopard-print, fur wheeled bags and matching briefcases, flashing gold python-embossed bags and patent white bostons. If the bags sound like a joke, zero in on their superb collection of men's jewelry. Exquisitely crafted in sterling silver without the chunky street look of some Western jewelry designers, there are link bracelets, skull rings, crystal and chain necklaces, and beautifully carved square pendants, all nicely presented and safely androgynous.

SAMANTHA THAVASA

WOMEN'S ACCESSORIES

2-3-3 Ginza, Chuo-ku, Tokyo (Others)
03-5159-0527
www.samantha.co.jp/
🕐 11:00–20:00
📅 Not fixed
📍 MAP 3-24   ¥|¥-¥|¥|¥

It's not the bags, but the sizzling collaborations that make this accessories brand a hit among Japanese *kawaii* OL types. Celebrity mom Victoria Beckham put her pencil to paper and sketched a Boston bag in croco embossed leather for a chic answer to baby bags. They now come in a bright red, purple, yellow, and black, and apparently Mama Victoria uses one too. Sisters Penelope and Monica Cruz have designed a canary yellow Boston bag with big pockets and a gold metal chain strap. However, their best-selling bag was not designed by any celebrity. Called Orlare, this soft structured bag in textile with thread trimming, comes with curved wooden handles and in many colors and patterns. The shop also has an accessories corner with extremely delicate, pretty designs in sterling silver and 18K gold—some of which have been designed by the tennis star Maria Sharapova. The label also does bag designs that are watered-down versions of creations from Luella, Marc Jacobs, and Prada. The colors here might be spectacular and even though everyone loves Victoria and Penelope, the materials remain cheap, the embossing looks fake, and serious tastemakers leave confused.

SAMSONITE BLACK LABEL

LUGGAGE

8-6-3 Ginza, Chuo-ku, Tokyo
03-3571-8151
www.samsonite.co.jp/
⊘ 11:00–20:00
🗋 No holidays
⌲ MAP 4-34   ¥·¥·¥

In a spirit of dashing defiance, Samsonite has introduced the sizzling new Black Label, a collection that brings the best of technology and stylish design to the airport baggage carrousel. Marc Newson's suitcase trolleys in fruity colors come in backpack, duffle bags, and 55 cm and 63 cm sizes. Alexander McQueen has lent his hands to the collection with trolley cases of two white and black designs, a bone imprint and a croc emboss. (The white styles tend to run out as soon as they hit the shelves, but the shop continuously stocks the black ones.) Vintage shapes have inspired the Classic Collection series of cases that puts practicality into what were originally steamer trunks, and they come in all sizes, including a special moon-shaped vanity. And finally, the Xlite, a boon for those who need to travel light: the ultralight, steel gray and black suitcases with spacey looks will ensure envy wherever you go.

SANTA MARIA NOVELLA

PERFUMERY/COSMETICS

Ginza Komatsu 1F, 6-9-5 Ginza,
    Chuo-ku, Tokyo
03-3572-2694
www.santa-maria-novella.co.jp/
⊘ 10:30–19:30
🗋 No holidays
⌲ MAP 4-35   ¥·¥–¥·¥·¥

Santa Maria Novella, an old world apothecary (originally started in a monastery in 1221), comes to the posh alleys of Ginza from Florence's Piazza di Santa Maria Novella. In sparkling new cabinets that still retain old world charm are potions and vials of elixirs, like Eau de Cologne in thirty different fragrances from sandalwood to patchouli, triple distilled pure fragrances of almost every possible flower, and the same hand-blended, hand-wrapped perfection is poured into soaps. The aftershave lotions for men promise a big night out with exotic fragrances including Russian cologne and lavender, shaving foam with olive oil and cacao butter, and pomegranate aftershave cream. Baby oils, cream perfumes, and baby liquid soaps all come in separate boy and girl fragrances, and the most exhilarating collection yet is for the house—with carnations, verbena, sandalwood, and rose for the burner, iris and pomegranate candles, and lavender tablets for the closet.

SARTO TECNICO

MEN'S BOUTIQUE/DRYCLEANER

2-2-3 Marunouchi, Chiyoda-ku,
Tokyo (Others)
03-5220-5600
www.bassettwalker.com/
11:00–20:00
Not fixed
MAP 7-21 ¥¥-¥¥¥¥

For a gentleman's shop that caters only to preppy styles, the ambience still feels quite young and trendy. They do jackets in colors like yellow, red, and orange, as well as regular suit styles in luxe fabrics. But the best thing here is not on sale on the hangers, it is actually the dry cleaning. The shop takes orders for gentle care cleaning using distilled water for everything including suits, shawls, leather shoes, jackets, and even fur, and delivers undoubtedly the best rehabbing for your clothes in town.

SAVOIR VIVRE

INTERIOR

AXIS Bldg. 3F, 5–17-1 Roppongi,
Minato-ku, Tokyo
03-3585-7365
www.savoir-vivre.co.jp/home.htm
11:00–19:00
Not fixed
MAP 12-38 ¥¥¥-¥¥¥¥

Savoir Vivre is the shop for quirky, extremely artistic objets for the house. Created by Japanese potters, the shop also serves as an exhibition gallery of talented potters and glassblowers. Here, Japanese artists take you on a nostalgic trip through hand-blown vintage carved glassware, antique cutlery and other things that you'd love to be gifted with. Low on price and high on creativity, the shop never disappoints. Regular visits are a must as the shop frequently organizes exhibition-cum-sales of upcoming artists.

SAYA

INTERIOR

Tokyo Midtown, 9-7-1 Akasaka,
Minato-ku, Tokyo
03-5413-0709
www.shop-saya.com/
11:00–21:00
Not fixed
MAP 12-39 ¥¥¥¥

A Tokyo design shop that at last explores home territory, with the first dedicated collection of the country's genius postwar product designer, Sori Yanagi. He was so prolific that he designed almost everything from the torch of the 1964 Olympic games to tractors. This shop stocks only his kitchen tools, though, such as his 1953 aluminum kettle, the 1250 cutlery series and others. But no shop like this would be complete without his most well known creation—the butterfly stool, which he designed in 1954 using his architectural sensibilities at a time when East and West were coming closer. The stool is designed so as not to injure the rice straw weaving of tatami floors. This *from Japan with love* collection is not just wonderfully edited, it comes at great prices too.

SAYEGUSA
KIDS'

7-8-8.Ginza, Chuo-ku, Tokyo
03-3573-2441
www.sayegusa.com/
🕐 10:30—19:30
📅 No holidays
📍 MAP 4-36   ¥ ¥ ¥ ¥-¥ ¥ ¥ ¥ ¥

Sayegusa remains the ultimate shopping destination for children's fashion, ages 0-12, in Tokyo. Set up in 1869, they are not only the suppliers of clothes for children of the Japanese imperial family but they stock collections from the latest and best of children's fashions from around the world. Lately, the accent has been on the whimsical cotton and denim collections from British label Cara-mel, and also the simple rustic dresses and cashmere from Marni. Shoes are a forte too, with the original Car shoes in several colors, children's Stride-Rite Mary Janes and Hunter rain boots. Sayegusa understandably is proud of their silk dresses and smoking and party outfits with matching handbags bags and velvet hats. Car coats, pea coats, trench coats, rain coats with umbrellas, outer wear from Napapijri, and other ideas like soft toys in felt, invite you to splurge. The basement has their collection of bespoke tailoring for girls' and boys' school uniforms or formal attire. A mighty collection for kids in desperate need of preppyness.

S BY GLOBE SPECS
MEN'S/WOMEN'S EYEWEAR/ ACCESSORIES

Andos Bldg. 3F, 1-7-5 Jinnan, Shibuya-ku, Tokyo (Others)
03-5728-5628
www.globespecs.co.jp/
🕐 11:00—20:00
📅 Not fixed
📍 MAP 8-38   ¥ ¥ ¥ ¥

S stands for statement and this shop makes you giddy with a superb collection of hats, eyewear, and accessories. They stock trilbies by the one-hundred-year-old Viennese hat maker Muhlbauer, bowlers, golf hats, floppy hats, and Tracy Watts' fedoras, recognizable as the same model worn by Madonna on the cover of her album *Music*. Combine this with real vintage Americana—necklaces and ear-rings in coral, turquoise, bakelite, lucite and hand-carved bone. For a contemporary kick, the very underground Derome Brenner can play with acetate like no one else, with retro-chic 50s style loops, bracelets, and rings. And as the parent company has the coolest eyewear shop in town you'll find great vintage eyewear with 70s Pucci, Cazal, Dior, Alain Mikli, and Anne et Valentin. S by Globe Specs also offers "La Loop," great statements in the form of chains that go around the neck and end in a loop in the front, for fashionably dangling your sunnies. "La Loop" makes these in matt sterling hammered links, braided leather, and stones such as agate, turquoise, and coral. Despite the tiny size of the shop, the collections remain dynamite, with perpetual cool.

SCYE
MEN'S/WOMEN'S DESIGNER

District United Arrows 2F, 5–17–9 Jingu-mae, Shibuya–ku, Tokyo
03–5464–2715
www.scye.co.jp/
⊙ 12:00–20:00 (Sat/Sun/Holidays 11:00–20:00)
🏢 No holidays
👠 MAP 6-77   ¥|¥|¥-¥|¥|¥|¥

Scye, pattern-cutters extraordinaire, make clothes inspired from vintage English tailoring. Try their white leather motorcycle jacket for speed, or the knit jacket with a winning straight silhouette. Their masterful draping and stylish creasing give each item its own special character. Mostly in white and ecru with pure clean and very classic lines, other great must-have items include jute dresses and simple cotton jackets. In spring make a beeline for their two-button pinstripe jackets and smart peacoats in cotton and linen.

SEE BY CHLOÉ
WOMEN'S DESIGNER

La Foret Harajuku 1F, 1–11-6 Jingumae, Shibuya-ku, Tokyo (Others)
03-3478-5781
www.chloe.com/
⊙ 11:00–20:00
🏢 No holidays
👠 MAP 5-63   ¥|¥|¥|¥

Chloé fans thank the gods for the See by Chloé diffusion line that is as fun and striking as Chloé, and infinitely more wallet pleasing. The See by Chloé white shift is a neat little dress with an embroidered bib and puffed sleeves. There are denim shorts and blouses with ruffles, lots of vintage-inspired dresses, high-waisted culottes, and jacquard turtleneck dresses. For nighttime there are party dresses made for sirens, with short hemlines you can pair with dark silk tuxedo jackets. If you are dazzled with all this and don't know where to splurge, close your eyes and rush for the perfect pair of black pants—choose from the longer wider option, the cropped option and the dark skinny jeans option.

SEMPRE

INTERIOR

5-13-3 Minami-Aoyama, Minato-ku, Tokyo (Others)
03-5464-5655
www.sempre.jp/
🕐 11:00–20:00 (Sun/Holidays untill 19:00)
📅 No holidays
🍴 MAP 1-88　¥¥-¥¥¥¥

The yellow flag outside marks this design milestone. Ten years or so ago, Sempre started out as a purveyor of simply nice tableware design. Today, the owner is a major voice in the design industry and has amassed really practical usable designs from all over the world. Wastepaper flower vases from the hot Philippine designer Mind Masters, designer rugs from Spanish designer Nani Marquina hand woven in India, and unusual in Tokyo—great jars of paint in many colors for walls, Romanian glass pieces and rolls of curtain cloth and sofa fabric. The total solution concept also offers extensive furniture and tableware solutions. The only problem with such great shops is that once you step in you want to live there and never leave.

SERGE THORAVAL

MEN'S/WOMEN'S ACCESSORIES

5-1-14 Jingumae, Shibuya-ku, Tokyo
03-5485-0271
www.hpfrance.com/serge_catalog/
🕐 11:00–20:00
📅 Not fixed
🍴 MAP 6-78　¥¥¥-¥¥¥¥

Serge Thoraval's tragic death in a motorcycle crash has not stopped his creations from reaching thinking people all around the world. This shop is dedicated to this self-taught metallurgist, whose best known creation is the maille series of silver mesh with crystals. They come in rings, bracelets, earrings, and pendants, and have spawned innumerable imitations. But for those who prefer something quiet, consider his poetic Cyrano de Bergerac seven ring set, the Bible series, the series of jewelry engraved with Paul Eluard's words, or simply the exquisite set of rings inspired by the five senses. It all has a breathtaking beaten-metal appearance and comes in sizes for men and women. The shop also undertakes special orders in gold that could serve as wedding bands with a superb style statement.

SERGIO ROSSI

MEN'S/WOMEN'S SHOES

3-2-3 Marunouchi, Chiyoda-ku, Tokyo (Others)
03-5220-7751
www.sergiorossi.com
🕐 11:00–20:00
📅 No holidays
🍴 MAP 7-22　¥¥¥¥-¥¥¥¥¥

Never too decorative, Sergio Rossi makes perfectly fitted boots, wedges, slip-ons, and pumps, with the occasional chain or button for decoration. If you're really in the mood to splurge, you can also order made-to-measure square-toe pumps, ankle boots with heels, knee-length boots, and a fantastic round-toe riding boot with a double side zip. Each of these trophies cost two million yen each. So for everyday wear you might want to stick to the simpler calf leather ideas in beige, black, pink and green that for some seasons are released in Klein blue, red white polka dot, copper, white mesh or dazzling gold.

SETU&KNIT

WOMEN'S BOUTIQUE

3-4-1 Ginza, Chuo-ku, Tokyo
03-3535-8061
None
11:00–19:00
Sun/Holidays
MAP 3-25
¥¥¥

Setu&Knit is a tiny little shop that has been stocking plus-year wool knits for a couple of decades now. The collections here favor older madams and are knitted for comfort, so they come in one size and balloon volumes and bell sleeves that are at once pretty, youthful and warm. So confident are they of the benefits of their fabric, they even suggest wearing the collection in summer.

SEXY DYNAMITE QUEEN WITH VIVIENNE WESTWOOD MUSEUM

VINTAGE

1-20-11 Jingumae, Shibuya-ku, Tokyo
03-3423-5737
www.sexydynamitelondon.com
11:00–20:00
Not fixed
MAP 5-64
¥¥-¥¥¥

You will find a great guide in owner Shinoda Makoto, a hardcore fan; he has been following Vivienne around since 1976 after meeting the Sex Pistols. Stocking the cult mini crinis, along with Vivienne creations from '88-'94, and other stuff which even Vivienne famously denies wearing anymore. Don't expect to find much of the recent Red and Gold labels, though.

SHANGHAI TANG

MEN'S/WOMEN'S BOUTIQUE

5-6-16 Ginza, Chuo-ku, Tokyo
03-3569-8801
www.shanghaitang.com
11:00–20:00
No holidays
MAP 4-37
¥¥¥¥

While all major Europe fashion houses have their profits firmly fertilized by Japanese soil, it took years for this most Asian of Asian brands to come to Tokyo. A sexy take on the olden languid days of tango-dancing, pre-communist Shanghai, all the clothes are lined in their trademark hot pink satin. Mini cheongsams, cashmere sweaters, mandarin jackets, notebooks and pajamas all made of classic Chinese silk. The hot colors, flowing fabrics and oriental weaves make you want to leave with at least something small for your next Asian sojourn. Consider the Mao watches, or the silver-plated dim sum baskets, the ma hwa teddy bears or the jasmine room perfume. Another favorite, notably among young mommies, is the hot red silk diaper bag and the colorful floral trainers. If you can't see yourself in these clothes, reconsider, because their jeans fit great and their clothes are distinctly less oriental in taste than previously.

SHARE SPIRIT
MEN'S/WOMEN'S DESIGNER

14-10 Hachiyama-cho, Shibuya-ku, Tokyo
03-3462-4390
sharespirit.jp/
🕐 11:00–20:00
📅 No holidays
🔱 MAP 2-49   ¥¥¥-¥¥¥¥

Designer, traveler, archaeologist and poet Hikaru Kitano's flagship offers a bohemian spirit with antique clothes from far flung desti-nations, painstakingly recreated and made wearable. A threadbare soldier's jacket fringed with antique Afghan coins, a 300-year-old Inca fabric of vicuna wool made into a sweater or a must-have leather bag with ancient Indian imagery, Kitano's creations are incredibly beautiful, glamorous and purposely stressed. All the leather is braided by his close friends from an Aztec village in Mexico—a place, it is rumored, where he's the sole foreigner to have ever visited

SHIBUYA FRONTIER
MEN'S/WOMEN'S SHOES

1-16-3 Jinnan, Shibuya-ku,
  Tokyo (Others)
03-3464-4579
www.shibuya-frontier.com/
🕐 10:00–21:00
📅 No holidays
🔱 MAP 8-39   ¥¥-¥¥¥¥

This dusty shop with shoes strewn all over is the city's favorite haunt for the elevated platform sole. It has been revered by every fashion insider, from Salvatore Ferragamo to the young Japanese *kogaru*. So while high platforms might be out of daily life now, this shop still stocks the most outrageous kinds—think Naomi Campbell, who fell down on the catwalk in eight-inch Vivienne Westwood platforms. The stock here extends to the realm of sports shoes (especially a huge range from American Buffalo Boots). Think platform athletic boots that go up to a staggering ten inches in height, and loads of other regular stuff—like cowboy boots in precious leathers.

SHINZONE

WOMEN'S BOUTIQUE

5-2-7 Jingumae, Shibuya-ku, Tokyo
03-5774-1450
www.shinzone.com/
11:00–20:00
No holidays
MAP 6-79 ¥¥¥-¥¥¥¥

Shinzone is a nice little basement boutique that puts a halt to any bling-bling fantasy by serving up simple things that are really important to the weekend closet. Linen shorts, silk trenchcoats, pale cotton cashmere knits, silk ruched camisoles, corduroy pants, skinny denims, and jute Bermuda pants Whatever the season, they always offer really comfortable day looks that pay no attention to aggressive femininity. For the men's collection, head to their Ginza branch.

SHIPS LITTLE BLACK

MEN'S/WOMEN'S BOUTIQUE

1-5-4 Ginza, Chuo-ku, Tokyo (Others)
03-3561-0552
m.shipsltd.co.jp
11:00–20:00
Not fixed
MAP 3-26 ¥¥-¥¥¥

Ships is the oldest fashion import shop in Japan. Set up more than three decades ago, the shop was once high on the fashion charts with a range of American casuals and Mulberry bags. In its current incarnation, Ships is a popular shopping destination for office ladies as they stock a style that is simple and basic, yet stylish. Famous for stocking knit sets of pullovers and cardigans all the year round, along with Mackintosh jackets, polka dots and striped camisoles with lace. Combine this with the best riding boots from French Sartor, Faliero Sarti's scarves in silk cashmere combinations, and pretty Pierre Hardy pumps, and the look is full of uncontrived style. The shop still remains loyal to the Mulberry label so you can find the Roxanne and other popular numbers. And if you decide to really pamper yourself, this is the only place in the world that sells loafers and tango shoes from Silvano Lattanzi in the softest of calf and lamb leather. They come with their own polish and pieces of leather to repair the sole, and are rumored to last a lifetime.

SHISEIDO

COSMETICS

8-8-3 Ginza, Chuo-ku, Tokyo (Others)
03-3572-3913
www.shiseido.co.jp/com/
11:00–21:00
No holidays
MAP 4-38 ¥¥-¥¥¥

Japanese cosmetics giant and sole distributor worldwide of cult perfume Serge Lutens, Shiseido have had many near mythical greats. Set up more than a hundred years ago, Shiseido were the first purveyors of fluoride toothpaste in Japan in 1888. More than a century later, they are well-known for their extensively researched and technologically advanced beauty care. Among the thousands of products on display here is the Eudermine lotion, in a beautiful red bottle, a more than one-century-old formula that provides perfect moisturizing balance for the skin. With the Japanese passion for milky white skin, Shiseido has also come up with the perfect blemish removers. Their age-defying SKII series is legendary for its use of Pitera, a blend of vitamins, amino acids, proteins, and organic acids that work together to bring about a seemingly miraculous rebirth of the skin through stimulation and renewal of the outer layer, allowing the skin's natural rejuvenation process to function at its most efficient level. Pitera is only sourced from one place in the world, a sake brewery in Japan. The extensive men's collection does not have the hype of the women's, but is highly rated especially for the emulsion.

SHOSAIKAN
STATIONERY

5-13-11 Minami-Aoyama, Minato-ku, Tokyo
03-3400-3377
www.shosaikan.co.jp
🕐 11:00–20:00
📅 Not fixed
🍴 MAP 1-89   ¥|¥-¥|¥

A trip to Shosaikan is a pilgrimage for connoisseurs of fine writing. Undoubtedly the world's best pen shop, with 2500 pens from 35 different brands, Shosaikan also stocks antique stationery, exquisite letter writing paper, ink, and pen accessories. To lovers of fine pens, Shosaikan's collection of limited editions from Faber Castell, Waterman, Montegrappa, and Parker is intoxicating. Looking for a real museum piece? The 1930 Alfred Dunhill-Namiki pen is available here with an 18k gold nib and lacquered embellished barrel. From the classic Mont Blanc range to Lamy, Aurora, Pilot, Cross, Visconti, Sailor, Cartier, Sailor, and Waterman, Shosaikan does not make light work of writing. Their wide selection of inks, like those from Must de Cartier, is impressive too, and comes in bottles that serve as excellent decoration on your desk. For those who have it all, the final word is the Japanese traditional Butokai pen—a bracelet that miraculously transforms into a pen with its own nib.

SHOYEIDO
INTERIOR/PERFUMERY

Pine Village 2F, 5-47-13 Jingumae, Shibuya-ku, Tokyo
03-5774-4406
www.shoyeido.co.jp
🕐 10:00–19:00
📅 Wednesdays
🍴 MAP 6-80   ¥-¥|¥|¥|¥

For some reason, home perfume and haute couture seems to be going hand in hand of late, and the interest in fragrant air at home has never been higher (think John Galliano , Bottega Venetta, or the more reclusive Lucien Pellat-Finet). But it is incense, not candles, that real fragrance connoisseurs and designers want, and this 300-year-old shop provides the same—in the Japanese variety of sticks, cones, and coils. Most of the fragrances are derived from precious woods, herbs, and leaves, and the best way to enjoy them is to burn them in ash, as they demonstrate in the shop. An easier method is to buy one of their plug-in fragrance diffusers. Incense pouches are available for clothes, wardrobes, cars, wallets, and even letters and visiting cards. The shop also runs demonstrations by appointment on the art of enjoying Japanese incense—called *kodo*—and how to best blend and layer fragrances.

SHU UEMURA

COSMETICS

5-1-3 Jingumae, Shibuya-ku,
Tokyo (Others)
03-3486-0048
www.shu-uemura.co.jp/
🕐 12:00–20:00
📅 Wednesdays
🎵 MAP 6-81   ¥¥-¥¥¥

Shu Uemura is a genius with the brush. Proof of this is in his foundation bar, eye-shadow bar, the tools of the trade that are on sale here and the unequivocal favorite, the lash bar. No woman leaves this shop without feeling and looking ecstatic. Colors have always been his forte. Take, for example, the Rouge Unlimited lipstick series that comes in 48 colors, including green, black, blue, yellow, white, red, and purple. The tiny room at the back stocks his complete range of cosmetics and other winners, like the deep seawater spray for the face and the high performance balancing cleansing oil packaged in four lively bottles with sketches from different artists like John Trembley and Ai Yamaguchi. Tips, tricks and tactics on how to wield the brush to your own face are given in one-on-one private classes upstairs.

SIDE BY SIDE

MEN'S/WOMEN'S BOUTIQUE

La Foret Harajuku 2.5F, 1-11-6 Jingumae,
Shibuya-ku, Tokyo
03-5775-1975
www.sidebyside.jp/
🕐 11:00–20:00
📅 No holidays
🎵 MAP 5-65   ¥¥¥-¥¥¥¥

This great ambassador of Cool Britannia stocks some of the best graduates of Central St. Martins and the hottest streetwear from Japanese designers. Colorful, printed Ts from Philip Normal are flying off the shelf along with unisex Japanese brand Alexander Lee Chang and the cult Noki's superb graphic shirts. The shop has achieved iconic status, having launched the careers of designers such as Marios Schwab and Daisuke Sakaguchi, a Londoner of Japanese origin whose grafitti-inspired oversized silver accessories have followers such as David Beckham and Elton John. Women can check out great knitwear from Japanese Mint design and SDTR Tokyo. Side by Side is the only shop where you can buy Top Shop's side line Top Man design. A note of caution, though—most of the pieces are one-offs made specially for this store, so sizes and quantities are seriously limited.

SIGERSON MORRISON

WOMEN'S SHOES

Roppongi Hills Keyakizaka St., 6-9-1
Roppongi, Minato-ku, Tokyo (Others)
03-5414-3893
www.sigersonmorrison.com
⊘ 11:00–20:00
▦ No holidays
⌐ MAP 12-40   ¥|¥|¥-¥|¥|¥

The trend in flat shoes started by and personified by Audrey Hepburn has made a comeback, thanks to a lot of people—including Sigerson Morrison. Every season they come up with flats in the juiciest of colors in pump styles in leather, patent, suede, and brightly colored vinyl. In winter they take on the luscious flavors of strawberry, pansies, dahlias, and ivory. While flat shoes are what they do really, really well, their heels are exquisitely crafted too, and keep the interest high in the same luscious colors.

SISLEY

MEN'S/WOMEN'S BOUTIQUE

4-11-6 Jingumae, Shibuya-ku,
Tokyo (Others)
03-5510-3166
www.sisley.com
⊘ 11:00–20:00
▦ Not fixed
⌐ MAP 5-66   ¥|-¥|¥

A Benetton label through and through right to the striking ads (the Sisley ones are about half-naked high-wattage girls), this label sells a bit more than basics at great prices. Oddly enough, the bad girl ads somehow don't translate into Sisley looks, which are preppy straightforward dresses, black and grey suits, cardigans and sweaters, A-line skirts, and—in the winter—a range of coats in many colors. Good quality at decent prices and absolutely without any danger to men.

SKECHERS

MEN'S/WOMEN'S/KIDS' SHOES

1-1-12 Kichijoji-honmachi, Musashino-
shi, Tokyo
0422-20-8530
www.skechers-jpn.com/
⊘ 11:00–20:00
▦ Not fixed
⌐ MAP 19-1   ¥|-¥|¥

Low on the fashion radar but high in fun content, low in price but super high on comfort, Skechers have been made famous by a shot of faux preppy, mini-clad Britney Spears jumping high in them. Sneakers with thick sporty soles, Skechers come in many colors and shapes, including a trainer mule that's perfect for weekends when you are in and out of the house. They also do great-for-biking men's leather boots and sandals and sneakers for kids.

SLEEPING FOREST

WOMEN'S BOUTIQUE

GB Bldg. 2F, 5-17-24 Jingumae, Shibuya-
ku, Tokyo
03-5766-3015
www.hpfrance.com/Shop/Brand/
sleepingforest.html
🕐 12:00–20:00
📅 No holidays
⌖ MAP 6-82

¥¥¥

Sleeping Forest is the girl's hope after shopping for the boyfriend at nearby Cannabis. This is a much more gamine version though, having been inspired from Walt Disney stories (imagine Mickey Mouse in an artsy, dark minimalist way). Delicate and ultra feminine collections from Obstinacy, Trovata, and Kin line the racks. With a penchant for lace, crochet, polka dots, and other essential girly trimmings, the shop might not be as lofty as Cannabis, but will not leave the fashionista disappointed with its vintage and classic romanticism. Menfolk have not been left behind here with a neat collection of clothes from German Frank Leder and Japanese brand Motel.

SLOW-FLOW

YOGA

Aoyama Bell Commons 3F, 2-14-6 Kita-
Aoyama, Minato-ku, Tokyo
03-3475-8102
www.slow-flow.com
🕐 11:00–20:00
📅 Not fixed
⌖ MAP 16-8

¥¥-¥¥¥

Just being here feels good; if yoga is your passion, this shop is your elixir. With a line of 100 percent organic cotton clothing among a huge selection of tops, fleeces, pajamas for both women and men, and outerwear for going to the gym, the place supplies a perfect wardrobe for inner reflection. Of course, not only do they have a superb collection of yoga mats and fashion friendly bags to carry them in, but also a series of yoga DVDs, music, aroma oils, and yogini soaps. There's even aromatherapy for the car-bound—a diffuser that plugs into the cigarette lighter of the dashboard.

SONIA RYKIEL

MEN'S/WOMEN'S DESIGNER

3-4-12 Ginza, Chuo-ku, Tokyo (Others)
03-3535-7071
www.soniarykiel.com/
🕐 11:00–13:30,14:30–19:30
📅 No holidays
⌖ MAP 3-27

¥¥¥¥¥

Madame Rykiel created her trademark striped sexy knitwear in the sixties; she was expecting and could not find a sweater to cover her burgeoning belly. As a symbol of French fashion, Sonia Rykiel is revered for her classic knits—sweaters, knit tunics, pants, and coats—all with unrivalled detailing, like perfectly balanced tucks, pinching, and ribbing. Her fabric lines are equally fashionable, complementing her knit lines with bias-cut dresses with big corsages and bows. While the designer herself is at the end of her career, watch out for her daughter, Natalie, who's trying something new and naughty!

SONY PLAZA

INTERIOR, ETC.

Sony Bldg. B2F/B1F, 5-3-1 Ginza, Chuo-ku, Tokyo (Others)
03-3575-2525
www.sonyplaza.com/
🕐 11:00–21:00
📅 No holidays
📍 MAP 4-39

¥-¥¥¥

An insanely large amount of imported stuff for your house, pet, nails, shoes, and all else. Be careful. Even if you don't need anything, you'll end up purchasing something here. You may find that it ends up being pretty useful, in fact, like the plastic nail polish protectors that stay put on your fingers while the paint dries, a beautiful *Havaianas* selection where you can mix and match colorful straps to the base, sock stickers that keep your socks up, and other sundry articles. No matter how much you resist, this shop will end up taking weight off your purse.

SOS

MEN'S/WOMEN'S SURF AND SKI SHOP

2-8-3 Jiyugaoka, Meguro-ku, Tokyo
03-3725-8169
www.sossportswear.com/
🕐 12:00–20:00
📅 Wednesdays
📍 MAP 11-13

¥¥-¥¥¥

This shop, in its pretty little Jiyugaoka surroundings, is run by two surf and ski enthusiasts who are more at home in the wilderness than in the heart of one of Tokyo's shopping districts. Their labor of love has been to offer the best of surfwear in the summer and skiwear in the winter, and most of it is imported from Sweden. (They are the only retailer in Tokyo for some of the most wanted brands in these sports.) Their biggest collection is from SOS (Sportswear of Sweden), who are particularly good at ski wear, with solid parka pant sets, ice shelter jackets, and stretch jackets and pants with water proof zips, goggle wipes and superb colors like concrete, mustard, dark orange, and purple—and beautiful flowery prints for women. They also stock midlayers from Houdini's collection of fleeces, shorts, bras, long johns, crew necks, boxers, headbands, and hats. If you insist on turning your piste into a catwalk then there is none other than J. Lindberg ski wear in white, black, and a touch of olive. There is also loads of gear for the consummate city player, including ultra lightweight primaloft jackets that are warmer than down jackets, super quick-drying T-shirts, and—if you have acclimatized to the idea of wearing sandals with socks—the shop has a huge variety of ankle-length ones, all handknit by a lovely 90-year-old Japanese lady.

SPIRAL

INTERIOR

5-6-23 Minami-Aoyama, Minato-ku, Tokyo
03-3498-1171
www.spiral.co.jp/
🕐 11:00–20:00
📅 No holidays
✆ MAP 1-90   ¥|¥|¥-¥|¥|¥|¥

Don't be fooled by the empty spaces. This shop is the hottest bed for experimental household design, with plenty of one-off creations that are only sold here. Brainchild of the car modeler Nichinan, the store also sells products from designer Kuramata Shiro. Leave with great solutions for everyday life, such as the KaYaRiKi mosquito coil stand –a sleek square with two slabs balancing the coil in the centre—adjustable hangers, toilet signs, and flower vases. Try also the Nautilius, a Star Wars-like travel clock in ultra light PVC, definitely the most stylish on the planet. As the aim is experimentation rather than profit, the low prices, high-design performance make it one of Tokyo's best kept design secrets.

SPIRAL MARKET

INTERIOR

Spiral Bldg. 2F, 5-6-23 Minami-Aoyama, Minato-ku, Tokyo
03-3498-5792
www.spiral.co.jp/market/
🕐 11:00–20:00
📅 No holidays
✆ MAP 1-91   ¥|¥-¥|¥|¥

Refreshingly free of typical design shop theatrics, Spiral Market offers clean, cheap and practical design solutions from stationery and toiletry to wooden toys, ribbons, wrapping, paper, flower vases and aromatherapy. Since the craze for haute Japanese pottery sees no sign of abating, discerning designers and collectors are coming here to stock up on the contemporary Japanese aesthetic at the best prices. Designs here buck the rough, chunky trend with simple colors and pretty shapes for glasses, bowls, mugs and plates, all arranged in an exhibition-cum-shop style display.

STEFANEL

WOMEN'S DESIGNER

Aoyama Bell Commons 3F, 2-14-6 Kita-Aoyama, Minato-ku, Tokyo (Others)
03-3475-8130
www.stefanel.it
🕐 11:00–20:00
📅 Not fixed
✆ MAP 16-9   ¥|¥|¥-¥|¥|¥|¥

Stefanel's location in the Bell Commons building might be as understated as its collection, but this is where regulars head when they want to get the looks for less. Winter sees knits that the label is best at. Knit camisoles, sweaters, cardigans, and coats line the racks along with a row of sensible boots and accessories. Summer sees a similar range in cotton, jute, and other natural fabrics that is perfectly office-friendly, with carefully paired pant and skirt suits in pastel colors, camisole tops, shirts, and skirts casual enough for after-five outings.

STEPHAN SCHNEIDER

MEN'S/WOMEN'S DESIGNER

6-1-3 Jingumae, Shibuya-ku, Tokyo
03-3486-0377
www.joix-corp.com/
🕙 11:00–20:00
📅 No holidays
MAP 6-82　¥|¥|¥-¥|¥|¥

Stephan Schneider's work at a passing glance could be mistaken as daywear and he would like it to be considered as such. But while this brooding Belgian romantic's (he is originally German but has trained and now lives in Antwerp) designs could be worn daily, it is anything but ubiquitous glam. Take for example his simple coordination that conveys a rich formality with tailored trousers and jackets. No obsession with details or overtly dynamic silhouettes but elegance in a stony palette with a bit of color here and there. Daily wear means consistency and comfort so he dares to use the same fabrics for men and women. This makes his womenswear sharp and powerful and brings beauty to menswear. Slightly grungy, very subversive and appropriately unshagalicious, it is, of course, a favorite among Tokyo's fashion invincibles, and so this is his only flagship outside Antwerp.

ST.JAMES

MEN'S/WOMEN'S/KIDS'
BOUTIQUE

1-34-26 Ebisu-nishi, Shibuya-ku, Tokyo
03-3464-7123
www.st-james.jp/
🕙 11:00–20:00
📅 No holidays
MAP 2-50　¥|¥-¥|¥|¥

No-nonsense stripes are what St. James is good at. This French knitwear label is well known for its marine stripes that come in all colors under the sun. They do 100% cotton jerseys and pullover knits in superb colors that can be matched with sensible outdoor shoes that they sell here especially Spanish ballerina flats. While the adults' styles remain a tad too simple, the same marine style in cotton looks great on kids 0-7 and comes with matching jackets and shorts.

ST. JOHN

WOMEN'S DESIGNER

5-6-13 Ginza, Chuo-ku, Tokyo (Others)
03-5537-2747
www.sjk.com
🕙 11:00–19:00
📅 No holidays
MAP 4-40　¥|¥|¥|¥-¥|¥|¥|¥|¥

When Kelly Grey said goodbye after 22 years and handed over the St. John's brand ambassadorship to Gisele Bündchen and Angelina Jolie, there was a lot of whispering around in the fashion world. Were their decades-old-perfect suit combinations going to suddenly sizzle? St. John was created in 1962 when model Marie Grey (Kelly

Grey's mum) made her own knit dress for her honeymoon. She then patented her trademark cloth, which uses wool and rayon fibers for crease-free, functional suits that have long been loved by women. Everything is made in their own factory, right down to the buttons. Not much has changed with its suits, thankfully, which have been worn by women like Hillary Clinton. Since 2006, they have been trying to shed their slightly frumpy office image and are gearing up to woo the younger generation. While they might be quite far away from launching a jeans collection, their couture and evening lines are bringing them new fans.

STOMP STAMP

KIDS'

Roppongi Hills Hill Side B2F, 6-10-2 Roppongi, Minato-ku, Tokyo
03-5413-3060
www.stompstamp.com/
🕐 11:00–20:00
📅 No holidays
🗺 MAP 12-41   ¥-¥¥¥¥

A convenient kid's shop that has looks for little Jennifer Annistons and Tom Cruises. The huge collection is arranged around the shop with Etro polos, jeans, sweaters, shirts, and jackets that could be styled from playschool to more formal moments. Shoes are fun here and include Hunter boots and Ugg Shearling slip-ons. While most of the styling is predictable, it's the accessories that are attention grabbing, with Juicy Couture, Swatch, and a whole line of amazing bags that make choosing for your kids very difficult.

STRASBURGO

MEN'S/WOMEN'S BOUTIQUE

3-18-1 Minami-Aoyama, Minato-ku, Tokyo
03-5772-6515
www.strasburgo.co.jp
🕐 11:00–20:00
📅 No holidays
🗺 MAP 1-92   ¥¥¥¥-¥¥¥¥¥

Strasburgo is certainly the best personal shopper you could have ever had. It boasts hand-picked designer casuals and formals from Givenchy, Nina Ricci, Alexander McQueen, Giambattista Valli, and Rochas, plus superb basic knits from Cruciani. If your budget allows you to buy just one thing, let it be a pair of killer formal trousers. Strasburgo stocks at least twenty different kinds every season; they make you look tall and slim and are perfect for any event. For an instant foot lift, there is none other than shoemaker Rene Caovilla with his bejeweled sandals, of which Strasburgo stocks around twenty varieties. Also find the nicest hats in town from Firenzere Marzi. The men's floor is upstairs, but you could safely give it a miss—unless you are the preppy type with a penchant for expensive, really conservative stuff.

STÜSSY

MEN'S/WOMEN'S CASUAL

4-28-2 Jingumae, Shibuya-ku, Tokyo (Others)
03-3479-6432
www.stussy.com
12:00–20:00
Not fixed
MAP 5-67
¥-¥¥

The Stussy tribe loves to DJ, go for raves, and generally hang out on the street. The oversized T-shirts and hoodies are a particular favorite, ideally worn with really low-waist baggy jeans, chunky accessories, and baseball hats tilted to the side (oh yes, and designer eyewear). Most of the stuff is decorated with the Stussy logo and men's and women's clothes are almost identical—but for the size.

SUIKINCHIKA-MOKUDOTTEN-MEIKAI

WOMEN'S BOUTIQUE/ ACCESSORIES

La Foret Harajuku 3F, 1-11-6 Jingumae, Shibuya-ku, Tokyo
03-5411-2705
www.hpfrance.com/suikin/
11:00–20:00
No holidays
MAP 5-68
¥¥-¥¥¥

Accessories here have an arts and crafts feel, albeit with a razor-sharp contemporary edge. Japanese nihonga paintings in gold and blood red on a bracelet provide the perfect splash of color for a lazy dress, lacquerware earrings are bright, shiny, feather light and so easy to wear. Bits and pieces of turquoise, silver bells, cord, horn, and bones are often threaded together to make necklaces and bracelets that have a certain amount of presence but don't dwarf your personality. And as this is Japan—meaning a love for all things delicate and ephemeral—the chunky silver jewelry often found in such shops in other parts of the world, here takes a turn toward the wonderfully light, with pretty chains and demure pendants. To go with all the jewelry, the shop also has a neat collection of washed-leather jackets and bags, wool and cotton skirts, plus dusty looking shoes for a superb look, ideal for that cocktail party at the end of, say, the Paris-Dakar rally.

SUNAO KUWAHARA

WOMEN'S DESIGNER

LaFuente Daikanyama Main Bldg. 1F, 11-1 Sarugakucho, Shibuya-ku, Tokyo (Others)
03-5728-2897
www.a–net.com
11:00–20:00
No holidays
MAP 2-51
¥¥¥-¥¥¥¥

Popular with Tokyo's arty, articulate, and sometimes nerdy types, Kuwahara is actually the designer of a really moody, sweet label, taking trends and cutting them up to suit his own tastes. In this beautifully laid out, spacious boutique with its wooden interior, he has, for example, taken the balloon trend and worked at it with great fervor, successfully disfiguring it into a double layered skirt with a jagged hemline, which keeps the volume but avoids the pumpkin look with a really pretty tulip shape, at once arty and beautiful. His jackets and sweaters too are deconstructed, often in subdued plaid but with surprises like chiffon detailing. His clothes have a vintage feel and never go out of fashion.

SUN'S COURT
INTERIOR

Hill Side Terrace C, 29-10 Sarugaku-cho, Shibuya-ku, Tokyo (Others)
03-5458-5950
www.sbfoods.co.jp/sunsc/
🕐 11:00–19:30
🗓 No holidays
📍 MAP 2-52

¥-¥¥¥

On offer are more than a thousand soothing ideas for those at work or play or on the move. The best of these are the Artechnicas range of cut-out garlands in metal that look great on any window or lamp; a huge range of herbal teas and tea makers to soothe frazzled nerves on any occasion; and Reisenthal shopping bags that provide neat solutions for the extra bit of shopping. The shop is full of a zillion ideas and might seem short of floor space but has enough gear to kick your life up a notch.

SURPLUS A.P.C.
MEN'S/WOMEN'S DESIGNER

1-25-1 Aobadai, Meguro-ku, Tokyo (Others)
03-3719-2921
www.apcjp.com
🕐 12:00–20:00
🗓 Wednesdays
📍 MAP 2-53

¥¥-¥¥¥

Too cool for school types make a bee-line for APC surplus when their *poche* feels a bit light. This APC outlet is where the best of previous collections is stocked at markedly low prices. And because this is APC, who cares if the collections are old? You might not be able to get the latest jacket, but at these prices, giving your basics wardrobe a complete overhaul becomes a viable option.

SUZUKI TAKAYUKI
(by order at WR Aoyama)
BRIDAL

3-12-16 Kita-Aoyama, Minato-ku, Tokyo
03-5468-2466
None
🕐 12:00–20:00
🗓 Not fixed
📍 MAP 6-84

¥-¥¥¥

Suzuki Takayuki makes made-to-order wedding dresses that take two to three months to complete. He was originally a designer for clothes for professional dancers, and it's reflected in his clothes, as his drapes—be they from the bust onward or a fitted bust with drapes from the waist—make every girl absolutely resplendent. He's best at simple confections, with a touch of lace, accessories, and antique pieces of cloth detailing around the borders. The designer also takes orders for men's wedding suits, replete with shirt and vest. And for genuine princesses, he goes all out—helping to find the right pearls, shoes and, if she wishes, even details like little antique buttons and corsages.

SWC
MEN'S ACCESSORIES

3-24-2 Jingumae, Shibuya-ku, Tokyo
03-5414-1211
www.swc-japan.jp/
🕐 11:00–20:00
📅 Year-end holidays only
📍 MAP 5-69   ¥|¥¥-¥|¥|¥

Now matter how long you scour the globe, you'll never find a better place than Tokyo to indulge a bit in men's jewelry. SWC is dedicated to platinum, white gold, and silver jewelry—each unique piece based on designs inspired from the wild west and gothic architecture. There are enough skull and fleur de lys designs to keep the sinners among us happy, and for saints, there is a huge array of simpler less decorative designs that use clean lines and fine black detailing. Looking for a nice leather wallet or bracelet to go with that jeans and hip cowboy boots look? Their collection of modern Native American Indian leather accessories could be your answer.

TAILOR CAID
MEN'S BESPOKE

3-28-15 Shibuya, Shibuya-ku, Tokyo
03-5467-3088
www.tailorcaid.com
🕐 11:00–20:00
📅 Not fixed
📍 MAP 8-40   ¥|¥|¥|¥

Tailor Caid's Yuhei Yamamoto says he is not about suits but about personalities, so he tries to get the best of your personality into your suit. When you enter his shop, he engages you in a conversation to gauge your likes dislikes and your lifestyle. He does not do the Savile Row sharpness, neither does he like the over-tailored Italian style. Yamamoto prefers the most classic styles, encouraging you to wear things that would last for ever so long. Most clients also get a viewing of Audrey Hepburn, Cary Grant, Frank Sinatra, Paul Newman, and Sean Connery films. What this means in tailoring terms is a relaxed fit of superb form and proportion. This relates well to his choice of unique fabrics, like the 100% wool woven on ancient looms that he advises for summer too, so the form doesn't vanish after a couple of months of use. You can even decide which buttons go with the coat, choose colors that suit your palette, pick textiles, and confess to him all the issues you might have had in the past with your suits. Tailor Caid also offers the finest linen and relaxed bespoke shirts, with more than twelve kinds of cuffs and collars.

TAKASHIMAYA
DEPARTMENT STORE

2-4-1 Nihonbashi, Chuo-ku, Tokyo (Others)
03-3211-4111
www.takashimaya.co.jp/
🕐 10:00–20:00
📅 Not fixed
📍 MAP 21-3   ¥|¥|¥-¥|¥|¥

Since 1829 this is where people go when they need anything from branded jewelry, to cosmetics, maternity clothes, and accessories, including Hermès, Coach and Louis Vuitton bags. While the selection here is a bit more predictable than Isetan, no one leaves disappointed as they stock collections from APC to Armani and everything in between. Next door you'll find bookstore Kinokuniya, with an excellent English language book selection on the sixth floor, and the DIY store Tokyu Hands with an impeccable range of goods and services.

TALBOTS
WOMEN'S BOUTIQUE

3-5-12 Kita-Aoyama, Minato-ku, Tokyo (Others)
03-5772-9013
www.talbots.com
🕐 11:00–20:00
▦ Not fixed
🚇 MAP 5-70

¥|¥|¥|¥

Talbots are proud retailers of classic clothing. Think Mrs Neighbor, with two grown-up kids and impeccable taste, shopping here for gabardine pants, prim skirts, jackets, cable turtlenecks, velour scrunch neck tops, jewel neck sweaters, knit jackets and suede and leather stack heeled pumps. She also likes their limited evening look too, silk pants, embroidered, keyhole-necked sweaters, and silk tops in gray and black. In summer, the jackets in white stretch satin cotton are beautiful, and the beaded knit dresses combined with jeweled thongs provides the perfect getup for a party. While the clothes might be impossibly preppy for most, their services are great—especially the superb stylist you can chat with on their website, who provides answers from Talbots wardrobe for all your style conundrums 24/7.

TAPPET BASSETT WALKER
MEN'S/WOMEN'S BOUTIQUE

Marunouchi Bldg. 2F, 2-4-1 Marunouchi, Chiyoda-ku, Tokyo (Others)
03-5224-7567
www.bassettwalker.com
🕐 11:00–21:00 (Sun/Holidays untill 20:00)
▦ Not fixed
🚇 MAP 7-23

¥|¥|¥|¥

The only shop perfectly geared for women in the office. Suits, shirts, knits from Cruciani, and classic British tailored coats that can be combined with office shirts from Barba of Napoli and Oriali from Florence. For men the look is preppy and tailored, and most jackets come with a waistcoat in the same print. They also carry men's jewelry, leather accessories, and shoes.

TEXSTYLE DEPOTS
FABRICS

4-17-3 Ebisu, Shibuya-ku, Tokyo
03-3449-1201
www.texstyledepots.com/
🕐 11.00–20:00
▦ Not fixed
🚇 MAP 10-6

¥|¥|¥-¥|¥|¥

This shop's collection of superb fabrics has lent a creative hand to many designers, students, and individuals in town. Rows and rows of neatly laid out nylons, wools, rayons, cashmere, silk, and polyester line the walls, and can be purchased in lengths more than half a meter. The collections here are sourced from all over the world, including Japan, and are more suited for formal high fashion outfits. Chanel-inspired beige tweeds in a combination of wool, cotton, nylon, and rayon to give volume and fall, Harris tweed for rustic minimalism, lace, organic cotton, suede look-alikes in polyester, denim up to seventeen oz (just like original 1920s denim), organic denim—even a Japanese nanotex fabric woven with germanium, that when worn claims to help you get in shape—are just some of the things you can find here. Polyesters sell best with their silky touch, fantastic drapes, and cheap prices. For a brush with art, take their Zuanka collection of antique prints of swirls, circles, and flowers that can be printed on either silk, polyester, or nylon, as you chose, and delivered on the spot. The shop also has their own collection of casual chic clothes for both men and women that are made with fabrics selected from their collection.

TGI/TELLUS
MEN'S/WOMEN'S SHOES

1-29-16 Jiyugaoka, Meguro-ku, Tokyo (Others)
03-3717-5848
dianashoes.co.jp/brand/tgi.html
🕐 11:00–20:00
📅 No holidays
🚶 MAP 11-14   ¥|¥|¥

Great shop for shoes and accessories that are bound to become perrenial faves. The shop stocks Tellus, a brand that has been providing comfort for Tokyo's pretty feet for a few decades. Arranged on beautiful antique displays, you'll find leather pumps, flats, and kitten heels in blue, brown, black, burgundy. and even animal prints. To spruce up your look, most of the shoes can be matched with scarves, wallets, umbrellas, and simple bags from the shop. For men, the TGI brand remains conservative, with shoes, belts, bags, accessories, cuff links, and handkerchiefs. As the shop has its own factories in Italy and Turkey, the prices remain reasonable. Simplicity rules and makes choices very easy.

THE GINZA
WOMEN'S BOUTIQUE

7-8-10 Ginza, Chuo-ku, Tokyo
03-3571-7731
www.shiseido.co.jp/theginza
🕐 12:00–20:00 (Sun/Holidays 11:00–19:00)
📅 No holidays
🚶 MAP 4-41   ¥|¥|¥|¥-¥|¥|¥|¥

The whole building serves as a showcase for the fashion philosophy of Japan's oldest cosmetics giant. The entire Shiseido collection greets you on the first floor and the staff invites you to sample at your leisure. Climb up one floor for bags, hats, and shoes that you could give a miss, for the third floor that is understandably partial to Japanese designer Mihoko Saito and other diffusion lines like See by Chloé, and some pretty stoles and scarves in colorful woven wool. Floors above feature fashion mainstays from Pucci,

Jill Sander, John Galliano, Lucien Pellat, Marni, Manolo Blahnik, Chloé, and Yves St Laurent. Explore well and you will come away with the hottest numbers of the season from top to toe.

THE NORTH FACE
MEN'S/WOMEN'S SPORTSWEAR

Omotesando Hills, 4-12-10, Jingumae,
  Shibuya-ku, Tokyo (Others)
03-5785-0565
www.thenorthface.com/
🕙 11:00–21:00
🗓 Not fixed
↧ MAP 5-71   ¥¥¥-¥¥¥¥

In this huge, woody flagship store you can find The North Face's sci-fi apparel, equipment, and outdoor gear for adventurous men and women, and winning combinations of ski, snowboard, and surf outfits that will make you look and feel (if not perform) like a winner under all sporting conditions.

THE ORIGINAL LEVI'S STORE
MEN'S/WOMEN'S DENIM

6-29-4 Jingumae, Shibuya-ku,
  Tokyo (Others)
03-3486-0770
www.levi.com
🕙 11:00–21:00
🗓 Not fixed
↧ MAP 6-85   ¥-¥¥

The humble denim jean was first born from a process in the late 19th century that involved riveting corners of workmen's pockets to make them stronger. This was undoubtedly the biggest revolution in the fashion industry—bigger than the mini, bigger than the cardigan and winning a photo finish with the trench coat. Call it a piece of history or a daily essential, this flagship stocks them all—the 501 to Vintage LVC. Levi's might sell simply denim but the service here is still sheer luxury.

THEORY
MEN'S/WOMEN'S DESIGNER

6-5-39 Minami-Aoyama, Minato-ku,
  Tokyo (Others)
03-5766-5270
www.link-theory.com
🕙 11:00–20:00
🗓 No holidays
↧ MAP 1-93   ¥¥¥

Theory is one of the most perfect and consistent brands in the world. Their understated chic and superb quality collections are not just office friendly, but could take you through a fabulous dinner when combined with the right kinds of accessories. Their straight cut tailored pants are rumored to have many fans in high places. You could wear these in the country or to the movies or for a meeting, with a jacket and a pretty top, and they are guaranteed to become your quintessential item for a very long time. The men's collection upstairs has both superbly tailored casuals and suits.

THE SOVEREIGN HOUSE UNITED ARROWS

MEN'S BOUTIQUE

3-3-1 Marunouchi, Chiyoda-ku, Tokyo
03-6212-2150
www.sovereign-house.jp/
🕐 11:00–20:00
📅 Not fixed
📍 MAP 7-24   ¥·¥·¥-¥·¥·¥·¥

This is really a proper young gentleman's store, starring impeccable service (that gets to a first name level just after two visits), a lot of fine cuts (reasonably priced suits in steel, blue, and grey, pinstriped and two-buttoned), cool accessories (Kent, Drake's gloves and Colombo cashmere scarves), and the best shoes in the world from John Lobb.

THIRD CULTURE

WOMEN'S BOUTIQUE

2-28-5 Ebisu, Shibuya-ku, Tokyo (Others)
03-5448-9138
www.3rd-culture.com/
🕐 11:00–19:00
📅 Sun/Holidays
📍 MAP 10-7   ¥·¥·¥·¥-¥·¥·¥·¥·¥

Third Culture is something of an enigma. You walk along a quiet, leafy street far away from the station, and suddenly you stumble across an unassuming little concrete shop that houses the town's biggest and best collection of Manolo Blahniks, with over twenty five kinds of Manolos, (in sizes of up to 39 for some of them). Most Manolos also come in three different heel sizes. But there is a lot of other beautiful stuff too, and owner Oda is very picky when it comes to dressing up his women. Giambattista Valli, D&G, Lanvin, Chloé, all smartly arranged around by categories—shirts, pants, skirts, coats, and dresses. Oda can be seriously waspish to browsers, but is a darling when you are seriously looking to shed weight off your wallet for what is truly one of the richest collections in this part of town.

THIRTEEN DESIGNS

MEN'S ACCESSORIES

2-2-19 Hiroo, Shibuya-ku, Tokyo
03-5766-4913
www.thirteen.co.jp
🕐 13:00–20:00
📅 No holldays
📍 MAP 10-8   ¥·¥·¥·¥-¥·¥·¥·¥·¥

Homegrown Thirteen Designs is one of the most iconic cult accessory designers for men. They were in business long before the word "skull" was linked with "accessory." Thirteen limited edition skull designs come to you every year, from skull rings in silver to skull bracelets, belts and hand-stitched exotic leather wallets. This destination has been a favorite with visiting rock royalty—most notably Guns n' Roses. Thirteen Designs still makes all its stuff in the room at the back, and while businessmen buy their stuff at department stores, this hidden flagship retains its cult underground status for the rock chic and those young at heart.

THREE DOG BAKERY

PETS

2-17-1 Jiyugaoka, Meguro-ku, Tokyo (Others)
03-3723-7070
www.threedog.co.jp
🕐 10:00–20:00
📅 No holidays
📍 MAP 11-15

¥|¥|¥

Three Dog Bakery was originally started to offer yummy, all natural treats to dogs and cats. This they do with great appetite, with a menu running from cookies to cakes with icing. But the store also has a pretty collection of dog-care products like honey paw cream and natural shampoos, and such a pretty dog would, of course, wear the finest knits and collars, of which they have a cute little collection in the corner.

TK

MEN'S DESIGNER

6-17-11 Jingumae, Shibuya-ku, Tokyo (Others)
03-5778-6255
web-tk.jp/
🕐 11:00–20:00
📅 No holidays
📍 MAP 6-86

¥|¥|¥

Street casual label TK, from designer Takeo Kikuchi, stirs up clothes with the right quantities of Japonisme and counterculture. Street style usually doesn't offer much that one can do to add details, but that is exactly what they are really good at. Military styles, embellishment with zippers for clothes, army boots, hats, and bags; all carry the same supercharge—and the occasional collaboration with cartoon detective character Arsene Lupin and the Japanese rock band Ulfuls.

T KUNIMOTO

WOMEN'S DESIGNER

B1F, 3-26-3 Jingumae, Shibuya-ku, Tokyo
03-3408-7746
www.tkunitomo.com
🕐 12:00–21:00 (Sun/Holidays untill 20:00)
📅 No holidays
📍 MAP 5-72

¥|¥|¥

T Kunimoto takes ancient Japanese and Chinese motifs and gives them a new lease on life. Combine that with old American and European classics, imagine inspiration from India, add his love for polka dots, and that is how his collection was born. Color, asymmetry and avant-gardism rule in bell skirts and asymetrical jackets with uneven collars and fancy sleeves. The brand surprisingly has a fashion following over three generations of women of the same family so nothing vampy or powerful, just pretty nouveau-boho.

TOCO PACIFIC
WOMEN'S BOUTIQUE

Juhachibankan Bldg. 3F, 3-18-17 Minami-
Aoyama, Minato-ku, Tokyo
03-5411-0589
🕐 11:00–20:00
📅 No holidays
📍 MAP 1-94   ¥/¥/¥

Some "it" bags come and go, but, for some reason, Balenciaga's classic tote always manages to stay around. This shop stores a lot of these chameleon bags in unique colors, along with totes and Luellas in unusual sizes. If you are bored with this FWC style, there are loads of other things for you to splurge on—a superb collection of Pucci bathing suits for beach babes, Sienna Miller's favorite Alexander McQueen skull scarves, shades from von Zipper that Madonna has been seen sporting, with white, black, and red frames, plus Christian Louboutin wedge espadrilles in many colors, and Chloé Paddingtons. The shop swears it stocks stuff you will never find at flagship stores.

TOD'S
MEN'S/WOMEN'S ACCESSORIES

5-1-5 Jingumae, Shibuya-ku,
Tokyo (Others)
03-6419-2055
www.tods.com
🕐 11:00–20:00
📅 Not fixed
📍 MAP 6-87   ¥/¥/¥/¥

Tod's shoes are encased in a superb feat of modern architecture in this Toyo Ito-designed, Zaha Hadid-outfitted mega flagship. What is showcased inside is equally spectacular. Diego Della Valle and a thousand other *marchigiani* send wonderfully comfortable shoes from their factory in the picturesque valley of La Marche, Italy. Tod's trademark driving shoes in all their many versions, including stacked and kitten heeled ones, hand bags and totes to match, and a whole series of accessories, including ostrich bracelets and belts, are at home here. Browse through while lounging on specially designed pony skin leather sofas. The first floor is dedicated to Tod's much-coveted accessories, the second floor has women's shoes and leather jackets and the third floor commands a neat men's collection and an impressive view of the street below.

TOGA
WOMEN'S DESIGNER

6-31-10 Jingumae, Shibuya-ku,
Tokyo (Others)
03-6419-8136
www.toga.jp
🕐 11:00–20:00
📅 No holidays
📍 MAP 6-88   ¥/¥/¥-¥/¥/¥/¥

Another exciting Japanese creator who just may be fashion's next icon. Regularly showing at the Paris collections, Toga is well known for her exotic and erotic dresses, accentuating a woman's figure like none other with light, flowy fabrics. This year her theme turns to the monastic—stoic, but full of hot sex appeal with very short hemlines in pastel and earthy colors in silk and cashmere fabrics, fringed and gathered at the seams with silhouette detailing accentuated by belts and corsets. Her stuff is made for strong women—cool, dispassionate, Sophia Loren types.

TOKYU HANDS
INTERIOR/DIY

12-18 Udagawa-cho, Shibuya-ku, Tokyo (Others)
03-5489-5111
www.tokyu-hands.co.jp
🕐 10:00–20:30
📅 Non fixed
🔖 MAP 8-41   ¥ ¥-¥ ¥ ¥ ¥

This is one of the reasons why Japanese design never fails to surprise. At the world's most urbane DIY shop, you can indulge in all your crafts needs from flowers to wood, textile, mechanics or leatherwork. DIY parts for every conceivable human activity—along with a huge selection of accessories and other quirky, creative items for your house, spread over more than eight floors of creative genius.

TOM, DICK AND HARRY
MEN'S ACCESSORIES

2-10-16 Shibuya, Shibuya-ku, Tokyo
03-3406-7547
www.leatherbag.co.jp/
🕐 11:00–20:00
📅 National Holidays
🔖 MAP 8-42   ¥ ¥ ¥-¥ ¥ ¥ ¥

Going to work with a fabulous briefcase in tow or boarding a flight with a neat weekend satchel is a real luxury. But watching your precious Goyard or Vuitton take a beating on the train or in the plane is a particularly nasty experience. So you may decide to invest in a sturdy series of highly crafted leather bags (wonderfully free of logos to boot). Shoulder bags, messenger bags, totes, pocket pouches, bowler bags, and card cases, plus their slim new travel bags to take care of your diminutive laptop, crease free Egyptian cotton shirts, and the slenderest of novels. TD&H gallantly offers to carry out whatever altering you might require so that your bag is constructed to perfectly suits your needs. Most bags can be reproduced in five different color combinations.

TOMORROW-LAND

MEN'S/WOMEN'S BOUTIQUE/
ACCESSORIES

1-23-16 Shibuya, Shibuya-ku,
  Tokyo (Others)
03-5774-1711
www.tomorrowland.co.jp/
🕐 11:00–21:00
🗓 Not fixed
⌕ MAP 8-43   ¥|¥|¥-¥|¥|¥

If you are desperately in search of a present, yet are lost for ideas, head here, where you'll find a great collection of fragrances from Penhaligon's of London, Tocca candles in wine and grappa flavors (unavailable elsewhere in town), and loads of vintage Baccarat at reasonable prices in mint condition. Downstairs, you'll stumble across Tomorrowland Tricot: a superb collection of very reasonable, fantastically cut knits for men, and other original pieces, including jerseys with cotton collars, fine cotton shirts, and suits and shirts from Loro Piana.

TOMMY HILFIGER

MEN'S/WOMEN'S DESIGNER

3F, 1-23-16 Shibuya, Shibuya-ku,
  Tokyo (Others)
03-3407-0188
global.tommy.com/opencms/opencms/
  tommy-japan/
🕐 11:00–21:00
🗓 No holidays
⌕ MAP 8-44   ¥|¥-¥|¥|¥

While the Ivy League look of chinos and Oxford shirts has thankfully gone, there still remains a thirst for Tommy Hilfiger's rugby shirts. But the fashion world is all excited as Hilfiger's business is no longer public: expect luxe weekend looks, fine wool cardigans, linen shirts, smart flat-fronted chinos and superb shoes. The lifestyle giant continues to peddle everything from jeans to shoes, sunglasses to handbags, scents to bathproducts, golfwear, swimwear, clothes for babies, and home furnishings for the parents.

TOPKAPI

WOMEN'S ACCESSORIES

Marunouchi Bldg. 2F, 2-4-1 Marunouchi,
  Chiyoda-ku, Tokyo (Others)
03-3216-3805
www.topkapi.co.jp/
🕐 11:00–21:00 (Sun/Holidays untill
  20:00)
🗓 Not fixed
⌕ MAP 7-25   ¥|¥|¥

In an unpredictable climate, you never want to leave home without a pair of gloves. So head to Topkapi for the most vivid and vibrant of fashion's must-have accessories. Topkapi makes gloves in all possible colors, shapes, and materials: quilted, knitted, woolen, lambskin, cashmere, golf inspired—and all at wonderful prices so you can happily color coordinate them with your entire wardrobe. In summer the collections give way to straw hats and bags.

TOPMAN/ TOPSHOP

MEN'S/WOMEN'S BOUTIQUE

La Foret Harajuku 2F, 1-11-6 Jingumae, Shibuya-ku, Tokyo
03-5414-3090
www.topshop.com
🕐 11:00–20:00
📅 No holidays
🏷 MAP 5-73   ¥|¥

The world's hottest fast fashion chain at last comes to town. The men's line Topman started in 1978 and the women's line Topshop soon followed. Both come together in this newly opened mecca to cool. It stocks the collection line Top Shop Boutique, the Top Shop Collaboration designer's collaboration, and the men's regular line. Whether you choose a plain V-neck cotton T, Celia Birtwell 60s print frocks, or their chunky shoes or sandals, you can be sure the store will keep you looking up to date. After all, such picture perfect shoppers as Kate Moss, Natalie Portman, and Nicole Kidman are known to stop by at the Oxford Street mecca to stock up on the latest.

TRAMANDO

WOMEN'S DESIGNER

Laforet Harajuku 1F, 1-11-6 Jingumae, Shibuya-ku, Tokyo
03-3404-3288
www.tramando.com/
🕐 11:00–20:00
📅 No holidays
🏷 MAP 5-74   ¥|¥|¥|¥

Under his label, Tramando, textile designer Martin Churba's collections have successfully traveled from the turf of chic Recoleta in his native Buenos Aires to a comfortable home in Tokyo. This shop is dedicated solely to him and his hi-tech romantic creations from the fabric he created—called Trosmanchurba. With a sculptural fall and lines so neat they put geometry to shame, Tramando's tops, skirts, and coats use multiple hues of colors on the same canvas for a painting-like effect on clothes—often with portraits printed on the entire length of cloth. The look is unparalleled and creates a futuristic romance effect adored by many (including the singer Björk).

TRAPU

WOMEN'S BOUTIQUE

4-13-12 Jingumae, Shibuya-ku, Tokyo
03-5772-3311
www.trap-u.com/
🕐 11:00–20:00
📅 No holydays
🏷 MAP 5-75   ¥|¥

So what is in the LA girl's closet? Not a lot of pricey high fashion stuff, but some great fun pieces like long tunics, tiny denim skirts, jeans, and vintage dresses with Von Zipper sunnies, psychedelic girl kitsch accessories, Hello Kitty funky diva bags, and *trait d'union* skull earrings. The really hard core, of course, kit themselves with CC Skye Chanel inspired metal chain leather bracelets that are so in just as Kabbalah is so out, and no one finishes the look better than knit boots from Liv, on sale here in candy colors. Tokyo girls have always had a fashion affair with LA celebs and this shop brings them the best.

TREE OF LIFE
AROMATHERAPY

6-3-8 Jingumae, Shibuya-ku, Tokyo (Others)
03-3409-1778
www.treeoflife.co.jp
🕐 11:00–20:00
🏬 No holidays
🍴 MAP 6-89   ¥¥-¥¥¥

Tokyo's best-kept ayurveda and aromatherapy secret offers every imaginable service in its five-story building. Hot favorites are, of course, the fifty different kinds of aroma oils, some of them—such as the venerated Japanese *hinoki* cypress—available only in Japan. You can also buy cosmetics and skin care products made from Bulgarian roses and Tunisian neroli. If you are a handmade soap fan, the place offers everything under the sun for you to indulge yourself. As if all this is not enough pampering, the store also offers rose and other facials along with complete ayurvedic treatments on its fourth floor.

TRIBECA
MEN'S BOUTIQUE

1-8-91 Jiyugaoka, Meguro-ku, Tokyo
03-3725-4608
www.ueno-shokai.co.jp/shop/shop_page/tribeca.html
🕐 11:30–20:30
🏬 No holidays
🍴 MAP 11-16   ¥¥¥

This tiny, well-situated Jiyugaoka shop is the perfect place for a bit of spontaneous weekend shopping for men's clothes. In neat displays, the shop promises articles for all days of the week. A range of fine cotton, wool, and velvet jackets with trousers in houndstooth and Prince of Wales checks. For the holidays: down jackets, Armani jeans, John Smedley knitwear, leather jumpers, and Mackintosh quilted wool coats. You can pull all this off with their selection of Orobianco totes, fine English leather brogues, or retro sneakers, and slim ties to regular-sized ties in fine wool twills and silk.

TRICO
INTERIOR

B1F, 6-9-1 Jingumae, Shibuya-ku, Tokyo (Others)
03-3486-1790
www.bytrico.com/
🕐 12:00–20:00
🏬 Wednesdays
🍴 MAP 6-90   ¥¥-¥¥¥¥

Trico's owners have perhaps the highest design standards in town, having turned all their shops into mini museums of modern design.

They scour the world for what is the quirkiest, funkiest, funniest, and the latest. Take, for example, Maxim Velcovsky's take on basic plastic cups in glass: Trico has the clear glass version. See the rug with a built-in umbrella stand. Check out Patrick Frey and Markus Boge's "Trick Stick," a gravity defying minimal coat hanger. Accustomed as you might be to funky design, this shop's international collections are definitely worth a visit.

TRIPPEN
MEN'S/WOMEN'S/KIDS' SHOES

3-34-8 Jingumae, Shibuya-ku, Tokyo (Others)
03-3478-2255
www.trippen.co.jp/
⊘ 11:00–20:00
▦ Not fixed
↧ MAP 5-76

¥ ¥ ¥

Varyingly inspired by the protective clothing of medieval horsemen, reptiles, and lonesome cowboys, Trippen is a trip to environmentally friendly shoes with ultramodern design. The shape of the foot and the materials always remains the same, and so the models seem similar every season. Both the men's and women's collections keep the same sole but the upper patterns change every season. Take, for example, the "Turn," a unisex design that takes a rectangular shape and turns it into a shoe, with the excess portion becoming a flap. Trippen shoes have a cool silhouette and often use multiple layers of leather, and, in keeping with the desire to protect nature, use the entire skins with all its imperfections. But if the shoes are too reptilian for you, stick to the kids' shoes and boots, which have great colors, extreme flexibility and a die-hard following among chic parents.

TSUMORI CHISATO
MEN'S/WOMEN'S DESIGNER

Shinbiyo Square 1 B1F, 4-21-25 Minami-Aoyama, Minato-ku, Tokyo (Others)
03-3423-5170
www.a-net.com
⊘ 11:00–20:00
▦ Not fixed
↧ MAP 1-95

¥ ¥ ¥ - ¥ ¥ ¥ ¥

Tsumori Chisato is the latest Japanese craze among Europe's arty types. She makes wildly graphic clothes with volume and colors, and a slight affectation of the boho chic laced with fairytales. She's always in sync with Tokyo street trends, and surrounds herself with artists—often working their pieces into her dresses and skirts through embroidery, heavy beading and painting. Of late she has been taking her cue from the northern lights of Scandinavia, with snow, sleds, girls in dresses, and cakes painted on loose tops and flowy dresses. Come winter, her sweaters are the best in town, with feminine details, earthy colors, and perfect lengths finished with great embroidery.

TUMI

MEN'S/WOMEN'S LUGGAGE

6-6-9 Ginza, Chuo-ku, Tokyo (Others)
03-5537-3880
www.tumi.com
⊘ 11:00–20:00
▦ No holidays
⌁ MAP 4-42 ¥|¥|¥|¥-¥|¥|¥|¥|¥

There are sexier versions of travel luggage around, but nobody can beat Tumi for their quality or the organizational skills offered by their luggage. Their business cases come with infinite pocket variations, detachable computer inserts, and rollerblade wheels, the golf bags cater for all climes, the duffles and totes fit comfortably overhead in the plane, and the new luggage restrictions at the airport will make you embrace their overnighters. If no amount of ballistic nylon functionality can convince you to rid yourself of your fashion urges, stick to their pricier but stylish leather series, and, for guys with a bike, Tumi does a series with Ducati that includes a backpack that even has space for a helmet.

UGG

MEN'S/WOMEN'S/KIDS' SHOES

Omotesando Hills Main Bldg. B2F, 4-12-10 Jingumae, Shibuya-ku, Tokyo (Others)
03-5785-0502
www.goldwin.co.jp/uggaustralia/
⊘ 11:00–21:00
▦ Not fixed
⌁ MAP 5-77 ¥|¥-¥|¥|¥

UGGs were originally shoes worn by surfers to beat the cold after a ride out on the waves. In their reinvention as fashion statements you can wear them with jeans or pair them with pretty dresses, with equal pizzazz. The classic boot in twin-faced sheepskin, with a natural sheepskin insole, comes in chocolate, chestnut, and mink, among other colors. They also make lace-up and tie-around boots, and if you find all this a bit too elephantine for your taste, try the loafers in patent leather or the wooden slip-ons, or the super comfy slip-ons for the house. They also make beautiful baby shoes in pink, sand, and light blue. Loafers for men, with removable sheepskin insoles, are a winner too. UGG is in full coquette mode with its line of thongs, espadrilles, and crocheted boots all lined with the trademark sheepskin and yes, these are supposed to be a great option for summer. To match your shoes, UGG also has more than 25 kinds of bags that include sheepskin shoppers, barrels, hobos, totes, messengers, and even wristlets.

UNDERCOVER

MEN'S/WOMEN'S DESIGNER

Blue Sanc Point C Bldg., 5-3-18 Minami-Aoyama, Minato-ku, Tokyo (Others)
03-3407-1232
None
⊘ 11:00–20:00
▦ No holidays
⌁ MAP 1-96 ¥|¥|¥|¥

Hard, edgy clothes from Japan's genius street-fashion pioneer, Jun Takahashi. His Undercover clothing line has been inspired by such things as victims, hostages, prisoners awaiting execution, and other ideas hard to digest. His difficult to describe collections are the essence of Japanese cool, but ripped, torn, strapped, masked, or ugly, his designs are all real collectors' items. The store, spread over three floors, stars his women's genius creations on the first floor and Undorcoverism for men on the second floor. The women's line is feminine with a lot of layering, soft fabrics, dresses and tops that have undergone his artistic embellishments with pearls, embroidery and other inspirations of the moment. The men's collection is straight rock chic street reality with vests, knits and superb stressed biker's jackets. Takashashi is as much a designer as an artist and the basement has his creations of stuffed dolls, toys, kids clothes, T-shirts and other accessories for the maximum impact of Undercover style.

UNIQLO
MEN'S/WOMEN'S/KIDS'
VOLUME SELLER

5-7-7 Ginza, Chuo-ku, Tokyo, (Others)
03-3569-6781
www.uniqlo.jp
🕐 11:00–21:00
📅 No holidays
🛗 MAP 4-43   ¥-¥¥

Uniqlo's global expansion might have become legendary, but its clothes never budge from the back-to-basics attitude. Since they sell absolutely everything at the cheapest possible prices in the best possible quality, people come here to shop for their fleeces in the winter, and come summer their colorful T-shirts keep it cool. The jeans are also a big draw, as are the men's and women's washable summer coats. Their huge palette of unisex ankle socks comes in more than 50 colors and the underwear selection is an opportunity to stock-up on unfussy basics. Uniqlo's stuff is all about pricing and styling, so be brutal when shopping here. If it doesn't work for you, it goes back on the shelf. The Harajuku location, renamed the UT store, is dedicated to hip T-shirts sold in even hipper packaging.

UNITED ARROWS
MEN'S/WOMEN'S BOUTIQUE

6-16-13 Jingumae, Shibuya-ku, Tokyo
(Others)
03-3797-9791
www.united-arrows.jp/
🕐 12:00–20:30 (Sat/Sun/Hol/11:00–20:30)
📅 No holidays
🛗 MAP 6-91   ¥¥¥¥

UA always stocks the best and latest of Christian Louboutin's purring pumps and sky high boots. For autumn and winter the staple is the leopard print for both pumps and boots. Or try the round suede pumps in luscious mocha and wine red. The shop is also famed for its loyalty to Balenciaga pants and Lanvin jackets, It shoes from Chloé and Balenciaga and reasonable Cath Kidson shopping and beach bags. Men's stuff remains a tad conservative, with Turnbull and Arthur checked shirts and brogues, so for a bit of slick UA brings it on with Comme des Garçons men's collection. And finally if you've shopped too much, the favorite Rimowa and UA hardcases will wheel your possessions to any corner of the globe.

UNITED BAMBOO

MEN'S/WOMEN'S DESIGNER

4-24-14 Jingumae, Shibuya-ku, Tokyo (Others)
03-3479-8171
www.unitedbamboo.com/
🕐 11:00–20:00
📅 No holidays
↑ MAP 5-78

¥|¥|¥|¥

Thuy Pham and Miho Aoki's new shop in Omotesando is arranged like a flea market with a great collection of memorabilia from collaborating artists and tons of United Arrows shoes. Here you can escape from the preppy trenches of select shops and discover their collections of draped tunics and dresses very often worn with a T-shirt inside. Check mutton jackets for men, skinny striped trousers, CDs, illustrations, objets, colorful silkscreen scarves from Tracy Nakayama, ankle length boots, sandals, and pumps all in a gallery-like display—offer a great weekend afternoon of browsing.

URBAN RESEARCH

MEN'S/WOMEN'S BOUTIQUE

6-19-21 Jingumae, Shibuya-ku, Tokyo (Others)
03-5468-6565
www.urban-research.com
🕐 11:00–20:00
📅 No holidays
↑ MAP 6-92

¥|¥-¥|¥

Inspired by military, equestrian, and vintage, this shop has an incredible collection of more than thirty brands of traditional, handmade shoes for both men and women, handpicked by the staff from all over the world and sold at very reasonable prices. The brand propagates a total look rather than individual pieces, so they suggest combining the shoes with a great slim fitting suit (such as those sold here by elusive Japanese designer Davit Meursault) and a Freitag bag, of which they have an impressive collection. For the more conservative there is a great selection of men's wash bags in leather and canvass. The women's collection is all about going back to basics, with hand-made lace tank tops and blouses combined with elegant collarless empire style coats with a knot in the front, or wraparound dresses in the color of dust teamed with quilted flat ballerinas. Look no further for the best in arty, earthy, and effort-less cool.

USAGI POUR TOI

WOMEN'S BOUTIQUE

GB Bldg.1F, Jingumae, Shibuya-ku, Tokyo
03-5766-3011
www.hpfrance.com/Shop/Brand/Usagi_pour_toi.html
🕐 12:00–20:00
📅 No holidays
↑ MAP 6-93

¥|¥|¥

Usagi pour toi is a private castle for women filled with delights waiting to be discovered: things like beautifully colored pumps, ultrafeminine tops, boyish shorts, jackets cut knife-sharp, classic and neutral tones with dashes of eccentric colors in dresses, skirts, and scarves—all painstakingly chosen by the shop's buyers. While style-meisters shop on the floors above, this shop attracts giddy gamines on the weekends with a boyfriend on their arm.

VALENTINO
MEN'S/WOMEN'S DESIGNER

5-4-6 Ginza, Chuo-ku, Tokyo (Others)
03-3569-2151
www.vbj.co.jp/
🕐 11:00–20:00
📅 No holidays
⌐ MAP 4-44   ¥|¥|¥|¥

Valentino fuses la dolce vita with archetypical looks that channel the icy yet alluring aura of iconic Hollywood bombshells. The "Master of the Dress" set up shop almost 50 years ago and his sumptuous designs suit old money and nouveau riche alike. Find exquisite evening dresses in his signature monochrome palette of white or unleash your inner siren in a scarlet gown. Also stocks the entire range of Valentino accessories, bags, sunglasses, and the much sought-after jeans and other casual elegant chic from R.E.D. Valentino.

VALEXTRA
MEN'S/WOMEN'S ACCESSORIES

6-5-1 Ginza, Chuo-ku, Tokyo
03-5568-7811
www.valextra.com/
🕐 11:00–20:00
📅 No holidays
⌐ MAP 4-45   ¥|¥|¥|¥-¥|¥|¥|¥

Recently, bags seem to be part of every magazine, billboard, catwalk, and conversation. And when an accessories maker comes along with only one or two bags per season, you respect them for their discretion, intelligence, and exquisite beauty (the result of no logos and freedom from trends). The hot sellers often come in snow-white leather with hand painted black edges and using soft white calf or luxe croc. The men's collection of business, weekend, and shopping bags are equally soft—the most stylish on the planet. The diaries and other small leather goods are great to give and get, but the Valextra bags are for those who want to go beyond Hermès.

VANESSA BRUNO
WOMEN'S DESIGNER

Senjo Bldg. 1F/B1F, 1-8-13 Jinnan,
    Shibuya-ku, Tokyo (Others)
03-3496-5514
www.vanessabruno.co.jp/
🕐 11.30–20.00
📅 No holidays
⌐ MAP 8-45   ¥|¥|¥|¥

This self-financed designer is somewhat of a cult in Japan and Europe and has brought a whole new meaning to dressing for the late-twenties-early-thirties city girl. Even those hovering happily outside fashion's radar have one of her sequined totes. But for her fans, she is somebody who knows how to dress a woman in great style with luxe fabrics, and, most importantly, without overspending. Draping is key, with low-necked tops cut away from the body without being too loose, and those skinny pants always tucked into super-gorgeous boots. In the shop all her clothes look tricky with plunging necklines, bare midriffs and sky high hemlines but when paired and worn with her skinny pants and a jacket, the look could be great by day and glammed with heels at night. Her stylish attitude, thankfully free of designer zeal, has made her the queen of spirit and mood.

VANNES

MEN'S/WOMEN'S ACCESSORIES

Greenfantasia Bldg. 1F, 1-11-11
   Jingumae, Shibuya-ku, Tokyo
03-3402-1751
None
🕐 11:00–21:00
📅 No holidays
⌕ MAP 5-79   ¥|¥|¥

Don't be fooled by this nondescript looking shop. Their low cost bags in cheap materials suit absolutely all budgets, and are a step ahead of trends. Their cult following makes all the Japanese fashion mag pages. Pair that polka dot scarf with a matching polka dot bag in cotton or, for the funkier at heart, get the Astro Boy Boston. If you're looking for a stylish bag to flaunt at the gym, Vannes has a range of hold-alls in silver, gold, and jungle print. Also head here if you need the right bag for just one evening. Prices make up for the unfriendly service.

VERSACE

MEN'S/WOMEN'S DESIGNER

4-1 Kioi-cho, Chiyoda-ku, Tokyo (Others)
03-3262-2777
www.versace.com
🕐 11:00–20:00
📅 Not fixed
⌕ MAP 13-3   ¥|¥|¥|¥

Versace's clothes are known to be loved by people with huge personalities (like Madonna, who also starred in a Versace campaign). Sister Donatella seems less electric but still makes "I-want-that-right-now" clothes. The corset in bone figures heavily in dresses both on the inside and the outside. Loads of mighty baroque print shirts and dresses are still around, with the seasonal empire dresses and cocoon shapes, plus Donatella is in better health than ever, which means her best is just around the corner.

VIA BUS STOP

WOMEN'S BOUTIQUE

Shibuya Seibu Dept. Store, Movida 2F-7F,
21-1 Udagawa-cho, Shibuya-ku,
Tokyo (Others)
03-5428-8215
www.viabusstop.com
🕐 10:00–20:00
🗓 Not fixed
📍 MAP 8-46

¥¥¥¥

Via Bus Stop, with its convenient location and expert collections, is the first port of call for many visiting celebrities. The shop unravels from the second floor upwards, with Japanese designer Seta Ichiro, Tocca, and Antonio Berardi. The section upstairs has women's casuals from Chalayan, Sharon Waucob, Trosman, and McQ. There is an entire floor dedicated to Alexander McQueen's creations for both men and women, including his superbly creepy skeleton accessories and a range of shoes. The men's casual collection has a beautiful section of Drake's scarves, hats and gloves, bags, and other accessories that are present-perfect. The topmost floor is dedicated to evening pleasures in Ungaro, Giambattista Valli, John Galliano, and Victor&Rolf.

VIA BUS STOP/ AUDOXIA

WOMEN'S ACCESSORIES

Shibuya Seibu Department store B3F, 21-
1 Udagawa-cho, Shibuya-ku,
Tokyo (Others)
03-5459-1981
www.viabusstop.com
🕐 10:00–20:00
🗓 Not fixed
📍 MAP 8-46

¥¥¥¥

While the upper floors stock designer creations, this basement shop is full of accessories of the moment, especially Chloé and Alexander McQueen. This is where you can splurge the most with women's shoes from Alessandro Dell'Aqua, Bruno Frisoni, new designer Ras from Spain, and superb bags with their own individual presence from lesser known brands.

VIA BUS STOP HOMME

MEN'S BOUTIQUE

1-4-8 Aobadai, Meguro-ku,
Tokyo (Others)
03-5728-6022
www.viabusstop.com
🕐 11:00–20:00 (Sundays opens from
13:00)
🗓 No holidays
📍 MAP 2-54

¥¥¥¥-¥¥¥¥¥

This shop efficiently covers all the must haves for a modern man's casual wardrobe. Neatly laid out on two floors, it always stocks the best street-wise collections from Alexander McQueen, Marc Jacobs, Bernhard Willhelm, Hussein Chalayan, Marni, Ungaro, and many styles of shoes—the trend of the moment being casual shoes inspired by extreme sports. Collection Privee's style of bags is appropriately stressed to match the rest of the look.

VICTORINOX

MEN'S BOUTIQUE/ACCESSORIES

La Porto 2F, 5-51-8 Jingumae, Shibuya-ku,
Tokyo (Others)
03-5766-1377
www.victorinox.co.jp/
🕐 11:00–20:00
📅 No holidays
📍 MAP 6-94   ¥|¥|¥|¥

Victorinox apparel comes only for men, in the spirit of their most famous accessory—the pocket multi tool knife. Dressy button shirts, razor sharp blazers, cotton or woolen pants, and a host of outerwear, including car coats and down jackets in black and brown, all skillfully styled. Most people come here, of course, for the knives, the varieties of which are increasing every year. But their sensible luggage, and night-vision watches are a big draw, too. If you have all this already, they also do USB memory drives, kitchen knives and torches all in red with the Swiss flag.

VIVA CIRCUS

WOMEN'S SHOES

2F, 6-12-23 Jingumae, Shibuya-ku, Tokyo
03-5774-0808
www.nej.co.jp
🕐 11:00–20:00
📅 No holidays
📍 MAP 6-95   ¥|¥-¥|¥|¥

This neat little shoe shop is divided into two segments: the part that stores nondescript looking bags and shoes and the really fun part—a wonderful selection of the coolest sneakers from around the world. For those with an urban crusader mentality these sneakers are as stylish as the sneaker school of cool gets, with retro collections from Puma, Adidas Silver Streak and Nike. Circus also resurrects sneakers with a collection that time might have forgotten with Quick sneakers in white leather that started making history way back in 1905, Toppers, the world's favorite shoes from Brazil, plus an extensive range from the homegrown brand Patrick with classic and vintage combinations of round toe sporty styles and Converse's basic white leather low tops. If you think your feet have graduated from sneakers to a more formal sole, this shop shall drag you back to sneaker heaven.

VIVA YOU

WOMEN'S DESIGNER

Marui City 4F, 1-21-3 Jinnan, Shibuya-ku,
Tokyo (Others)
03-5728-7435
www.vivayou.jp
🕐 10:00–20:00
📅 No holidays
📍 MAP 8-47   ¥|¥-¥|¥|¥

Toshikazu Iwaya is best known for his salacious label Dresscamp. Few know that he is also the brain behind Viva You, a place that brings his hard-hitting, cutting edge sensibilities to the world at much more reasonable prices. This shop features sharp silhouettes with detailing like knit dresses cut low on the back, I-line silhouettes of the moment that are not only narrow but sharp and with voluminous sleeves, wide pants and bold volume details, and vivid colors with a particular fascination for red and blue. All this, and at prices that are just a fraction of his catwalk label.

VIVIENNE TAM
WOMEN'S DESIGNER

5-5-6 Minami-Aoyama, Minato-ku, Tokyo (Others)
03-5468-5743
www.viviennetam.com
🕐 11:00–20:00
📅 No holidays
📍 MAP 1-97

¥|¥|¥

Vivienne Tam fans storm their way in here not just for the China chic but for the really sexy, baby-doll silhouettes that are often in silk and skim above the knee. Hot colors, embroidery, and silk screening breathe dragon fire into her clothes. This bright red boutique stocks collections that are entirely made in Japan, which unfortunately means that finding sizes can sometimes be very challenging. If the dresses don't fit, stick to the accessories, especially the bags that follow the same hot, sexy patterns as the clothes.

VIVIENNE WESTWOOD
MEN'S/WOMEN'S DESIGNER

5-49-2 Jingumae, Shibuya-ku, Tokyo (Others)
03-5774-5939
www.viviennewestwood.com/
🕐 11:00–20:00
📅 No holidays
📍 MAP 6-96

¥|¥|¥|¥ - ¥|¥|¥|¥|¥

She's sixty-four and still the queen of punk, and obsessing about her is almost a tradition in Japan. Vivi girls and boys (as Vivienne's fans are known in Japan) join the leagues of cosplay Lolitas to shop at this and the many other stores in Harajuku that stock Vivienne vintage and a very reasonable pret-a-porter collection available only in Japan. Also find Anglomania, a collection referenced from her earlier collections, tweed, check, plaid jackets, trousers and skirts along with shoes and the complete range of accessories from stockings to Vivi Planet brooches, Libertine, Boudoir, Anglomania perfumes and a neat little make-up bar in the corner. The extensive men's collection is in the basement and stocks her knit lines, suits, shirts, a good collection of graphic Ts, and accessories.

WACOAL DIA
LINGERIE

7-6-16 Ginza, Chuo-ku, Tokyo
03-5537-0850
www.wacoaldia.com
🕐 11:00–20:00 (Sun/Holidays untill 18:00)
📅 Mondays
📍 MAP 4-46

¥|¥|¥|¥

Lingerie doesn't get more perfect than this. Wacoal Dia is the exclusive collection from Japan's largest lingerie maker. Inspired by regular street clothes and created by haute couture designer

Atsuko Kamio, tank tops come with tiny pleated frills on the straps, spandex mesh full sleeves and velvet center front folds, which can thankfully even be worn on the streets with any of their silk camisoles. Broad strips of net take the place of bra straps that support light lacy cups and are paired with Brazilians or strings in ultra fine silk with light layers of lace. Silk waist corsets given you a slimming appearance, as do their beautiful bustiers. They also do a fine collection of bras suited for halter necks. For those wanting to try all this on, the entire basement floor (closed to men) is devoted to changing rooms with enough space to lounge around in real style and comfort.

WAKEUP

INTERIOR/WOMEN'S
ACCESSORIES

1-15-8 Jinnan, Shibuya-ku, Tokyo
03-3461-2195
None
🕐 12:00–21:00
📅 No holidays
🍴 MAP 8-48   ¥|¥

Warm and bright shades of fuschia welcome you at the entrance as the shop whisks you on a trip through Vietnam, Cambodia, Laos, Nepal, Mexico, and other trippy, freewheeling places. What you get back from this trip is not the backpacking toting, incense burning, cotton scarf, baba-cool look, but elegant and eclectic solutions for you and your house. Glassware, mugs, vases, and silver accessories for all occasions; brilliantly colored scarves, horn jewelry, woolen blankets and flotsam and jetsam from countries with color and spice. The room at the back stocks kilims from Turkey, unusual tiger motif carpets from Nepal, and a selection of exotically colored table lamps.

WASALABY

INTERIOR

2-9-19 Jiyugaoka, Meguro-ku, Tokyo
03-3717-9191
www.wasalaby.com
🕐 11:00–19:00
📅 Wednesdays
🍴 MAP 11-17   ¥|¥-¥|¥|¥|¥

Wasalaby is a unique, museum-like space that sells exquisite collections of Japanese pottery that is at once traditional and contemporary. It stocks those creators who have lent a touch of their own style to traditional Japanese kiln techniques. Collections in fine wood, lacquer, and hand-blown glass are meticulously chosen by the shop owner so they can be mixed and matched to offer the most unique tableware. The best in this shop, however, is the finest white porcelain in a matte finish by star potter Taizo Kuroda. Each piece is truly a work of art, and costs almost as much.

WATASHI NO HEYA

INTERIOR

2-9-4 Jiyugaoka, Meguro-ku, Tokyo
03-3724-8021
www.watashinoheya.co.jp
🕐 11:00–20:00
▦ Not fixed
ʃ MAP 11-18   ¥|¥-¥|¥|¥

A painfully popular shop, whose selection of bright ideas for dining, kitchen, and bedroom are eagerly sought by Tokyoites. Most people come here for quick ideas to spruce up the house: furniture, lighting, rugs, bathmats, slippers, and imported home fragrances. But the true stars are the items of Japanese style—bowls, glass, lacquer, and quirky little Japanese paper ideas. Stocking both high and low, there is enough gear here to help turn dream homes into reality.

WHIZ

MEN'S CASUAL

J-Hill Side 2F, 3-15-4 Jingumae, Shibuya-
    ku, Tokyo
03-5785-2644
None
🕐 12:00–20:00
▦ Not fixed
ʃ MAP 5-80   ¥|¥-¥|¥

Two street labels separated by a fence offer fun interiors for the urban prowlers who come shopping here every weekend. Smart and in neutral colors, the shop is particularly good at cotton jackets that look fitted—such a clever trick and *so now* even among top labels like Aquascutum, Zegna and Boss. The shop offers them in beautiful colors—neutral enough to go with everything and highly appropriate for warmer climates and heat-regulated buildings. The T-shirts come in red and blue and sailor stripes and are a hot favorite among the twenty- and thirtysomethings.

WJK

MEN'S/WOMEN'S BOUTIQUE

La Foret Harajuku 2.5F, 1-11-6 Jingumae,
    Shibuya-ku, Tokyo
03-3401-6390
www.wjk.jp
🕐 11:00–20:00
▦ Not fixed
ʃ MAP 5-81   ¥|¥|¥

In its fair sized men's collection, WJK stocks some superbly minimal Japanese designers, and is a great place to stock up on simple, high quality basic Ts, jeans, hooded jackets, and shirts. Check out the quality lamb leather biker jackets from Japanese designer AKM. The modest women's line follows the men's line, and vies for equal attention with very smart pantsuits and the choicest hooded jackets. Also a great place for people who don't like too much color.

WOLFORD
WOMEN'S LEGWEAR

Tobu Ikebukuro Department Store, 1-1-25 Nishi Ikebukuro, Toshima-ku, Tokyo
03-3981-2211
www.wolford.jp/index.html
🕙 10:00–20:00
📅 Not fixed
📍 MAP 17-3   ¥|¥-¥|¥|¥

No woman can say no to anything from Wolford, undoubtedly the world's finest hosiery. The tops, body, and sweaters in the finest of wools—like merinos, cashmeres and perfect fits in polyesters—are comfortable, warm, and last forever. The stockings come in many sizes, designs, and colors, and are famously run-free. Also a great place for all men for whom finding a gift for women is a challenge.

WOOD YOU LIKE COMPANY
INTERIOR

5-48-1 Jingumae, Shibuya-ku, Tokyo (Others)
03-5468-0014
www.woodyoulike.co.jp
🕙 11:00–20:00
📅 No holidays
📍 MAP 6-97   ¥|¥|¥-¥|¥|¥

Wood You Like Company says goodbye to the cult of status furniture. What is here is just a huge array of handcrafted furniture, each piece of heirloom value, taking months to make. The best of centuries-old wood carpentry techniques combined with contemporary designs results in furniture perfectly suited for the urban pad. There are plenty of unpretentious but clever series of chests, mirrors, shelves, tables, benches, kitchen stools, and beds. As everything is made in the company's own factories, prices remain reasonable and you can bespoke your furniture with a choice of woods—cherry, walnut, maple, and oak (as oak is the least favourite of woods in Japan, prices are remarkably low). The quality is so high that the shop proudly asks buyers not to cover tables with a table cloth or use coasters for drinks: despite the stains or scratches, the wood recovers with just a swipe. The service is excellent and for detailed explanations in English, ask for Ms Kawai who is happy to share with you her encyclopedic knowledge of woods.

WR
WOMEN'S BOUTIQE

3-12-16 Kita-Aoyama, Minato-ku, Tokyo (Others)
03-5468-2466
🕙 12:00–20:00
📅 Not fixed
📍 MAP 6-98   ¥|¥-¥|¥|¥

If you've got a yen for mixing high and low, WR is your ticket. Say, a great selection of jeans from Levi's Red, beautifully stressed draped offerings from Rick Owens, a few must buys from Japanese designers Suzuki Takayuki and simple tanks, Ts and dresses, designed by the shop themselves. Spread over two floors with thumping club music, here is where beautiful young things shop for style without the price. On the ground floor the dresses, Ts and tops are perfect for layering, and for completing the look with jeans. Head upstairs for a selection of irresistible designers like AF Vandervost, Anne Valérie Hash and others. The shop also takes orders for wedding dresses from Suzuki Takayuki.

WUT BERLIN
WOMEN'S BOUTIQUE

Parco Part 2, B1F, 3-7 Udagawa-cho, Shibuya-ku, Tokyo
03-5489-0771
www.hpfrance.com/Shop/Brand/Wut_berlin.html
🕐 10:00–21:00
🗓 No holidays
📍 MAP 8-49   ¥｜¥｜¥

This shop celebrates the big Germanic leap into fashion, with collections from some of the brightest stars from Berlin and around. Bitten Stetter, Macqua, Parawahn, Kaviar Gauche, and Carola Plochinger are just a few who offer industrial cutting-edge shades of black, grey, and beige combined with superbly finished tailored details like knife pleats, standing lapels, pleating, gathering, and just a bit of lace and buttons for a soft touch. Each item is beautifully crafted and—even though a bit mechanical—manages to convey romance without frill and flounce.

Y-3
MEN'S/WOMEN'S DESIGNER

5-3-20 Minami-Aoyama, Minato-ku, Tokyo (Others)
03-5464-1930
www.adidas.com/y-3/
🕐 11:00–20:00
🗓 No holidays
📍 MAP 1-98   ¥｜¥｜¥｜¥

Avant-garde designer Yohji Yamamoto and team Adidas got together and painted sportswear with three long black and white stripes. And as the master of scissors Yamamoto was involved, the look had to be really tailored. The look for men ranges between tailored pants and vests worn casually with white shirts, to sporty hoodies, glossy down jackets, and fine woolen drawstring pants. The women's look strays far from his touch and hardly goes beyond simple pleated skirts, leather jackets, and hoodies. It's a great experiment of couture with sports but how do you wear it? It's a question that leaves even the stylists baffled.

YAB-YUM
MEN'S/WOMEN'S DESIGNER

Shibuya Parco Part1 4F, Udagawa-cho, Shibuya-ku, Tokyo (Others)
03-6415-1562
www.yab-yum.com/
🕐 10:00–21:00
🗓 Not fixed
📍 MAP 8-50   ¥｜¥｜¥

This Anglo-Japanese label based in Tokyo is inspired by the pastoral, laced with Victoriana vintage. Still remaining quite free of commercialism and artificiality, designers Patrick Ryan and Mami Yoshida create complex layers and mismatched outfits in dusty colors. For women, the skirts come in oversized forms, worn with socks and flats and tops that look comfortable and neutral. Overall the feel is organic, prewar, and reserved for model sizes.

YASUYUKI ISHII
MEN'S DESIGNER

2-20-8 Ebisu-nishi, Shibuya-ku, Tokyo
03-3770-6137
www.yasuyukiishii.jp
🕐 12:00–20:00
📅 No holidays
📍 MAP 2-55   ¥¥¥¥-¥¥¥¥

Before setting up his own label, Yasuyuki Ishii enjoyed a fully fledged career as an artist. His artistic sensibilities made him strive to remain underground, despite having opened his first shop in Daikanyama. Not far from the station in a difficult-to-find small apartment in a residential building, his world is full of manly accessories, boot cut jeans, and lots of croco and python, including hard-to-find items like python pants and a whole series of rider's jackets. Shirts are acid washed and mostly black, jackets in leather or velvet sometimes accompanied by a fur collar, mouton jackets and superb Rocaille underwear decorated with skulls. The shop is also painted black, and with the staff also decked out in near goth make up and clothes, you'll find yourself transported into a world that still head-bangs on the weekends.

YOHJI YAMAMOTO
MEN'S/WOMEN'S DESIGNER

5-3-6 Minami-Aoyama, Minato-ku, Tokyo (Others)
03-3409-6006
www.yohjiyamamoto.co.jp/
🕐 11:00–20:00
📅 No holidays
📍 MAP 1-99   ¥¥¥¥¥

Yohji Yamamoto's avant-garde craft makes him the designer of designers—meaning he's loved by everyone from Sonia Rykiel to Karl Lagerfeld and a long list of fashion leaders. All his collections—Yohji Yamamoto for men and women, Yohji Yamamoto Noir, Y's, and Y's for men—are stocked in this shop, decorated in a minimal industrial aesthetic. But it is his collection line, Yohji Yamamoto, that reflects his finest creations. The androgynous look with mannish silhouettes like skirts and dresses paired with trousers is Yohji's favorite. Seriously anti-pretty, his clothes—yards of black gabardine poetically layered and draped—are visions of his ideal woman. Some say that the master has been leaning towards femininity but there's nothing to worry about: every bit of chiffon he uses is still finished off with Dr. Martens at the feet. The men's line is slightly different, with a relaxed silhouette loose enough to look stylish but never too baggy. The colors sometimes stray from black into browns and beiges.

YUKIKO HANAI

WOMEN'S DESIGNER

Nissei Akasaka Bldg. 1F, 8-1-19 Akasaka,
Minato-ku, Tokyo (Others)
03-3404-5791
www.hanai.co.jp/
🕐 11:00–19:00
📅 Sun/Holidays
🚇 MAP 16-10   ¥¥¥¥-¥¥¥¥¥

Tokyo's grand dame of fashion makes women glow. She makes billowing gathered dresses in white and red, with lots of fabulous flowers and frills. Cloudy white shirts with tiered ruffles are never too big or heavy as she combines volume with off-shoulder dresses and very big hats. You'll also find lace skirts, puff-sleeved dresses, tank tops, and Sabrina pants. If you have pretty shoulders her stuff is definitely for you. This flagship stocks all her brands: Yukiko Hanai Prestige, Yukiko Hanai, Yukiko Hanai Prosumer, YHClassico by Yukiko Hanai.

YUKI TORII

MEN'S/WOMEN'S DESIGNER

5-7-16 Ginza, Chuo-ku, Tokyo (Others)
03-3574-8701
www.yukitorii.co.jp/
🕐 11:00–20:00 (Sun/Holidays untill
19:00)
📅 Not fixed
🚇 MAP 4-47   ¥¥¥¥-¥¥¥¥¥

Yuki Torii's style suits absolutely everybody. It all depends on how you wear it. She makes ultra feminine basics in beautiful fabrics: dresses in white, grey, and red that could be matched with a furry capelet for a younger look, or one of her three-quarter-length jackets for events where you must hobnob with a different crowd. Most of her tops are tailored and constructed, with refined detailing like lace, embroidery, and piping, so it looks good at work and even better with jeans on the weekend. To these, she has added gorgeous coat dresses, tightly belted with huge puff sleeves and voluminous lapels. Most of her outfits can be easily worn in the winter as well, combined with her trademark ruffled jacket or fuzzy knit cardigan coats. Her clothes are impeccably styled, seemingly effortless, and impossibly pretty.

YUMI KATSURA

BRIDAL

1-25-3 Minami-Aoyama, Minato-ku,
Tokyo
03-3403-7831
www.yumi-katsura.co.jp
🕐 11:00–19:00 (Sun/Holidays untill
18:00)
📅 Wednesdays
🚇 MAP 16-11   ¥¥¥¥-¥¥¥¥¥

Yumi Katsura is the biggest wedding designer in town, with a fan base in New York as well. While her windows are decorated with bridal uniforms that Scarlet O'Hara might have worn, ask inside and they will show you rows of superbly crafted, ultra-modern, expensive wedding gowns with embroidery, lace, and beads in innumerable designs.

YVES SAINT LAURENT

MEN'S/WOMEN'S DESIGNER

Omotesando Hills 1F, 4-12-10 Jingumae,
   Shibuya-ku, Tokyo (Others)
03-5785-0750
www.ysl.com/
🕐 11:00–21:00
📅 No holidays
📍 MAP 5-82   ¥|¥|¥|¥

Since Pilati took over this venerable brand in 1995, he has replaced
Ford's hard-edged chic with historic styles, such as the superb
skinny waisted tunics with huge belts that shed years off everyone.
Combined with the must-have Muse bag, YSL is suddenly back on
the fashion radar. If all the choice confuses, stick to the basic best
combination of YSL circa 1970—a white shirt, cuffed trousers, and
platforms, for a great office look.

ZADIG & VOLTAIRE

MEN'S/WOMEN'S/KIDS'
DESIGNER

Roppongi Hills West Walk 2F, 6-10-
   3 Roppongi, Minato-ku, Tokyo (Others)
03-3408-3408-4811
www.zadig-et-voltaire.com
🕐 11:00–20:00
📅 No holidays
📍 MAP 12-42   ¥|¥|¥

Zadig &Voltaire does their whole collection in black, white, grey,
beige, and khaki, yet somehow succeeds in giving a vision of a
sunny holiday, cobbled streets, vistas, and delectable cuisine. The
look is not sharp, but a casual, refined combination of relaxed
shapes for both men and women with jeans, jackets, shirts, and
sweaters, and there is a cute little collection for kids that helps gives
the entire family a place in the sun.

ZAKKAYA

INTERIOR

Miyazaki Bldg. B1F, 6-28-5 Jingumae,
   Shibuya-ku, Tokyo
03-3407-7003 (fax only)
www2.ttcn.ne.jp/zakka-tky.com
🕐 11:00–20:00
📅 Not fixed
📍 MAP 6-99   ¥|¥|¥

A totally Japanese phenomenon, *zakka* means small, cool lifestyle
ideas. It could be an ashtray with a message, or a fun telephone.
What you get in this shop you will not get anywhere else: small
ideas in extremely good Japanese taste to spruce up the forgotten
spaces in your house. Unevenly textured mugs, plates, and bowls,
antique glass jars, handwoven, handsewn shopping bags in strong
earthy colors and little nonchalant pieces of this and that, beautifully laid out in an industrial-meets-Zen environment.

ZARA

MEN'S/WOMEN'S/KIDS' BOU-
TIQUE

25-10 Udagawa-cho, Shibuya-ku,
Tokyo (Others)
03-5728-4310
www.zara.com
🕐 11:00–20:00
📅 No holidays
🍴 MAP 8-51

¥|¥-¥|¥|¥

Thirty thousand fashionable items make it to Zara's hangers every year, which means that collections change at least twice a week! While most of them might be watered down versions of catwalks, if you want looks for less (and sizes that fit) Zara is heaven. You'll find a great collection of trouser suits for all seasons in many different colors. Shoes, bags, sunglasses, excellent service, and a tax-free rebate are also part of the fun of shopping here. The kid's collection is available at their Ginza and Shinjuku shops.

(ERMENEGILDO) ZEGNA

MEN'S DESIGNER

2-13-5 Kita-Aoyama, Minato-ku,
Tokyo (Others)
03-3405-4130
www.zegna.com/
🕐 11:00–20:00
📅 No holidays
🍴 MAP 17-12

¥|¥|¥|¥

Zegna has been combining class and tradition for years. Of late, this has been augmented with a lot of creative moves, such as coming up with Z Zegna, a young but slick casual line inspired by the love of jazz, films, and all things urbane by creator Alessandro Sartori. Their genius can also be seen in providing a sporty flip to the more traditional winter coat for the spring/summer season. Zegna weaves their fabrics first before designing. 100% traditional fabrics, like wool, are given a modern twist, such as in beige wool twills, multicolored wool checks, or even brown and blue large check wool. They infuse this with innovation, like in a wool jacket with brass buttons on the outside. Fused on the inside is a 100-percent linen safari jacket for a great city look. The other great things here are the accessories—jackets and coats with scarves that are striped on one side with blocks of color on the other, patterned ties, and belts that switch from calfskin to suede superbuck.

THE MAPS

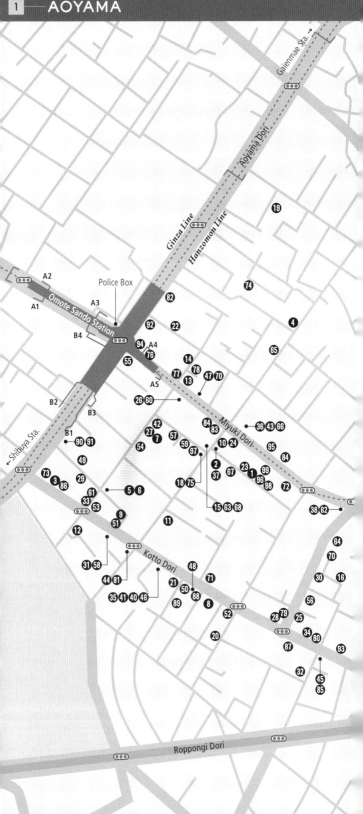

233

Kyu-yamate Dori

Nakameguro Sta.

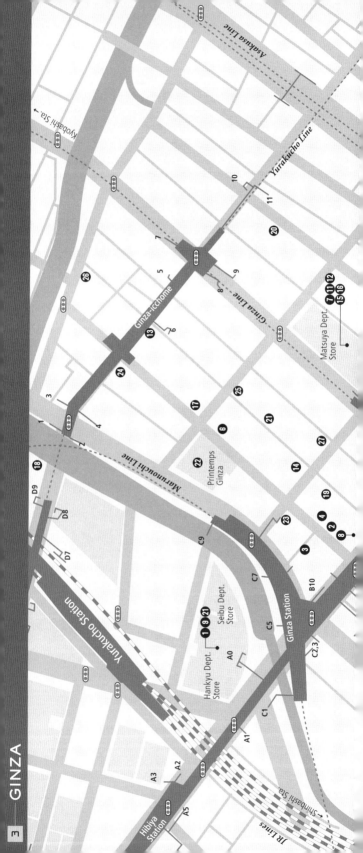

3 — GINZA

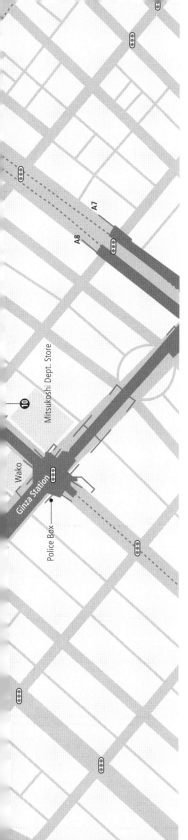

Police Box

Ginza Station

Wako

Mitsukoshi Dept. Store

A8

A7

10

1. ANNE KLEIN
2. ANYA HINDMARCH
3. BEAUX-ARTS MELS
4. BRIONI
5. CHANEL
6. CHRISTIAN LACROIX
7. DESIGN COLLECTION
8. EMILIO PUCCI
9. (SALVATORE) FERRAGAMO
10. GENTEN
11. JUNKO SHIMADA
12. KENZO
13. LONGCHAMP
14. M0851
15. MATSUYA
16. MIKIHOUSE
17. MIKIMOTO
18. MUJI
19. NEW YORKER
20. OBJ EAST
21. PAUL & JOE
22. PRINTEMPS GINZA
23. RESTIR
24. SAMANTHA THAVASA
25. SETU&KNIT
26. SHIPS LITTLE BLACK
27. SONIA RYKIEL

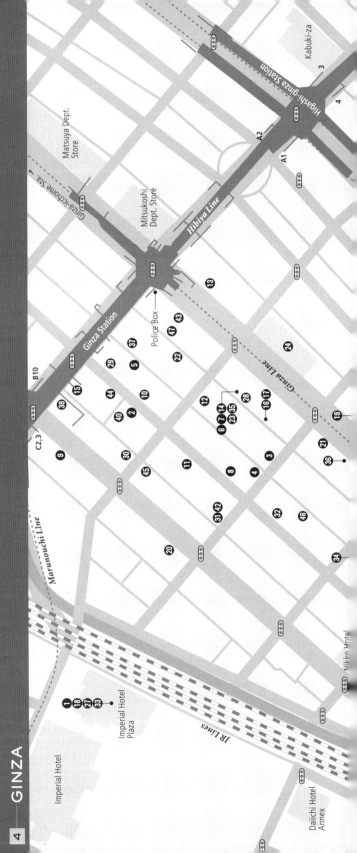

Matsuya Dept. Store

Ginza-ichome Sta.

Mitsukoshi Dept. Store

Hibiya Line

Kabuki-za

Higashi-ginza Station

3

4

A2

A1

Ginza Station

B10

Police Box

Ginza Line

C2,3

Marunouchi Line

JR Lines

Imperial Hotel

Imperial Hotel Plaza

Daiichi Hotel Annex

Nikko Hotel

1 18 27 33

9 39 15 40 2 44 30 45 20 10 28 5 37 22 47 43 13 12 6 7 14 23 35 16 17 25 24 19 21 36 11 8 4 3 31 42 32 46 34

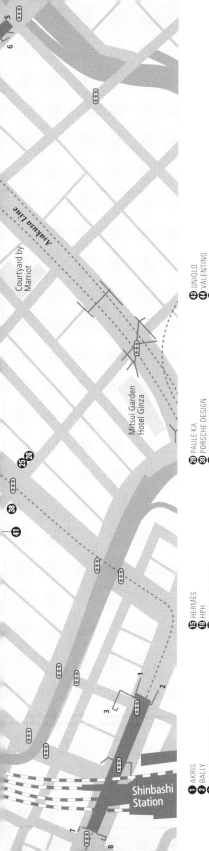

Shinbashi Station

Courtyard by Marriot

Asakusa Line

Mitsui Garden
Hotel Ginza

1 AKRIS
2 BALLY
3 BARNEYS NEW YORK
4 CANALI
5 CHA NO GINZA
6 CONCENTO H.P. FRANCE
7 DIPTYQUE
8 DUNHILL
9 EDDIE BAUER
10 EPOCA THE SHOP
11 ETRO
12 FOXEY
13 GEOX
14 GINZA KOMATSU BOUTIQUE

15 HERMÈS
16 HPH
17 JUANA DE ARCO
18 KRIZIA
19 LANVIN
20 LA PERLA
21 LLADRO
22 MARIAGE FRERES
23 MARIANELLI
24 MATSUZAKAYA
25 MONT BLANC
26 MORIMAE
27 NARCISO RODRIGUEZ
28 OJEWEL

29 PAULE KA
30 PORSCHE DESIGN
31 RENE CAOVILLA
32 ROBERTA DI CAMERINO
33 ROYAL CHIE LAVISH
34 SAMSONITE BLACK LABEL
35 SANTA MARIA NOVELLA
36 SAYEGUSA
37 SHANGHAI TANG
38 SHISEIDO
39 SONY PLAZA
40 ST. JOHN
41 THE GINZA
42 TUMI

43 UNIQLO
44 VALENTINO
45 VALEXTRA
46 WACOAL DIA
47 YUKI TORII

239

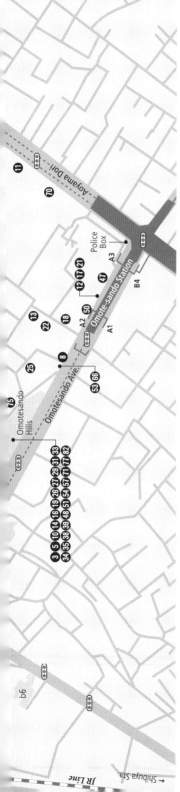

Shibuya Sta.
JR Line
← Shibuya Sta.

b6

Omotesando Hills

Omotesandō Ave.

Omote-sando Station
A2 A1
A3
B4
Police Box

Aoyama Dori

1 ADDITION ADELAIDE
2 AINZ TULPE
3 AMADANA
4 ANGE
5 ANN DEMEULEMEESTER
6 BAPE KIDS
7 BEAMS HOUSE INTERNATIONAL GALLERY
8 BENETTON
9 BIRKENSTOCK
10 BOTTEGA VENETA
11 BROOKS BROTHERS
12 CELINE
13 C2 LABO
14 DELFONICS

15 DIESEL
16 DOLCE & GABBANA
17 DONNA KARAN
18 EDIT FOR LULU
19 EM DESIGNS
20 FAT
21 FENDI
22 FRENCH CONNECTION
23 GAP
24 GAP KIDS
25 GARCIA MARQUEZ GAUCHE
26 GIEVES AND HAWKES
27 GIRLS END KIWA
28 GRAPEVINE BY K3
29 HAN AHN SOON

30 HANJIRO
31 HEDDIE LOVU
32 HP FRANCE BOUTIQUE
33 HP FRANCE BIJOUX
34 ISABELA CAPETO
35 JIMMY CHOO
36 K-DIARY
37 KIRA KIRA PROJECT
38 KIWA SYLPHY
39 KYOSHO
40 LA FORET
41 LAMP HARAJUKU
42 LAZY SUSAN
43 LE COQ SPORTIF
44 LEELA

45 LE LIGNE ROSET
46 LHP
47 LOEWE
48 MAC
49 MARIMEKKO
50 MARINA RINALDI
51 MARKS AND WEB
52 MICAN HP FRANCE EXCLUSIVE
53 MORGAN DE TOI
54 NAPAPIJRI
55 OPTICIEN LOYD
56 PUMA
57 QUIKSILVER
58 RALPH LAUREN
59 REALMAD HECTIC

60 REBIRTH
61 REVOLVER
62 SAMANTHA KINGZ
63 SEE BY CHLOÉ
64 SEXY DYNAMITE QUEEN WITH VIVI-ENNE WESTWOOD MUSEUM
65 SIDE BY SIDE
66 SISLEY
67 STUSSY
68 SUIKINCHI KAMOKUDOTTENMEIKAI
69 SWC
70 TALBOTS
71 THE NORTH FACE
72 T KUNIMOTO
73 TOPMAN/TOPSHOP

74 TRAMANDO
75 TRAPU
76 TRIPPEN
77 UGG
78 UNITED BAMBOO
79 VANNES
80 WHIZ
81 WJK
82 YVES SAINT LAURENT

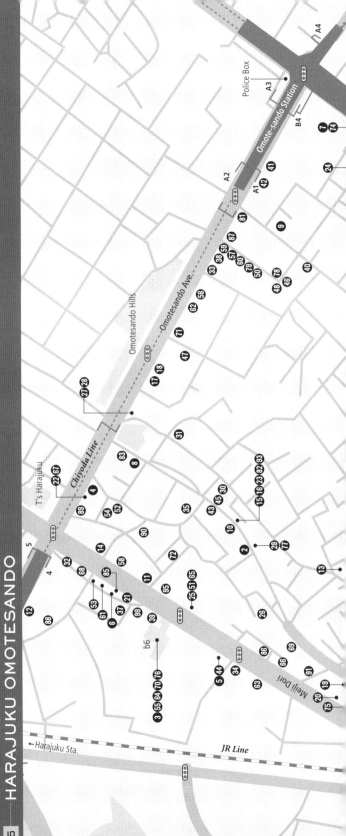

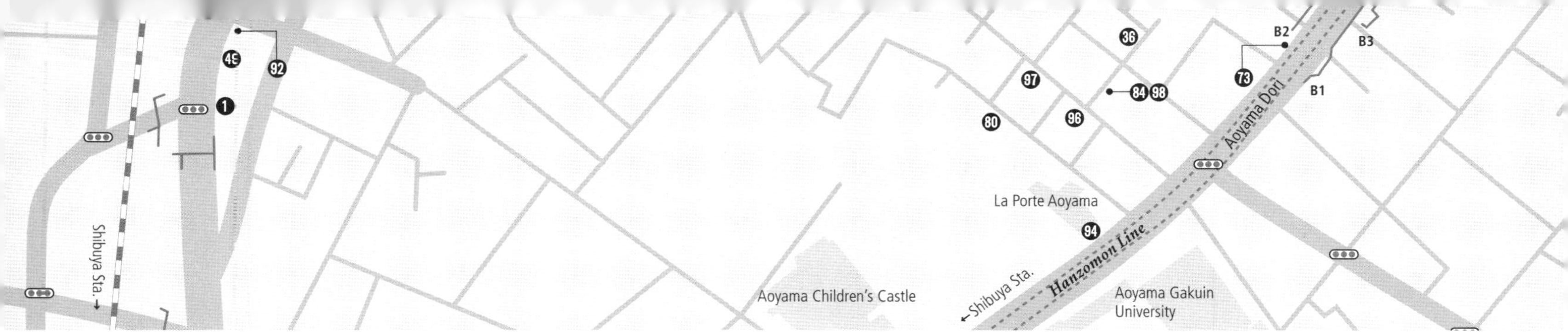

(1) 45RPM
(2) ADIDAS ORIGINALS
(3) ADORNOR
(4) AGNÈS B VOYAGE
(5) AIGLE
(6) ALBA ROSA
(7) AND A
(8) ANNA SUI
(9) ANTIK BATIK
(10) ARMANI CASA
(11) ASH AND DIAMONDS
(12) BANG AND OLUFSEN
(13) BANNER BARRET
(14) BASE STATION
(15) BBS TOKYO
(16) BOMB OF THE YEAR
(17) BRUNO MAGLI
(18) BURBERRY
(19) BURBERRY BLACK LABEL
(20) BURBERRY BLUE LABEL
(21) CA4LA
(22) CAMPER
(23) CANNABIS
(24) CHRISTOPHE COPPENS
(25) CIAOPANIC
(26) DEVICE TOKYO
(27) DIOR
(28) DIOR HOMME
(29) DISTRICT UNITED ARROWS
(30) DKNY
(31) DUAL
(32) EDWIN
(33) EMPORIO ARMANI
(34) EXR
(35) FACTORY
(36) FLAIR
(37) GABRIELLE PECO
(38) GALLARDA GALANTE
(39) GAS JEANS
(40) GISÈLE PARKER
(41) GUCCI
(42) HANAE MORI
(43) HH STYLE
(44) HIROMICHI NAKANO
(45) HOPE CHEST
(46) HP DECO
(47) IL BISONTE
(48) JAMIN PUECH
(49) JILL STUART
(50) JOHN SMEDLEY
(51) JUDGEMEK
(52) KOTUCA
(53) LE SPORT SAC
(54) LIMI FEU
(55) LOIS CRAYON
(56) LOUIS VUITTON
(57) LUCIEN PELLAT-FINET
(58) MANGO
(59) MAX & CO
(60) MIHARA YASUHIRO (SOSU)
(61) MILK
(62) MISSONI
(63) MISS SIXTY
(64) MOLAB
(65) MYSTIC
(66) NAUTICA
(67) NINE WEST
(68) NO CONCEPT BUT GOOD SENSE
(69) PATAGONIA
(70) PAUL & JOE ACCESSORIES
(71) PAUL STUART
(72) Q-POT
(73) RMK
(74) ROEN
(75) ROYAL FLASH
(76) RYUGI
(77) SCYE
(78) SERGE THORAVAL
(79) SHINZONE
(80) SHOYEIDO
(81) SHU UEMURA
(82) SLEEPING FOREST
(83) STEPHAN SCHNEIDER
(84) SUZUKI TAKAYUKI
(85) THE ORIGINAL LEVI'S STORE
(86) TK
(87) TODS
(88) TOGA
(89) TREE OF LIFE
(90) TRICO
(91) UNITED ARROWS
(92) URBAN RESEARCH
(93) USAGI POUR TOI
(94) VICTORINOX
(95) VIVA CIRCUS
(96) VIVIENNE WESTWOOD
(97) WOOD YOU LIKE COMPANY
(98) WR
(99) ZAKKAYA

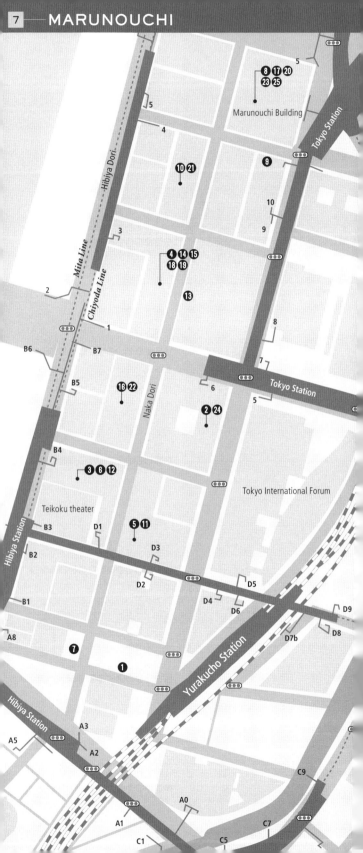

Marunouchi Building

Tokyo Station

Hibiya Dori

Mita Line

Chiyoda Line

Naka Dori

Tokyo Station

Tokyo International Forum

Teikoku theater

Hibiya Station

Yurakucho Station

Hibiya Station

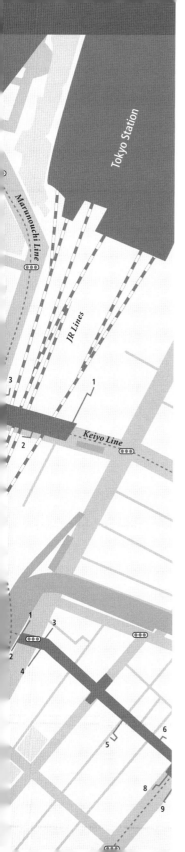

1. ALAIN FIGARET
2. AQUASCUTUM
3. BACCARAT
4. CHARLES JOURDAN
5. COCCINELLE
6. CORNELIANI
7. DARJEELING DAYS
8. DES PRÉS
9. EDIFICE et IENA
10. FACIAL INDEX
11. GEORG JENSEN
12. GIANFRANCO FERRE
13. HITMAN
14. ILLUMS
15. JEAN PAUL GAULTIER
16. JOHN LOBB
17. MAKER'S SHIRT
18. MARNI
19. OPAQUE
20. PORTER
21. SARTO TECNICO
22. SERGIO ROSSI
23. TAPPET BASSETT WALKER
24. THE SOVEREIGN HOUSE UNITED ARROWS
25. TOPKAPI

NHK

22

8

29 46

39

9

36 49

40

37

19 7

20 34 51 31 2

50

42 6

Parco 14

12 30 48

4

11 25 26

24 47

15 32

Tokyu Dept. Store 52 Seibu Dept. Store

27 28

23 Bic Camera

A3

16 3 6 7 7a

1 18 35 4

A1 Hachiko
Ext
A2

Shibuya Station
(Inokashira Line)

Shibuya Station

33

Mark City

Inokashira
Line

3

Cerulean Tower

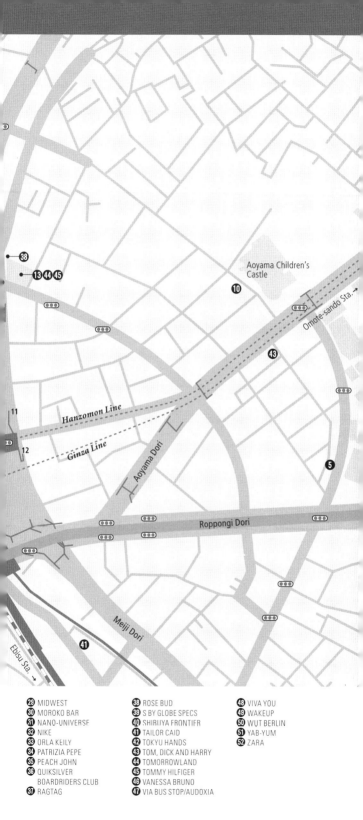

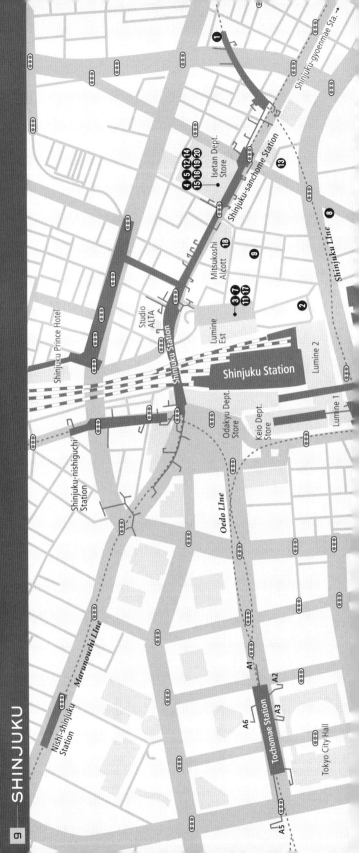

Shinjuku-gyoenmae Sta.

❶

Shinjuku-sanchome Station

❶③

❹❺⓬⓮
⓯⓰⓳⓴
Isetan Dept.
Store

❽

Shinjuku Line

⓮

❾

Mitsukoshi
Alcott

❸❼
⓫⓱

❷

Studio
ALTA

Lumine
Est

Shinjuku Station

Shinjuku Prince Hotel

Shinjuku Station

Lumine 2

Odakyu Dept.
Store

Keio Dept.
Store

Lumine 1

Shinjuku-nishiguchi
Station

Oedo Line

Marunouchi Line

A1

Nishi-shinjuku
Station

A6

A2

A3

Tochomae Station

Tokyo City Hall

A5

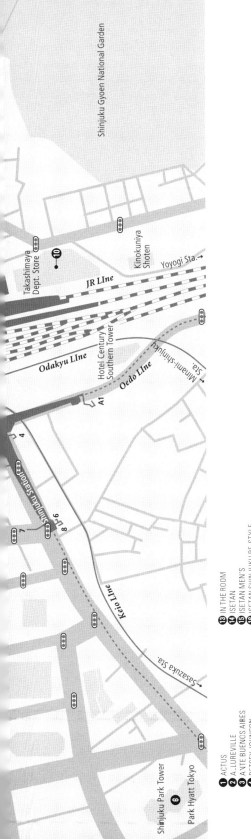

Shinjuku Gyoen National Garden

Takashimaya Dept. Store

Kinokuniya Shoten

Yoyogi Sta.→

JR LIne

Odakyu LIne

Hotel Century Southern Tower

Minami-shinjuku Sta.→

Oedo Line

A1

Shinjuku Station

Keio Line

Sasazuka Sta.→

Shinjuku Park Tower

Park Hyatt Tokyo

① ACTUS
② A.LUREVILLE
③ A'ITE BUENOS AIRES
④ BETSEY JOHNSON
⑤ BONPOINT
⑥ CONRAN SHOP
⑦ DESTINATION TOKYO
⑧ DIABRO
⑨ GEM KAWANO
⑩ GERARD DAREL
⑪ HPFRANCE WINDOW GALLERY
⑫ ICB

⑬ IN THE ROOM
⑭ ISETAN
⑮ ISETAN MEN'S
⑯ ISETAN SHINJUKU RE-STYLE
⑰ LAX
⑱ LE TANNEUR
⑲ MOSCHINO
⑳ RE-STYLE KIDS

249

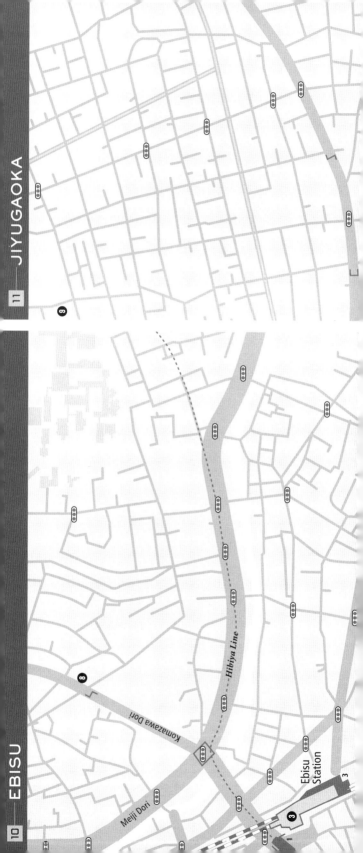

Meiji Dori

Komazawa Dori

Hibiya Line

Ebisu Station

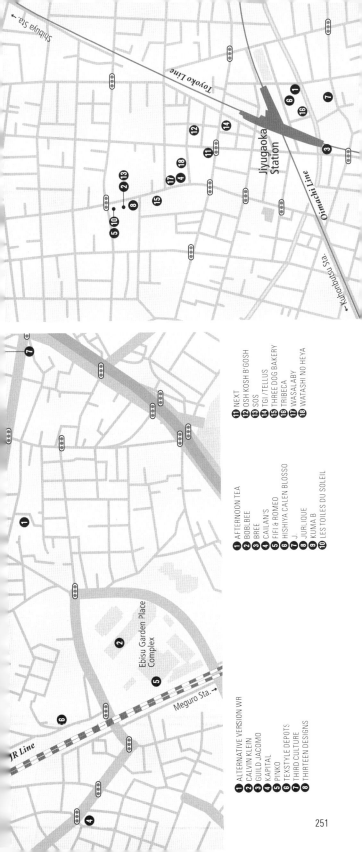

1. AFTERNOON TEA
2. BOB.BEE
3. BREE
4. CAILAN'S
5. FIFI & ROMEO
6. HISHIYA CALEN BLOSSO
7. J.
8. JURLIQUE
9. KUMA B
10. LES TOILES DU SOLEIL

11. NEXT
12. OSH KOSH B'GOSH
13. SOS
14. TGI / TELLUS
15. THREE DOG BAKERY
16. TRIBECA
17. WASALABY
18. WATASHI NO HEYA

1. ALTERNATIVE VERSION WR
2. CALVIN KLEIN
3. GUILD JACOMO
4. KAPITAL
5. PINKO
6. TEXSTYLE DEPOTS
7. THIRD CULTURE
8. THIRTEEN DESIGNS

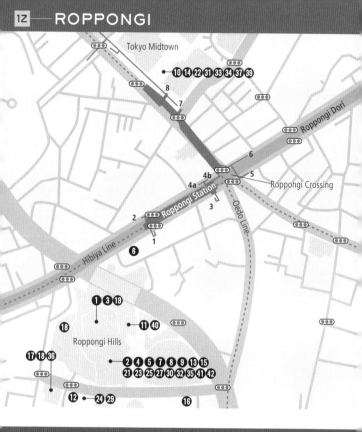

Tokyo Midtown

⑩ ⑭ ㉒ ㉛ ㉝ ㉞ ㉟ ㊲ ㊴

8

7

Roppongi Dori

6

5

Roppongi Crossing

4b

4a

Roppongi Station

3

Oedo Line

2

1

Hibiya Line

⑥

① ③ ⑲

⑱

⑪ ㊵

Roppongi Hills

⑰ ⑱ ㊱

② ④ ⑤ ⑦ ⑧ ⑨ ⑬ ⑮
㉑ ㉓ ㉕ ㉗ ㉚ ㉜ ㉟ ㊶ ㊷

⑫ ㉔ ㉙

⑯

② ③

Hotel New Otani

①

Yurakucho Line

Namboku Line

9b

9a

5

6

Marunouchi Line

D 7

C

B

Nagatacho Station

8

Hanzomon Line
Ginza Line

Benkei-guchi

San'no-guchi

Akasaka-mitsuke Station

① BILLIONAIRE
② GIORGIO ARMANI
③ VERSACE

1. ADORE
2. AGITO
3. AI BY ATSUKO IGA
4. ARMANI JEANS
5. ARTH
6. BANANA REPUBLIC
7. CALZALONE
8. CLASSICS THE SMALL LUXURY
9. COLE HAAN
10. E. MARINELLA NAPOLI
11. EMMA HOPE
12. ESCADA
13. ESTNATION
14. FABERÐCASTELL
15. HANWAY
16. HARRODS
17. HIROFU
18. HUGO HUGO BOSS
19. HYSTERIC GLAMOUR
20. IMMUDYNE
21. JOHANNA HO
22. JOSEPH
23. KEITA MARUYAMA TOKYO PARIS
24. KITON
25. L.E.D. BITES
26. LE GARAGE
27. LEONARD
28. LIVING MOTIF
29. LORO PIANA
30. LULU GUINNESS
31. MORABITO
32. MULBERRY
33. NICOLAI BERGMANN SUMU
34. OBJET STANDARD
35. ONITSUKA TIGER
36. ORREFORS KOSTA BODA
37. RICHARD JAMES
38. SAVOIR VIVRE
39. SAYA
40. SIGERSON MORRISON
41. STOMP STAMP
42. ZADIG & VOLTAIRE

14 — AZABUDAI

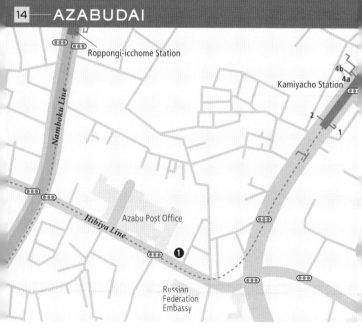

Roppongi-icchome Station

Kamiyacho Station

Nambuku Line

Azabu Post Office

Hibiya Line

Russian Federation Embassy

1. LISTE ROUGE

FUTAKO-TAMAGAWA

15

Takashimaya
Dept. Store

❶

Shibuya Sta.

Den-en-toshi Line

Oimachi Line

Highway 246

Futako-tamagawa Station

❶ BELT&BELT

GAIENMAE

16

Aoyama-icchome
Station

❿

D

2

1

❺ ❹ ❷

5

Ginza Line

4

2

❿⓬ 3

Gaienmae Station

1a 1b

❸ ❻ ❼

❽ ❾

❶

Oedo Line

Aoyama Cemetary

⓫

4

3

Nogizaka
Station

5

6

❶ ALESSI	❻ L'ARTISAN PARFUMEUR	⓫ YUMI KATSURA
❷ BERLUTI	❼ PAOLA FRANI	⓬ (ERMENEGILDO) ZEGNA
❸ CIBONE	❽ SLOW-FLOW	
❹ DORMEUIL	❾ STEFANEL	
❺ GIVENCHY	❿ YUKIKO HANAI	

Tobu Dept. Store

Ikebukuro Station

Seibu Dept. Store

Marunouchi Line

JR Lines

Yurakucho Line

Ikebukuro Lines

❶ ADIDAS PERFORMANCE CENTRE   ❷ OILILY   ❸ WOLFORD

to Shibuya

Ikejiri Sta.

Highway 246

Den-en-toshi Line

Mishuku Crossing

Sangenjyaya Station

❶ GLOBE

❶ SKECHERS

❶ IKEA

256

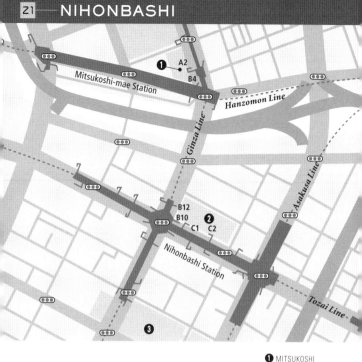

❶ MITSUKOSHI
❷ MONITOR MIND
❸ TAKASHIMAYA

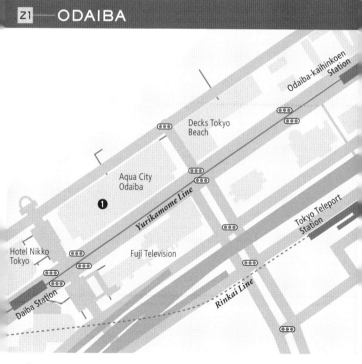

❶ J. CREW

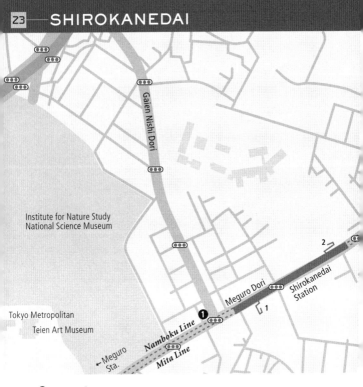

Gaien Nishi Dori

Institute for Nature Study
National Science Museum

Tokyo Metropolitan
Teien Art Museum

Namboku Line

Mita Line

← Meguro
Sta.

Meguro Dori

Shirokanedai
Station

❶

❶ MINA PERHÖNEN

THE CATEGORIES

- ACCESSORIES: MEN'S
- ACCESSORIES: WOMEN'S
- AROMATHERAPY
- BESPOKE
- BONSAI
- BOUTIQUE: MEN'S
- BOUTIQUE: WOMEN'S
- BRIDAL
- CASUAL: MEN'S
- CASUAL: WOMEN'S
- CIGARS
- COSMETICS
- DANCEWEAR
- DENIM: MEN'S
- DENIM: WOMEN'S
- DEPARTMENT STORES
- DESIGNER: MEN'S
- DESIGNER: WOMEN'S
- DIET
- DO-IT-YOURSELF
- DRIVING ACCESSORIES
- DRUGSTORE
- DRYCLEANER
- EYE WEAR
- FABRICS
- FUR
- HATS: MEN'S AND WOMEN'S
- HANDKERCHIEFS
- HEALTHCARE
- INFANTS
- INTERIOR
- JAPANESE DESIGNERS
- JEWELRY
- KIDS'
- KNITWEAR: MENS/WOMEN'S
- LEGWEAR: MEN'S
- LEGWEAR: WOMEN'S
- LINGERIE
- LUGGAGE
- MATERNITY
- PERFUMERY
- PETS
- SECOND-HAND: MEN'S AND WOMEN'S
- SHOES: KIDS'
- SHOES: MEN'S
- SHOES: WOMEN'S
- SPA
- SPORTSWEAR: MEN'S
- SPORTSWEAR: WOMEN'S
- STATIONERY
- SURFWEAR/SURFGEAR
- SURF AND SKI: MEN'S AND WOMEN'S
- TEA: JAPANESE
- TEA SALON
- TOYS
- UMBRELLAS
- UNDERWEAR: MEN'S AND WOMEN'S
- VINTAGE
- VOLUME SELLER: MEN'S/WOMEN'S/KIDS'
- YOGA

ACCESSORIES: MEN'S
AGNÈS B VOYAGE
AIGLE
ART-BERG DO
BALLY
BELT & BELT
BOBLBEE
BREE
CHROME HEARTS
CLASSICS THE SMALL LUXURY
COACH
CONCIERGE GRAND
EM DESIGNS
GARNI
GEORG JENSEN
GLOBETROTTER
GOYARD
HIROFU
HIROKO HAYASHI
HISHIYA CALEN BLOSSO
HPH
HUNTING WORLD
IL BISONTE
ISABURO
KATE SPADE
KIRA KIRA PROJECT
LAZY SUSAN
L.E.D. BITES
LE DEPOT MILLES FILLES
LE SPORT SAC
LE TANNEUR
LONGCHAMP
LOUIS VUITTON
M0851
MARIMEKKO
MIKIMOTO
PORSCHE DESIGN
PORTER
SAMANTHA KINGZ
SAMSONITE BLACK LABEL
S BY GLOBE SPECS
SERGE THORAVAL
SWING THE CAT
THIRTEEN DESIGNS
TOD'S
TOM, DICK AND HARRY
TOMORROWLAND
VALEXTRA
VANNES
VICTORINOX

ACCESSORIES: WOMEN'S
AGNÈS B VOYAGE
AI BY ATSUKO IGA
AIGLE
ANTITESI
ART-BERG DO
BALLY
BELT & BELT
BOBLBEE
BREE
CHROME HEARTS
CLASSICS THE SMALL LUXURY
COACH
COCCINELLE
CONCIERGE GRAND
EM DESIGNS
GARCIA MARQUES
GARNI
GENTEN

GEORG JENSEN
GIRLS END KIWA
GLOBETROTTER
GOYARD
GUMPS
HIROFU
HIROKO HAYASHI
HISHIYA CALEN BLOSSO
HP FRANCE BIJOUX
HP FRANCE BOUTIQUE
HP FRANCE WINDOW GALLERY
HUNTING WORLD
ISABURO
JAMIN PUECH
KATE SPADE
KIRA KIRA PROJECT
LAZY SUSAN
LE DEPOT MILLES FILLES
LE SPORT SAC
LE TANNEUR
LONGCHAMP
LOUIS VUITTON
LULU GUINNESS
M0851
MARIMEKKO
MIKIMOTO
MORABITO
MULBERRY
OILILY
ORLA KEILY
PAUL & JOE ACCESSORIES
PORSCHE DESIGN
PORTER
Q-POT
ROBERTA DI CAMERINO
SAMANTHA THAVASA
SAMSONITE BLACK LABEL
S BY GLOBE SPECS
SERGE THORAVAL
SUIKINCHIKAMOKUDOTTEN-
  MEIKAI
SWC
TOD'S
TOMORROWLAND
TOPKAPI
VALEXTRA
VANNES
VIA BUS STOP/AUDOXIA
WAKEUP

AROMATHERAPY
BELLINROSTON
DIPTYQUE
LUSH
MARKS AND WEB
TREE OF LIFE

BESPOKE
BOSTON TAILORS
GIEVES AND HAWKES
LISTE ROUGE
MAKER'S SHIRT
RICHARD JAMES
TAILOR CAID

BONSAI
MORIMAE

BOUTIQUE: MEN'S

10 CORSO COMO COMME DES GARCONS
17 DIX SEPT DESIGN GALLERY
5351
ADAM ET ROPE HOMME
ADDITION ADELAIDE
AMERICAN RAG CIE
AND A
APC
ATTIC
B'2ND
BALLANTYNE
BANANA REPUBLIC
BAPE EXCLUSIVE
BBS TOKYO
BEAMS
BEAMS HOUSE INTERNATIONAL GALLERY
BENETTON
BOMB OF THE YEAR
CAILAN'S
CANALI
CANNABIS
CHANGES UNITED ARROWS
CIAOPANIC
COLOUR BY NUMBERS
CORNELIANI
CP COMPANY
DANIEL CREMIEUX
DARJEELING DAYS
DECADE
DESIGNWORKS CONCEPT STORE
DESTINATION TOKYO
DEVICE TOKYO
DORMEUIL
DOVER STREET MARKET
DUNHILL
EDDIE BAUER
EDIFICE ET IENA
ESTNATION
EUGENIE
EXR
FACTORY
FAT
FLOAT
FRENCH CONNECTION
GAP
GAS JEANS
GEM KAWANO
GIANFRANCO FERRE
GIULIANO FUJIWARA
HARRODS
HPH
HUGO BOSS
HUGO HUGO BOSS
IPHIL
JAEGER
J. CREW
JOSEPH
JUDGEMEK
JUICY COUTURE
JUVENILE DELINQUENT
LANVIN
L'ECLAIREUR
LHP
LIFT ECRU
LIFT ETAGE
LOEWE
LOUIS VUITTON
LOVELESS
MIDWEST
NANO-UNIVERSE
NARA CAMICIE
NAUTICA
NEW YORKER
NEXT
NONNATIVE
REALMAD HECTIC
REBIRTH
RESTIR
ROYAL FLASH
RYUGI
SARTO TECNICO
SHANGHAI TANG
SHIPS LITTLE BLACK
SIDE BY SIDE
SISLEY
ST.JAMES
STRASBURGO
TAPPET BASSETT WALKER
THE SOVEREIGN HOUSE UNITED ARROWS
TOMORROWLAND
TOPMAN/TOPSHOP
TRIBECA
UNITED ARROWS
URBAN RESEARCH
VIA BUS STOP HOMME
VICTORINOX
WHIZ
WJK
ZARA

BOUTIQUE: WOMEN'S

10 CORSO COMO COMME DES GARCONS
16 AOUT
17 DIX SEPT DESIGN GALLERY
5351
ADDITION ADELAIDE
ADELAIDE
ADORE
ADORNOR
AFTERNOON TEA
AGOSTO
AKRIS
ALBA ROSA
ALLUREVILLE
ALTERNATIVE VERSION WR
AMERICAN RAG CIE
AND A
ANTE BUENOS AIRES
ANTIK BATIK
ANYA HINDMARCH
APART BY LOWRYS
APC
AQUAGIRL
AQUAGIRL ON THE STREET
ASH AND DIAMONDS
ATTIC
B'2ND
BALLANTYNE
BANANA REPUBLIC
BANNER BARRET
BAPY
BEAMS
BEAMS HOUSE INTERNATIONAL
BEAUX-ARTS MELS
BENETTON
BROWNIE BEE

CAILAN'S
CANNABIS
CARLIFE
CHANDELIER
CHANGES UNITED ARROWS
CIAOPANIC
COLOUR BY NUMBERS
COMPTOIR DES COTONIERS
CONCENTO H.P. FRANCE
CORIOLIS
CP COMPANY
CROON A SONG
DECADE
DESIGNWORKS CONCEPT STORE
DESTINATION TOKYO
DES PRÉS
DEUXIEME CLASSE
DEVICE TOKYO
DIABRO
DOUBLE STANDARD CLOTHING
DOVER STREET MARKET
DRAWER
DUAL
EDDIE BAUER
EDIFICE ET IENA
EDIT FOR LULU
EGOIST
ENCHAINEMENT UNI
EPOCA THE SHOP
ESCADA
ESTNATION
EUGENIE
EXR
FACTORY
FILO DI SETA
FLAIR
FLOAT
FOUNDFLES
FOXEY
FRENCH CONNECTION
GALLARDA GALANTE
GAP
GAS JEANS
GEM KAWANO
GERARD DAREL
GIANFRANCO FERRE
GINZA KOMATSU BOUTIQUE
GISÈLE PARKER
GOLDIE H.P. FRANCE
GRAPEVINE BY K3
HELIOPOLE
HERMAPHRODITE
HUGO BOSS
HUGO HUGO BOSS
ICB
INTERMIX TOKYO
IRIÉ
ISETAN SHINJUKU RE-STYLE
JAEGER
JANTZEN
J. CREW
JOSEPH
JOURNAL STANDARD LUXE
JUDGEMEK
JUICY COUTURE
KAMI
KIWA SYLPHY
KRIZIA
LA GRANDE AQUAGIRL
LAMP HARAJUKU
LANVIN

L'ECLAIREUR
LEONARD
LEELA
LIFT ECRU
LIFT ETAGE
LOEWE
LOIS CRAYON
LOUIS VUITTON
LOVELESS
MANGO
MARINA RINALDI
MARTINIQUE
MICAN HP FRANCE EXCLUSIVE
MIDWEST
MILKFED
MONITOR MIND
MOROKO BAR
MYSTIC
NAIVEWATER
NANO-UNIVERSE
NARA CAMICIE
NAUTICA
NEW YORKER
NEXT
PINKO
RESTIR
REVISITATION
ROSE BUD
ROYAL FLASH
RYUGI
SALOTTO
SETU&KNIT
SHANGHAI TANG
SHINZONE
SHIPS LITTLE BLACK
SIDE BY SIDE
SISLEY
SLEEPING FOREST
ST.JAMES
STRASBURGO
SUIKINCHIKAMOKUDOTTEN-
  MEIKAI
TALBOTS
TAPPET BASSETT WALKER
THE GINZA
TOMORROWLAND
TOCO PACIFIC
TOPMAN/TOPSHOP
TRAPU
UNITED ARROWS
URBAN RESEARCH
USAGI POUR TOI
VIA BUS STOP
WJK
WR
WUT BERLIN
ZARA

BRIDAL
KUMA B
YUMI KATSURA

CASUAL: MEN'S
AMERICAN APPAREL
BENETTON
CIAOPANIC
GAP
MUJI
NO CONCEPT BUT GOOD SENSE

NONNATIVE
RE-BIRTH
REAL MAD HECTIC
STÜSSY
UNIQLO
WHIZ

CASUAL: WOMEN'S
AMERICAN APPAREL
BENETTON
CIAOPANIC
EXR
GAP
MISS SIXTY
MUJI
NO CONCEPT BUT GOOD SENSE
STÜSSY
UNIQLO

CIGARS
ACANTA

COSMETICS
COSME KITCHEN
DOVER STREET MARKET
JURLIQUE
MAC
RMK
SANTA MARIA NOVELLA
SHISEIDO

DANCEWEAR
CHACOTT

DENIM: MEN'S
45RPM
DIESEL
DIESEL DENIM GALLERY
EDWIN
EVISU
HEDDIE LOVU
KAPITAL
LAX
MARITHÈ AND FRANCOIS
  GIRBAUD
THE ORIGINAL LEVI'S STORE

DENIM: WOMEN'S
45 RPM
DIESEL
DIESEL DENIM GALLERY
EDWIN
EVISU
HEDDIE LOVU
KAPITAL
LAX
MARITHÈ AND FRANCOIS
  GIRBAUD
THE ORIGINAL LEVI'S STORE

DEPARTMENT STORES
109
BARNEYS NEW YORK
ISETAN

ISETAN MEN'S
LA FORET
MATSUYA
MATSUZAKAYA
MITSUKOSHI
OPAQUE
PRINTEMPS GINZA
TAKASHIMAYA

DESIGNER: MEN'S
AGNÈS B
AGNÈS B HOMME
ALAIN FIGARET
ANN DEMEULEMEESTER
APOC
AQUASCUTUM
ARMANI JEANS
ATO
BALI BARRET
BOTTEGA VENETA
BRIONI
BROOKS BROTHERS
BURBERRY
BURBERRY BLACK LABEL
BURBERRY BLUE LABEL
CABANE DE ZUCCA
COMME DES GARCONS
COSTUME NATIONAL
DIOR HOMME
DKNY
DOLCE & GABBANA
DONNA KARAN
DRESSCAMP
EMPORIO ARMANI
ETRO
FENDI
GIORGIO ARMANI
GREEN
GUCCI
HELMUT LANG
HERMÈS
HIROMICHI NAKANO
HYSTERIC GLAMOUR
JEAN PAUL GAULTIER
JIL SANDER
J.LINDEBERG
JUNYA WATANABE
KEITA MARUYAMA TOKYO PARIS
KENZO
KITON
LUCIEN PELLAT-FINET
MARC JACOBS
MARNI
MARTIN MARGIELA
MERCIBEAUCOUP
MIHARA YASUHIRO (SOSU)
MIU MIU
NAOKI TAKIZAWA
NEIL BARRET
PAUL & JOE
PAUL SMITH
PAUL STUART
PRADA
RALPH LAUREN
REVOLVER
ROEN
SCYE
SHARE SPIRIT
SONIA RYKIEL
STEPHAN SCHNEIDER

SURPLUS A.P.C.
THEORY
TK
TOMMY HILFIGER
TSUMORI CHISATO
UNDERCOVER
UNITED BAMBOO
VALENTINO
VERSACE
VIVIENNE WESTWOOD
Y-3
YAB-YUM
YASUYUKI ISHII
YOHJI YAMAMOTO
YVES SAINT LAURENT
YUKI TORII
ZADIG & VOLTAIRE
(ERMENEGILDO) ZEGNA

DESIGNER: WOMEN'S
AGNÈS B
ALAIN FIGARET
ALBERTA FERETTI
ALEXANDRE HERCHCOVITCH
ANNA SUI
ANN DEMEULEMEESTER
ANNE FONTAINE
ANNE KLEIN
ANTEPRIMA
APOC
AQUASCUTUM
ARMANI JEANS
ATO
BALI BARRET
BETSEY JOHNSON
BLUMARINE
BOTTEGA VENETA
BRIONI
BROOKS BROTHERS
BURBERRY
BURBERRY BLACK LABEL
BURBERRY BLUE LABEL
CABANE DE ZUCCA
CELINE
CHANEL
CHARLES JOURDAN
CHLOÉ
CHRISTIAN LACROIX
COMME DES GARCONS
COSTUME NATIONAL
COURRÈGES
CYNTHIA ROWLEY
DIANE VON FURSTENBERG
DIOR
DKNY
DOLCE & GABBANA
DONNA KARAN
DRESSCAMP
EMILIO PUCCI
EMPORIO ARMANI
ETRO
FENDI
GIORGIO ARMANI
GIVENCHY
GREEN
GUCCI
HANAE MORI
HAN AHN SOON
HELMUT LANG
HERMÈS

HIROMICHI NAKANO
HYSTERIC GLAMOUR
ISABELA CAPETO
JEAN PAUL GAULTIER
JILL STUART
JIL SANDER
J.LINDEBERG
JOHANNA HO
JUNKO SHIMADA
JUNYA WATANABE
KEITA MARUYAMA TOKYO PARIS
KENZO
KITON
LILITH
LIMI FEU
LUCIEN PELLAT-FINET
MARC JACOBS
MARNI
MARTIN MARGIELA
MAX MARA
MAX & CO
MERCIBEAUCOUP
MICHAEL KORS
MIHARA YASUHIRO (SOSU)
MILK
MINA PERHÖNEN
MIU MIU
MORGAN DE TOI
MOSCHINO
NANETTE LEPORE
NAOKI TAKIZAWA
NARCISO RODRIGUEZ
NEIL BARRET
NICOLE MILLER
NO CONCEPT BUT GOOD SENSE
OBJET STANDARD
PAOLA FRANI
PATRIZIA PEPE
PAUL & JOE
PAULE KA
PAUL SMITH
PAUL STUART
PLEATS PLEASE
PRADA
RALPH LAUREN
RENATO NUCCI
ROEN
RYKIEL WOMAN
SEE BY CHLOÉ
SCYE
SHARE SPIRIT
SONIA RYKIEL
STEFANEL
STEPHAN SCHNEIDER
ST. JOHN
SUNAO KUWAHARA
SURPLUS A.P.C.
SUZUKI TAKAYUKI
THEORY
THIRD CULTURE
T KUNIMOTO
TOGA
TOMMY HILFIGER
TRAMANDO
TSUMORI CHISATO
UNDERCOVER
UNITED BAMBOO
VALENTINO
VANESSA BRUNO
VERSACE
VIVA YOU

VIVIENNE TAM
VIVIENNE WESTWOOD
Y-3
YAB-YUM
YOHJI YAMAMOTO
YVES SAINT LAURENT
YUKIKO HANAI
YUKI TORII
ZADIG & VOLTAIRE

DIET
IMMUDYNE

DO-IT-YOURSELF
TOKYU HANDS

DRIVING ACCESSORIES
LE GARAGE

DRUGSTORE
AINZ TULPE

DRYCLEANER
SARTO TECNICO

EYE WEAR
ALAIN MIKLI
CRADLE
FACIAL INDEX
GLOBE SPECS
J. F. REY
OBJ EAST
OPTICIEN LOYD
S BY GLOBE SPECS

FABRICS
TEXSTYLE DEPOTS

FUR
ROYAL CHIE LAVISH

HATS: MEN'S AND WOMEN'S
ARTH
CA4LA
CHRISTOPHE COPPENS

HANDKERCHIEFS
CLASSICS THE SMALL LUXURY

INFANTS
PSLING

INTERIOR
17 DIX SEPT DESIGN GALLERY
ACTUS
AFTERNOON TEA
AGITO
ALESSI
AMADANA

ARMANI CASA
ARTEMIDE
B&B ITALIA
BACCARAT
BALS
BANG AND OLUFSEN
BBS TOKYO
CASSINA IXC
CATHERINE MEMMI
CIBONE
COLLEX LIVING
CONCIERGE GRAND
CONRAN SHOP
DESIGN COLLECTION
DOVER STREET MARKET
DROGA
FRANC FRANC
GLOBE
HH STYLE
HP DECO
IKEA
ILLUMS
IN THE ROOM
J.
KARTELL
KIRA KIRA PROJECT
KNOLL
LAZY SUSAN
LE LIGNE ROSET
LES TOILES DU SOLEIL
LIVING MOTIF
LLADRO
LOFT
MARIAGE FRERES
MARIMEKKO
MUJI
NICOLAI BERGMANN SUMU
ORREFORS KOSTA BODA
RAFFINE LIVING
REPUBLIC OF FRITZ HANSEN
SAVOIR VIVRE
SAYA
SEMPRE
SHOYEIDO
SONY PLAZA
SPIRAL
SPIRAL MARKET
SUN'S COURT
TOKYU HANDS
TRICO
WAKEUP
WASALABY
WATASHI NO HEYA
WOOD YOU LIKE COMPANY
ZAKKAYA

JAPANESE DESIGNERS
APOC
COMME DES GARCONS
GREEN
HANAE MORI
HYSTERIC GLAMOUR KIDS
ISSEY MIYAKE/NAOKI TAKIZAWA
JUNYA WATANABE
LIMI FEU
MERCIBEAUCOUP
MIHARA YASUHIRO(SOSU)
MILK
MINA PERHÖNEN
OBJET STANDARD

PLEATS PLEASE
ROEN
SOSU MIHAYA YASUHIRO
SUNAO KUWAHARA
SUZUKI TAKAYUKI
T KUNIMOTO
TOGA
TSUMORI CHISATO
UNDERCOVER
Y-3
YASUYUKI ISHII
YOHJI YAMAMOTO
YUKIKO HANAI
YUKI TORII

JEWELRY
OJEWEL

KIDS'
ANTIK BATIK
APRICA
BAPE KIDS
BONPOINT
CARAMEL
GAP KIDS
HYSTERIC GLAMOUR
LE CHARME DE FIFI ET FAFA
MIKIHOUSE
NEXT
OSH KOSH B'GOSH
PATAGONIA
RE-STYLE KIDS
ROYAL FLASH
SAYEGUSA
ST.JAMES
STOMP STAMP
ZADIG & VOLTAIRE
ZARA

KNITWEAR: MENS/WOMEN'S
BALLANTYNE
JOHN SMEDLEY
LORO PIANA
MISSONI

LEGWEAR: MEN'S
CALZALONE

LEGWEAR: WOMEN'S
CALZALONE
COPO
PIERRE MANTOUX
WOLFORD

LINGERIE
GABRIELLE PECO
JUANA DE ARCO
LA PERLA
MARIANELLI
PEACH JOHN
WACOAL DIA

LUGGAGE
SAMSONITE BLACK LABEL
TUMI

MATERNITY
ANGE

PERFUMERY
L'ARTISAN PARFUMEUR
SANTA MARIA NOVELLA
SHOYEIDO

PETS
FIFI & ROMEO
HARNESS DOG
THREE DOG BAKERY
RYUGI

SECOND-HAND: MEN'S AND WOMEN'S
RAGTAG

SHOES: KIDS'
ABC
CAMPER
CAMPER BABY AND KIDS
GEEOX
SAYEGUSA
SKECHERS
TRIPPEN
UGG

SHOES: MEN'S
ABC MART
ADIDAS PERFORMANCE CENTRE
ADIDAS ORIGINALS
ALFREDO BANNISTER
BERLUTI
BIRKENSTOCK
BRUNO MAGLI
CAMPER
COLE HAAN
(SALVATORE) FERRAGAMO
GEOX
HITMAN
J.M. WESTON
JOHN LOBB
K-DIARY
NIKE
ONITSUKA TIGER
SERGIO ROSSI
SHIBUYA FRONTIER
SKECHERS
TGI/TELLUS
TRIPPEN
UGG

SHOES: WOMEN'S
ABC MART
ADIDAS PERFORMANCE CENTRE
ADIDAS ORIGINALS
ALFREDO BANNISTER
BIRKENSTOCK
BRUNO MAGLI
CAMPER
COLE HAAN
EMMA HOPE
(SALVATORE) FERRAGAMO
GEOX

GUILD JACOMO
HITMAN
JIMMY CHOO
KALISTE UN DIMANCHE A VENISE
K-DIARY
KOTUCA
NIKE
NINE WEST
ONITSUKA TIGER
RENE CAOVILLA
SERGIO ROSSI
SHIBUYA FRONTIER
SIGERSON MORRISON
SKECHERS
TGI/TELLUS
TRIPPEN
UGG
VIVA CIRCUS

SPA
CZ LABO

SPORTSWEAR: MEN'S
ADIDAS PERFORMANCE CENTRE
ADIDAS ORIGINALS
K-DIARY
LACOSTE
LE COQ SPORTIF
NAPAPIJRI
NIKE
PATAGONIA
PUMA
THE NORTH FACE

SPORTSWEAR: WOMEN'S
ADIDAS PERFORMANCE CENTRE
ADIDAS ORIGINALS
K-DIARY
LACOSTE
LE COQ SPORTIF
NAPAPIJRI
NIKE
PATAGONIA
PUMA
THE NORTH FACE

STATIONERY
DELFONICS
FABER-CASTELL
MONT BLANC
SHOSAIKAN

SURFWEAR/SURFGEAR
QUIKSILVER
QUIKSILVER BOARDRIDER'S CLUB

SURF AND SKI
SOS

TEA: JAPANESE
CHA NO GINZA

TEA SALON
MARIAGE FRERES

TOYS
BILLIKEN
KYOSHO

UMBRELLAS
HANWAY

UNDERWEAR: MEN'S AND WOMEN'S
CALVIN KLEIN UNDERWEAR
RESTERÖDS

VINTAGE
ANGELICO PERRO
BRAND BANK
CABOURG
HANJIRO
HOPE CHEST
SEXY DYNAMITE QUEEN WITH VIVIENNE WESTWOOD MUSEUM

VOLUME SELLER: MEN'S/ WOMEN'S/KIDS'
BASE STATION
UNIQLO

YOGA
MOLAB
SLOW-FLOW

ACKNOWLEDGEMENTS

Thanks go to my editor Gregory Starr for his unending patience, and the extremely talented design team at Kodansha International. The entire staff at HP France, especially Regina Komesu and Miki Nagai who, under instructions from their kind president Takanao Muramatsu, shepherded me through Ginza and Omotesando. Thanks for all the help given to me by Juan Jesus Rabanal, Yuki Aso, Natsuko Ikeda, Vincent Nida, Minato Kawai, Mika and Ryo Fujita, Alexandre, Kojin Kaneda, Kensuke Murate, Julien Sepheriades, Laura Corsico, Tatsuyoshi Hashikawa, Mathias Bouée, Yuhei Yamamoto, Chihiro Fukumoto, Sonoko Ishikawa, Xavier Destribats and Jean-Marc Dameron. Finally thanks to all the anonymous shop staff for sharing their knowledge.

（英文版）トーキョー・スタイル・ファイル
Tokyo Style File

2007 年 7 月 25 日　第 1 刷発行

著　者　　ジャハンヴィー・ダメロン・ナンダン
発行者　　富田 充
発行所　　講談社インターナショナル株式会社
　　　　　〒 112-8652 東京都文京区音羽 1-17-14
　　　　　電話　03-3944-6493 （編集部）
　　　　　　　　03-3944-6492 （マーケティング部・業務部）
　　　　　ホームページ　www.kodansha-intl.com
印刷・製本所　大日本印刷株式会社